Teaching Physical Education in the Primary School

Also available from Continuum

Teaching Physical Education 5–11, Tony McFadyen and Richard Bailey
Getting the Buggers Fit, Lorraine Cale and Joanne Harris

Teaching Physical Education in the Primary School

A Developmental Approach

Ian Pickup and Lawry Price

continuum

Continuum International Publishing Group
The Tower Building   80 Maiden Lane, Suite 704
11 York Road   New York, NY 10038
London
SE1 7NX

www.continuumbooks.com

Reprinted 2008

British Library Cataloguing-in-Publication Data
A catalogue record for this book is available from the British Library.

ISBN: 0826487602 (paperback)
            0826487599 (hardcover)

Library of Congress Cataloging-in-Publication Data
A catalog record for this book is available from the Library of Congress.

Typeset by Fakenham Photosetting Limited, Fakenham, Norfolk
Printed and bound in Great Britain by The Cromwell Press, Trowbridge, Wiltshire

Contents

For Jo, William and Anna (I.P.)

For Lois, Amy and Jack (L.P.)

With gratitude to family, colleagues and students for support, encouragement, inspiration and guidance during the writing of this book.

Preface

Our work in primary Initial Teacher Training (ITT) and teacher professional development has brought us into contact with student and practising teachers, headteachers, parents, subject leaders and pupils over a number of years. We have seen shining examples of meaningful, purposeful and relevant teaching in the physical domain and have no doubt that when taught well, physical education can make a significant and enduring contribution to the broader education of all children.

It is clear that the very best practice is cognizant of the full range of individual factors that can impact on children's motor development and this text sets out to introduce trainee primary teachers to the theory and practical application of a 'developmental' approach to the subject. We have attempted to illustrate how teachers can apply specific principles when delivering statutory curricula physical education and provide pointers for practice that can help teachers to achieve the outcomes of high quality physical education required by current 'policy' rhetoric in the United Kingdom. Above all else we hope to encourage reflective practice among future and current primary teachers and urge all teachers to adopt an approach to the subject that truly 'starts from the child'.

Ian Pickup and Lawry Price
Roehampton University
September 2006

The Role of *Physical* in Primary Education

Chapter outline

A sound mind in a sound body is a short but full description of a happy state in this world.

John Locke

Introduction

This chapter places physical education at the heart of the primary school curriculum by raising awareness of the role the subject can play in the lives of all children and young people. It draws on policy documents and evidence from a range of sources to advocate an enhanced status for the subject in today's primary schools. In an age where there are considerable pressures on timetabling, facilities, human resources and pupil attainment, primary school teachers and managers must become champions for physical education to ensure that all children have opportunities to 'learn to move' and 'move to learn'. This dual focus on learning in and through physical education provides an ideal opportunity for children to learn in each developmental domain and unlock their potential for lifelong physical activity through meaningful, worthwhile and individually relevant learning experiences.

Key points

- The state and status of primary physical education in today's schools needs to be improved through advocacy, reflective teaching and the development of personal philosophies for the subject amongst class teachers.
- The primary school age phases provide a vital opportunity for children to become physically educated.
- A teaching approach that values the subject's contribution to whole-child development and is relevant to the learning needs of all children can help to achieve the above.
- Physical education has the potential to be a central component of the primary curriculum and can contribute to learning in all developmental domains.

The body, movement and learning

When children begin their primary school education, movement has already played a central and significant role in their lives. In infancy and early childhood, children gradually gain control over their bodies so that they can begin to move in a variety of ways to explore the world in which they live. Young children demonstrate a remarkable variety and versatility of movement as they interact with their environment, other children, siblings and adults. In early years settings, physical play (both indoors and out) will have formed an integral part of each day and most young children will demonstrate a seemingly limitless desire to be 'on the move'.

Many writers have philosophized about perceived links between the mind and body and most educators now agree that the body – 'the physical self' – cannot be divorced from the broad learning process. It has been suggested that physical activity stimulates the development of generic cognitive or learning skills (Barr and Lewin, 1994) and some have gone as far as suggesting that increased physical activity improves cognitive functioning, concentration and academic performance. In early years and primary classrooms, we often see children who appear 'clumsy', struggle to hold pencils efficiently, or seem unable to sit in a way that helps them to concentrate and 'work'. Basic sensory and motor components (e.g.

body awareness, coordination of body sides, motor planning, perception of movement, fine motor control and touch) are also thought to influence learning and behaviour. This goes beyond the aims and goals of physical education *per se* and suggests that motor competence can help children to access all learning experiences. This area is generally under-researched but one which perhaps holds the key for future developments of teaching and learning in the physical domain.

Commonly used educational terminology includes 'multisensory learning' and 'kinaesthetic learning', each of which hints at a link between cognitive learning and the physical self. If we momentarily allow ourselves to forget the subject-based content of school curricula, generic skills such as problem solving, collaborating and sharing and communicating with others are all necessary life skills that can be learned through the engagement of the *whole* child – with the physical self central to the process. Learning in the physical domain, then, plays a significant role in child development. Not only are the skills learned applicable to a variety of lifelong physical activities, but wider learning within social, affective and cognitive domains can also make a major contribution to the lives of all children.

As children grow and develop, daily opportunities for physical activity appear to decline. Changes to the fabric of modern society have resulted in reduced space, time and open access to informal physical activity in local communities for children of primary school age. The reduction in green spaces and prevalence of a 'no ball games allowed' attitude, together with increased traffic and parental concerns regarding child safety in the community, have contributed to a dramatic reduction in spontaneous, sustained and regular activity in the daily lives of many primary aged children. In the educational context, some also believe that the culture of childhood (with play and physicality at its core) is at odds with the culture of schooling (Bailey, Doherty and Pickup, 2007). How often do we hear teachers asking young children to 'sit still' and to 'stop fidgeting' whilst they are asked to sit on a carpet at the start of each day?

We argue throughout this chapter that developmentally appropriate physical education can contribute to learning in all developmental domains. The application of the body to the learning process in the broadest sense can reap benefits beyond only developing physical skills and sound health. Our notion of what constitutes quality physical education is, therefore, more than an opportunity to escape the routines and pressures of 'proper' learning that takes place in the classroom, or to 'let off steam'. For many primary teachers, this view of physical education is a major departure from day-to-day practice and we hope that this book can help pre-service and in-service teachers to reflect on their own teaching and learning. Although the broad concept of 'movement learning' (Bailey and Pickup, 2007) merits further exploration, the contents of this book focus on the theoretical and practical knowledge required for primary teachers to deliver developmentally appropriate physical education experiences within the curriculum.

The current status of primary physical education

At a time of worldwide concern regarding the health and physical fitness of children and young people, and compelling evidence concerning the positive educational value of physical activity and sport, physical education as a curriculum subject is suffering apparently low status within many primary schools. This low status manifests itself in a number of ways, and in our frequent and regular visits to schools we see:

- limited curriculum time afforded to physical education;
- lack of coverage of all National Curriculum activity areas;
- cancellation of physical education lessons for a variety of reasons;
- physical education being 'outsourced' to non-qualified teachers;
- priority for facilities given over to other activities at certain times of the year;
- limited budget allocated to physical education;
- subject leader role afforded comparatively low status;
- limited professional development opportunities for all school staff.

Despite a long-standing international commitment to the subject as a 'fundamental right' for every child (UNESCO, 1978), and the presence of physical education as a foundation subject in the prevailing National Curriculum (DfEE/QCA, 1999), primary physical education certainly appears to be a poor relation to the 'core' subjects of English, Maths and Science. The impact of the National Literacy and Numeracy Strategies (DfEE, 1997 and 1999) in England is thought to have been particularly damaging to physical education, with an estimated half a million hours of teaching lost as a consequence of reduced timetable commitments to physical education (Speednet, 2000).

Concerns have also been raised within outcomes and reports of the Second World Summit for Physical Education (see the Magglingen Commitment for Physical Education at www.icsspe.org), the Independent Sports Review in the UK (ISR, 2005), and a position statement issued by representatives of the UK physical education profession (BAALPE, CCPR, PEAUK, PE ITT Network, 2005). Each of these documents suggests that the problem is centred largely on the training and professional development of teachers.

Despite a recent government investment of over of £1 billion through the Physical Education, School Sport and Club Links (PESSCL) strategy (DfES/DCMS, 2003), primary physical education is thought to be delivered by teachers who 'still go into schools without adequate Initial Teacher Training to teach physical education' (BAALPE, CCPR, PEAUK, PE ITT Network, 2005, p. 5). Whilst the government, Training and Development Agency for Schools (TDA) and providers of primary Initial Teacher Training (ITT) must review the time allocated to physical education within the primary ITT curriculum, practising teachers, subject leaders and headteachers must also critically reflect on their own views and perceptions of the subject and review the status that it is afforded in day-to-day practice.

Practitioners are encouraged to reflect on the role of physical education within their own views of what *education* itself is seeking to do. A Piaget-like view of education as creating people capable of doing new things, or concurring with Dewey's notion of the educative process as a spur for further education, may provide useful starting points for philosophical reflection. Further approaches have seen education as a process leading to personal autonomy based on reason (Dearden, 1968) or as a process which 'grips a child by his moral coat collars and lifts him up to see over the crowd to the task of personal responsibility for being human' (Morris, 1966, p. 116, cited in Andrews, 1979, p. 4).

Although these views are not new, they hold resonance for those working in primary schools, particularly within the context created by the Every Child Matters 'agenda' (DfES, 2003a). It is our firm belief that high quality physical education can contribute to the broad canvas of education by making a unique contribution to the physical, social, cognitive and affective development of every child. Whether concerned with the teaching and learning of specific physical skills or the use of physical skill development as a conduit for wider learning objectives, high quality physical education has an irrefutable role to play in primary education.

When physical education is positioned at the centre of school life, the impact on 'whole school' issues and broad educational attainment is evident. The Qualifications and Curriculum Authority (QCA) underline the wider significance of well-taught physical education in schools:

> When a PE curriculum is most effective, the ripple effect is felt far beyond sport and dance. The commitment, enjoyment, desire to improve and confidence that are engendered by high quality PE become an integral part of the learner and are transferred to other areas of study, leisure and work. (QCA, 2005, p. 17)

Learning to move – moving to learn

In January 2005, the UK physical education profession issued a position statement to summarize the value, role and unique place of the subject in the school curriculum. The central features of this statement revolve around two distinct elements of the subject – 'learning to move' and 'moving to learn' – together with the idea of developing 'physical literacy', especially pertinent to the primary school context:

> The aim of Physical Education is systematically to develop physical competence so that children are able to move efficiently, effectively and safely and understand what they are doing. The outcome – physical literacy – is as important to children's education and development as numeracy and literacy. (BAALPE, PEAUK, CCPR, PE ITT Network, January 2005, p. 8)

The position statement describes the unique, dual approach to learning offered by physical education. 'Learning to move', it is argued, includes the learning of skills, techniques and understanding required to take part in a range of physical activities. 'Moving to learn' uses physical activity as a context for learning, with a wide range of potential outcomes across all developmental domains. The statement suggests that the subject has a further four characteristics which give credence to its educational value:

- It is the only educational experience where the focus is on the body, its movement and physical development. It helps children learn to respect and value their own bodies and abilities, and those of others.
- Through improving physical competence, it positively enhances self confidence, self esteem, engagement and behaviour, and educational attainment through more positive attitudes to learning.
- It provides the skills, understanding and confidence for engagement in activity which is the basis for healthy, enjoyable, active lifestyles.
- It contributes to integrated development of mind and body, and enhances social and cognitive development. (ibid., p. 8)

The notion and meaning of 'physical literacy' has been developed most recently by Margaret Whitehead, who has taken a philosophical approach to explaining the role that movement plays in developing human capacities. Physical literacy has been partly defined as:

> The motivation, confidence, physical competence, understanding and knowledge to maintain physical activity at an individually appropriate level, throughout life. (Whitehead, 2006)

Links between physical literacy (theorized as a lifelong learning concept) and curriculum physical education have also been explored, and the important role of primary school physical education within the formation of competences and attitudes towards physical activity stressed (Whitehead with Murdoch, 2006). For some, considering the idea and importance of physical literacy provides an opportunity to rethink the educational value and structure of physical education and to evaluate how National Curriculum physical education can be best implemented or changed (Haydn-Davies, 2005).

The learning to move and moving to learn approaches to physical education offer educational benefits beyond just allowing children to take a break from the routines of the classroom, or for 'letting off steam', in providing a focus for learning that is enjoyable, motivational, sociable, physical, cognitive, interactive, challenging and fully accessible by all. An outcome of physical education, then, should be children and young people who are willing to participate in healthy, active lifestyles and who have a range of skills that allows ongoing, lifelong participation at an individually appropriate level.

This dual model is similar to other frameworks for the subject, most notably the idea of education *about*, *through* and *in* movement used by Arnold (1979) and Bailey (1999).

Whichever framework we choose to use as a model for our own practice, it is clear that physical education should be an educational priority where pupil learning and achievement are at the heart of the school-based teaching process. Teaching and learning in the physical domain through curricular physical education has a significant and unique contribution to make to the education of every child. The body and its capability of working within a range of practical contexts is the unique focus of the subject, yet well-taught physical education does not neglect child development in cognitive, social and affective domains in the pursuit of physical excellence that may or may not be achievable by all children.

The link between mind and body has been well documented for centuries in a range of philosophical and psychological literature. Recent trends in the primary classroom have included the introduction of 'brain gym', which claims to strengthen neurological pathways (and ultimately pupil attainment, concentration and behaviour) through a variety of body and mind actions (Dennison and Dennison, 1989; Hannaford, 1995). Whilst the scientific base for such claims needs to be viewed with care, links between mind and body are areas of clear potential for a subject where a dual focus is on physical and cognitive processes. If bodily actions within five- or ten-minute classroom activities are welcomed and thought to be educationally relevant by primary practitioners in the form of 'brain gym', then surely similar, if not greater, connections should be made in physical education lessons where the body is *the* major conduit for learning.

Although there is not yet conclusive evidence to confirm a definite link between cognitive development and physical education in school, findings to date suggest that the link may exist (Sallis and Owen, 1999). Indeed, some evidence suggests that where schools teach more physical education, and focus on the quality of what is done, pupils' attitudes to learning, attendance, behaviour and generic attainment increase across the school (QCA, 2005).

As physical education is a curriculum subject in its own right, *learning* must be at the heart of what we aim to do as physical educators – an underlying principle that goes far beyond simply providing opportunities for children to have a break from the routine of the classroom or prepare a minority of pupils for performance in sports competitions. Particularly when time available for physical education within a hectic weekly schedule is limited, every available minute must be maximized to facilitate learning, by placing an emphasis on careful planning, knowledge of children's learning needs born out of formative assessment and due consideration to issues of progression and continuity across all four Key Stages.

Movement *for* learning

Movement is thought to play a key role in early learning. The foundations of social behaviour are laid in the early years and movement opportunities provide many of the first socializing experiences as children interact with others in their new environments (Nichols, 1990). Being physically engaged is what helps children to construct their own view of the world at a physical and cognitive level (Bruner and Haste, 1987) and facilitates children to take an inventive, active role to reconstruct tasks and reinforce their own understanding (Wood, Bruner and Ross, 1976; Smith, 1993).

This 'social learning' includes an understanding of appropriate behaviour, often within boundaries and frameworks determined by others and depends on the successful building of relationships with peers, teachers and carers. Where the teacher's role is specifically geared to facilitating, shaping and influencing learning outcomes, children can show greater versatility, increased skilfulness and clarity of intent (Davies, 2003).

There is also strong evidence for the enhancement of children's self-esteem through participation in physical activity (Fox, 1988, 2000). Structured play and physical education programmes appear to contribute to the development of self-esteem in children and it has been suggested that self-esteem is influenced by an individual's perception of competence or adequacy to achieve (Harter, 1987). Enjoyment experienced during physical activity can reinforce self-esteem, which in turn can lead to enhanced motivation to participate further (Sonstroem, 1997).

Learning in the physical domain, therefore, must be seen as more than just being able to throw and catch a ball, or perform a particular gymnastics roll. The physically literate child will interact with sensitivity and ease to others in group situations, and will appreciate the expressive quality of movement in her/himself and in others (Whitehead, 2001). Fisher (2000) recognizes, however, that children will not cooperate with each other simply because it is in the teacher's plans; they will collaborate and communicate when they see the need to do so.

The movement context provided by well-taught physical education therefore needs to be carefully designed to capture these principles and the teacher must consider appropriate strategies and styles that are engaging, motivational and relevant. Fostering an intrinsic desire to learn in the physical domain must be uppermost in the teacher's mind and should not be restricted by a narrow view of physical education as being the subject that only happens outdoors or in the school hall. Careful cross-curricular planning and the identification of appropriate learning intentions can fully capture the subject's potential to contribute to learning and development across all domains.

Learning and National Curriculum physical education

Current National Curriculum for Physical Education (NCPE) (DfES/QCA, 1999) documentation sets out the knowledge and understanding that children are expected to learn in the subject throughout the four Key Stages. These strands are mapped across four 'aspects', namely:

- Acquiring and developing skills
- Selecting and applying skills, tactics and compositional ideas
- Evaluating and improving performance
- Knowledge and understanding of fitness and health.

These strands have clear links to learning in the physical (e.g. developing skills), social (e.g. working with others to plan and evaluate performances), cognitive (e.g. problem solving) and affective (e.g. fostering positive attitudes to healthy lifestyles through raising self-esteem) domains, and their inclusion within curriculum documentation ought to encourage teachers to include such learning intentions within plans. An emphasis on skill acquisition and refinement in the early stages of learning cannot operate independently from wider learning about pro-social behaviour, sharing space and helping one another.

The four aspects should be referenced in the planning, teaching and assessment process, whatever the activity area, and should not be dominated by a sole focus on specific sports techniques. Careful inspection of the NCPE materials will help the teacher to understand that six activity areas (Games, Gymnastics, Dance, Outdoor and Adventurous Activities, Athletics, and Swimming and Water Safety) are categorized in such a way that allows flexibility and differentiation to meet particular needs (the words 'football' and 'netball' for example, do not appear explicitly). In providing a broad and balanced curriculum across the activity areas, the aim should be to introduce children to a wealth of experiences, but to also seek common ground, transferability of fundamental skills and conceptual understanding across different contexts for movement.

In the school setting, physical education is part of the educational process. In a wider sense, through extracurricular and community activity, it can also introduce pupils to the rich cultural heritage of sport, recreation, exercise and dance in our society. In the pursuit of ensuring both the movement vocabulary and an entitlement to participation in its activities for all pupils, physical education is a facilitator in providing regular and vigorous opportunities for all round learning experiences within the physical dimension. We must, however, be careful not to claim too much for the subject or to be blinkered in our views as to its aims. It is clear that physical education, for many, has become a subject to avoid rather than rejoice in and our own work with non-specialist primary teachers suggests that the educational value of physical education remains misunderstood or unrealized by many 'beginning teachers', who in all probability have themselves had firsthand experience of the NCPE as pupils.

If, for example, physical education exists solely to develop physical fitness, then the nature, timing and content of delivery should reflect that aim. According to current advice from the Department of Health (DoH, 2004), children should be moderately to vigorously active for one hour a day to achieve health benefits. Very few schools have the time available to achieve this in curriculum time. Similarly, if the subject exists solely to identify and nurture talented children as future champions, then models more akin to sports coaching and training could legitimately be introduced.

The exact nature of the educational benefits of physical education and school sport has been the focus of a recent academic review, conducted through the British Education Research Association's Physical Education and Sport Pedagogy 'special interest group' (Bailey *et al.*, in press). The main summary points of this review provide cautionary guidance to all physical education practitioners and a 'call to arms' for further research to be conducted within the subject. Whilst research suggests that there are positive links between cognitive, affective, social and physical development and physical education and school sport, not enough is known about the *processes* of teaching and learning through which these links come about.

Teaching and learning in primary physical education

The 'super skills' of learning are thought to include the disposition to learn; play and physical activity are thought to be important in developing these skills among young children (Bruce, 1991). Further dimensions of learning beyond physical education-specific subject content are those of 'metacognition' and 'meta-learning' – often simply defined as 'thinking about thinking' and 'learning to learn'. Physical education is a subject that provides opportunities for children to solve problems, plan strategies, choreograph actions and sequences, and analyse their own work and that of others. The skilful teacher can capitalize on these opportunities to help children to develop skills, language and thought processes that have far-reaching applications to a wide range of contexts beyond the physical education lesson.

A focus on learning in physical education also suggests that we consider the range of styles in which children learn. Put succinctly, children do not all learn in the same way, and physical education has clear potential to appeal to visual, auditory and kinaesthetic learners, as well as those considered to be blessed with visual, spatial, verbal, logical, bodily, musical, interpersonal or intrapersonal intelligences (Gardner, 1993).

In spending each day with the same class, the primary teacher is in a unique position of being able to get to know his/her children exceptionally well, and insights gleaned across all subjects will enable the planning of tasks to match the learning needs of each child. Part of this process in physical education needs to acknowledge the need to use a variety of stimuli for movement and a range of teaching styles and strategies to promote learning. In using a range of contexts and spaces, a variety of objects and equipment and in providing a focus on expressing emotions and feelings through movement, the physical education 'classroom' offers an environment that should be truly appealing to all learners.

Developments in the psychology of learning have focused on the social context in which learning takes place. Vygotsky (1978) provided a theoretical framework that emphasized the fundamental role of socialization in developing cognition. The principle of 'scaffolding' emphasizes the importance of interaction between the learner and others whereby children can solve a certain range of problems only by interacting cooperatively with others. Physical education lessons provide children with potential for a range of social interactions – with partners, in small groups, with teachers, teaching assistants, visiting coaches and as a whole class or school group – which can be planned to maximize potential for learning in the social domain.

In order to help to bring about learning, the teacher, together with others in the classroom context, can provide pupils with clues to appropriate responses through verbal or non-verbal communication, provision of resources such as task cards, posters and word-banks or setting new problems through questioning. Equally, children will offer support and assistance to scaffold the work of others, as long as the learning context is designed to facilitate cooperation and communication between peers. This has clear implications to task design and lesson planning, choice of teaching style or strategy. At a simplistic level, long queues of children waiting to take a turn would not seem to be an appropriate use of 'constructivist' learning time in physical education.

To further exemplify the links between broader theory and physical education, Bloom's (1956) taxonomy of the cognitive domain (comprising of knowledge, comprehension, application, analysis, synthesis and evaluation) can be seen to have relevance to physical education (this is just one of a range of possible frameworks that could be used to emphasize such potential and has been chosen here because of the similarity in terminology used within its framework and the key concepts of NCPE). Bloom's categories are listed in Table 1.1 in order of perceived complexity, and it could be argued that quality physical education experiences provide children with a wealth of opportunity to develop 'higher order' thinking skills within analysis, synthesis and evaluation.

Learning episode 1.1: Scaffolding of learning

A group of ten-year-old children are playing a small-sided invasion game that they have created using a specified space and a free choice of equipment. The 'rules' they have agreed are that the game is 4 v 4, and that it is a throwing and catching game using a large, soft, spongy ball. The objective of their game is for each team to score a point by throwing the ball into a large hoop positioned at each end of the pitch. The game runs for approximately 5 minutes before the children clearly get frustrated as no-one has yet managed to score a point. The observing teacher engages the group in a discussion about this problem and uses questioning to help the children improve their performance as a group. This questioning centres on ways in which the game could be changed to enable more points to be scored, based on a poster that the teacher has displayed on a wall next to the playground. The 4 points on the poster relate to space (bigger or smaller), task (making it different), equipment (different ball) and people (numbers involved on each team). Considering these questions for a moment, one child suggests to the others that instead of 4 v 4, that they play 5 v 3 so that the 5 attackers have a better chance of scoring. Consensus of opinion follows and within seconds the attacking team have scored.

Table 1.1   Bloom's cognitive domain and physical education

Category	Key words	Skills demonstrated	Primary PE examples
Knowledge: Recall data or information.	defines, describes, identifies, knows, labels, lists, matches, names, outlines, recalls, recognizes, reproduces, selects, states	• observation and recall of information • knowledge of dates, events, places • knowledge of major ideas • mastery of subject matter	• Pupils can identify and list major muscle groups • Pupils write labels to go on task cards showing games skills • Pupils remember the safety rules for swimming at the start of the new term
Comprehension: Understand the meaning, translation, interpolation and interpretation of instructions and problems. State a problem in one's own words.	comprehends, converts, defends, distinguishes, estimates, explains, extends, generalizes, gives examples, infers, interprets, paraphrases, predicts, rewrites, summarizes, translates	• understanding information • grasp meaning • translate knowledge into new context • interpret facts, compare, contrast • order, group, infer causes • predict consequences	• At the start of the lesson, pupils are able to predict effects of warming up • In athletic activities, pupils estimate how far they can run in 10 seconds • Working in groups, pupils compare other children's skill sequences
Application: Use a concept in a new situation or unprompted use of an abstraction. Apply what was learned in the classroom into novel situations in the workplace.	applies, changes, computes, constructs, demonstrates, discovers, manipulates, modifies, operates, predicts, prepares, produces, relates, shows, solves, uses	• use information • use methods, concepts, theories in new situations • solve problems using required skills or knowledge	• In OAA activities, pupils work in groups to solve problems • Pupils transfer gymnastic sequences from floor to apparatus • Pupils demonstrate their work to others

Category	Key words	Skills demonstrated	Primary PE examples
Analysis: Separates material or concepts into component parts so that its organizational structure may be understood. Distinguishes between facts and inferences.	analyses, breaks down, compares, contrasts, diagrams, deconstructs, differentiates, discriminates, distinguishes, identifies, illustrates, infers, outlines, relates, selects, separates	• seeing patterns • organization of parts • recognition of hidden meanings • identification of components	• Pupils identify categories of movements and list actions their partners make in dance activities • Pupils select one aspect of a skill performance to work on • Pupils compare and contrast the work of others
Synthesis: Builds a structure or pattern from diverse elements. Put parts together to form a whole, with emphasis on creating a new meaning or structure.	combines, compiles, composes, creates, devises, designs, explains, generates, modifies, organizes, plans, rearranges, reconstructs, relates, reorganizes, revises, rewrites, summarizes, tells, writes	• use old ideas to create new ones • generalize from given facts • relate knowledge from several areas • predict, draw conclusions	• Pupils plan a sequence of movement in response to a musical stimuli • Pupils combine actions and strategies to outwit opponents • Pupils use knowledge originally gained in gymnastic activities to jump higher in games activities
Evaluation: Make judgements about the value of ideas or materials.	appraises, compares, concludes, contrasts, criticizes, critiques, defends, describes, discriminates, evaluates, explains, interprets, justifies, relates, summarizes, supports	• compare and discriminate between ideas • assess value of theories, presentations • make choices based on reasoned argument • verify value of evidence • recognize subjectivity	• Pupils evaluate and improve own performance having first devised a set of success criteria • Pupils decide on the best strategy to apply to achieve the desired goal • Pupils explain how they have improved their performance

Physical education for all children

If we accept that for many children school is the only context in which they can be physically active and engaged in structured sport (Telama *et al.*, 1997), then the importance of inclusive curricula physical education can be seen to have a critically important role within children's learning. Whilst today's curriculum requirements in England are focused on six activity areas, a renewed focus on the subject's role in lifelong learning, the development of 'physical literacy' and the fostering of affective, cognitive, social and physical skills is necessary to ensure that physical education plays a meaningful, relevant, exciting, purposeful and appropriate role in the education of all children.

The primary school years should, on average, provide around 500 hours of physical education learning across Key Stages 1 and 2 (assuming two lessons per week, each term, for six years). If we add to this total, a 'sixth' of all learning in the current 3–5 Foundation

Stage and take into account out of school hours learning (OSHL), the enormous potential for the subject during early and later childhood becomes apparent. For those charged with leading and developing the primary curriculum and developing associated schemes of work, a pertinent question should be 'what do we want children to be able to do and know at the end of 500 hours of learning?'

This is a significant chunk of time, and when viewed within a targeted, long-term approach to curriculum mapping, it would seem that we currently expect far too little of our children in primary physical education. Planned-for progression from one year group to the next, across transition stages and between schools should enable optimum development in children's knowledge, skills and understanding across the full range of activity areas within curriculum physical education. Equally, it should take into account the full range of social, biological and psychological factors that can impact on children's learning in the physical domain and build on prior experiences in and out of the school setting.

Learning episode 1.2: Is this progression?

A class of Year 6 children arrive at the school hall for a gymnastic activities lesson, their sixth lesson in sequence on the theme of linking actions and using asymmetry. They arrive at the hall as the Year 3 class leave, a transition they are used to as the hall is well used at this school. The Year 6 and Year 3 class teachers have agreed that the first class will get the apparatus out while the Year 6 class will put the apparatus away, thus saving time for more activity. The Year 6 warm up ensues (although space is limited owing to the six preset stations *in situ*) based on a 'full body stretch' that the class learned in Year 4. Once the teacher has finished leading this activity, the children are allocated a 'station' to work at in their small groups in order to practise and refine the movement sequences that have been developed to incorporate asymmetry over the past 5 weeks. Consider the extent to which the learning experience described allows for progression of prior learning and identify any constraints that could be rectified by the teachers.

In the United Kingdom, primary schools have a 'captive audience' of children aged 5 to 11. Curriculum physical education can therefore be seen as the only context for learning in and through physical activity that is fully inclusive. Community sports clubs and school-based extracurricular activities are, by definition, exclusive domains that, for a variety of reasons, are not accessible by all pupils. This has an implication for the identification and development of talented pupils in physical education, where it is suggested that the widest base of participation in physical activity is within primary school curriculum time. High quality physical education teaching in the primary school will ensure that movement experiences are matched to specific needs of individual children, wherever they may sit along a developmental continuum of perceived ability.

Physical growth, development and health

The early and later childhood age phases represent a period of relatively steady physical growth and development (see Chapter 3) and are considered by some to be the greatest window of opportunity for physical skill acquisition and development. The refinement of movement capabilities in the primary years provides a base from which all later physical activity and sport participation can follow throughout life (Gallahue and Ozmun, 1998; Malina, 1996), something that cannot be ignored if an objective for physical education is to promote an enduring and lifelong love of physical activity and sport.

Worryingly, research evidence suggests that, although physical education is consistently ranked as an enjoyable subject by the majority of primary pupils, many later become disaffected from the subject and choose to drop out of physical activity entirely. This is particularly true of girls, although it is clear that the way in which the subject is taught has a direct bearing on perceptions, attitudes and resulting behaviours. In the face of evidence regarding increasing incidents of childhood obesity and associated health concerns, the school environment must do everything it can to promote positive attitudes to healthy and active lifestyles. Recent estimates suggest that, worldwide, one in five children is overweight, with approximately 400,000 others joining this list each year (International Obesity Task Force, 2005). Although there are acknowledged problems concerning the validity of common measures of body mass and the need for sensitivity in handling such issues by teachers (Evans *et al.*, 2005) childhood obesity has been described as a 'pandemic' of the new millennium (Kimm and Obarzanek, 2002).

Research shows that young people who engage in regular physical activity are more likely to make healthy lifestyle choices, including decisions that relate to diet, alcohol and drugs. Whilst we must acknowledge that concepts relating to children's body weight are complex sociological, psychological and biological issues, the promotion of physical activity for all children through quality, enjoyable, relevant and meaningful experiences of physical education in school can play a pivotal role within the wider health education agenda.

The development of physical competences and fostering of positive attitudes towards physicality and the 'embodied self' are the truly unique contributions that quality physical education can offer to the lives of all children. However, as learning in the physical domain is inextricably linked to social, cognitive and affective aspects, wider educational objectives for the subject are possible and desirable. The physical domain may, for some children, be the best context within which to learn – not just with regards physical skills but also knowledge and understanding from across and beyond the formal curriculum.

Movement experiences provide young children with some of their first opportunities for social interaction, problem solving and developing self-esteem, a component of the affective domain that is said to be the most important measure of psychological well-being (Biddle, 1999). Fox (1988, 2000) advocated the role of sports and physical activity participation in enhancing self-esteem, which in turn is thought to lead to enhanced motivation to partic-ipate in similar activities in the future (Sonstroem, 1997).

The primary class teacher

It is clear that teachers approach the subject from a wide range of perspectives and precon-ceptions. We know from our own work in ITT and Continuing Professional Development (CPD) that some pre and in-service teachers feel insecure with regards subject knowledge and simply do not feel confident to teach this very demanding subject away from the confines of their 'normal' classroom. In extreme cases, trainees recount negative experi-ences of the subject and there is little wonder that there may be an initial reluctance to embrace the subject and its enormous potential for teaching and learning.

It is also clear, however, that when the subject is rightly positioned as an inclusive vehicle for learning and as a conduit for child development, even the most reticent trainees begin to appreciate its value and worth. A primary aim of this book is to assist teachers in their work in physical education despite any negative preconceptions founded on earlier life experiences. We hope the text will help to develop subject knowledge and pedagogy and to provide a springboard for the positioning of physical education as one of the most important aspects of pupil learning. Because we approach the subject from a 'develop-mental' perspective, it is also hoped that a 'child upwards' approach, as opposed to a 'sports down model' can influence not only practice in the Foundation Stage, Key Stages 1 and 2, but also through into secondary school years.

Physical education is the only subject that truly engages the whole child and provides a wide range of learning contexts, environments and situations beyond the four walls of the primary classroom. This provides challenges to practitioners who may be justly concerned with class management and safety issues. Whilst these are essential components of effective physical education teaching, bringing about learning must be the main focus and the starting point for the teacher; if this is addressed through careful task and lesson planning, use of appropriate teaching strategies and focused 'assessment for learning', then it could be argued that safe practice and well-behaved children will follow.

Whilst the words physical education and sport are often used interchangeably, we must underline the importance of the word *education* in physical education and the unique contribution that curriculum physical education can make in the education of all children. Sport can be viewed as an outcome of well-taught physical education, or used as an activity approach within a balanced physical education curriculum; 'Sport Education' has also gathered pace and popularity in recent years as a structured and well-rationalized concept (Siedentop, Hastie and van der Mars 2004). However, in ensuring that physical education is placed at the heart of the curriculum, real breadth and balance of experience in individually relevant contexts (some of which may indeed be or become sporting pursuits) can be encouraged.

Government policy and the child

Recent Government policy in the United Kingdom has focused on children, exemplified by the *Every Child Matters* White Paper (DfES, 2003a) and ensuing Children Act (DfES, 2004), which has created a framework around five key goals for every child to achieve, regardless of background:

- Be healthy
- Stay safe
- Enjoy and achieve
- Make a positive contribution
- Achieve economic well-being.

The focus on health is clearly relevant to the physical educator, and those working across the full range of subjects in the primary school should consider too the contribution that their teaching and learning can make to each aim.

As policy makers continue to discuss ways in which education, health and social services can provide integrated, seamless provision and schools take on increased responsibility for children from early years through to upper primary years, we think that the status of physical education in some primary schools has been somewhat reduced. It would seem clear that physical education is extremely well positioned to make a significant contribution to the outcomes of Every Child Matters and those seeking to raise standards in the primary school context should seek connections between subject matter and such wider educational objectives.

The context created by the Children Act provides the profession with an enormous opportunity to rethink physical education from the child's perspective rather than 'from sport downwards'. The growing body of evidence relating to movement and cognition, behaviour, self-esteem and social interaction provides a further spur to policy makers not to neglect a fundamental natural resource that we all have for learning in – and through – our bodies.

The National Physical Education, School Sport and Club Links (PESSCL) strategy was launched by DfES/DCMS in April 2003 to promote the notion of equality through delivery of high quality physical education and school sport (HQPESS). The overarching objective of the strategy is to increase the percentage of 5 to 16 year olds who spend a minimum of two hours a week on HQPESS within and beyond the curriculum. This ambitious strategy includes the ongoing development of school sport partnerships, professional development for in-service teachers, response to the needs of gifted and talented children and young people, an investigation (led by QCA) to disseminate examples of best practice, an initiative to encourage young people to become involved in leadership roles, enhancement of school swimming and fostering of school-club links.

The DfES (2003b) has produced a model to illustrate the components of HQPESS. The model is represented in Figure 1.1. The 'Teaching and learning' components of the model will be the immediate focus of a teacher's own practice in the subject. The model can also be used to reflect on physical education professional development during and beyond ITT.

Figure 1.1 High Quality Physical Education and School Sport (adapted from DfES, 2003b)

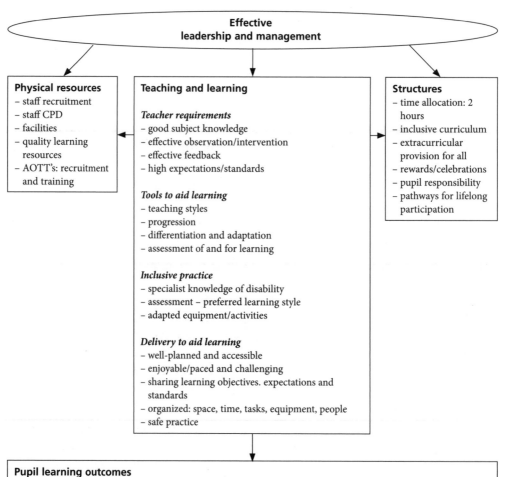

The aims and goals of physical education

There is little doubt regarding the central importance of movement and physical activity in the lives of children and young people. Bailey (1999) asks us to consider the following recent research findings:

- Physical activity play is the first appearing and most frequently occurring expression of play in infants.
- Children in all cultures around the world engage in both spontaneous and rule-governed forms of physical activity.
- Most children would rather take part in physical activities than in any other endeavour.
- They would prefer to succeed in those activities than in classroom-based work.
- Physical competence is a major factor influencing social acceptance in children of all ages and both sexes.
- Regular physical activity can make significant positive contributions to physical, mental and emotional well-being in children.

If we are to provide worthwhile, meaningful, individually relevant and fully inclusive physical learning experiences for children we must consider the wide range of factors that impact on children's learning in the physical domain. This includes events and processes that take place before and during birth and throughout infancy and childhood periods. The physical education planning process must therefore 'start from the child' and build on what each child can already do, moving learning forward to fulfil individual potential in all domains.

Our approach fits within a developmental perspective to teaching and learning. Gallahue and Donnelly (2003) have defined developmental physical education as:

> Physical Education that emphasizes the acquisition of movement skills and increased physical competence based on the unique developmental level of the individual. It recognizes and incorporates the many contributions that systematic, sensitive teaching can make to both the cognitive and affective development of the individual. Developmental Physical Education encourages the uniqueness of the individual and is based on the fundamental proposition that, although motor development is age related, it is not age dependent. (Gallahue and Donnelly, 2003, p. 12)

The basic aim of school-based physical education is to provide activities and experiences that enhance and encourage learning to move and it thereby relies on learning through movement. Gallahue's (1996) assertion that 'a portion of every school day ... should be set aside for large muscle activities' is a model that provides for this to happen in practice. Separating out the difference between the 'learning to move' and 'moving to learn' aims can also be presented as follows:

- the learning to move aim of physical education is based on acquiring and developing fundamental movement skills and helping to maintain and enhance physical fitness;

• the moving to learn aim of physical education is predicated on the fact that effectively taught quality provision of physical education positively affects both the cognitive and the (social-emotional) development of children.

In an integrated and fully educative sense, the emphasis has to be on providing a quality physical education experience from as early as possible in children's development. The process of 'becoming physically educated' by learning to move and learning through movement has been defined in the North American context as follows:

> A physically educated person HAS learned skills necessary to perform a variety of physical activities, IS physically fit, DOES participate regularly in physical activity, KNOWS the implications of and the benefits from involvement in physical activities, and VALUES physical activity and its contributions to a healthy lifestyle.

(NASPE, 1992)

If what is represented here are goals and objectives of our physical education, then we must recognize that a goal is what we aim for and expend effort in achieving. In educational terms, goals are long-term processes, measured through the attainment of a series of objectives. An objective is the means by which we achieve a goal or set of goals. Objectives, therefore, are the observable, measurable or quantifiable statements that guide the individual teacher to select appropriate educational strategies that help their children attain their goals.

A quality physical education programme will establish clearly defined goals and objectives for its intended recipients and the programme designed to provide this will reflect a consistent effort towards the fulfilment of such. Within this the acquisition of movement skills is a primary goal of a developmental approach to teaching physical education. This goal focuses on helping children to become:

• Skilful movers
• Knowledgeable movers
• Healthy movers
• Creative and expressive movers

… in a range and variety of fundamental and increasingly sophisticated (ultimately 'specialized') movement skills.

The goal of 'fitness' maintenance and enhancement focuses on helping children become not just movers who can perform effortlessly, but also ones who are healthy, are informed about what and why they are doing activities, and are enthusiastic and committed movers – all of which contribute to promoting an active lifestyle.

The cognitive learning goals of developmental physical education centre on helping children become both effective multisensory learners and active learners. The role of movement in this process presents it as a viable medium for both perceptual-motor and cognitive concept learning. Similarly, affective development can be fostered by helping children achieve the behaviour goals of becoming self-discovering and cooperative learners. By promoting all of the above goals, teachers can both appreciate and use movement skills teaching as an effective tool to enhance self-esteem, encourage positive socialization, and acknowledge its role in character development.

The following diagram illustrates, for quick reference purposes, the aims and goals of what we interpret developmental physical education to be.

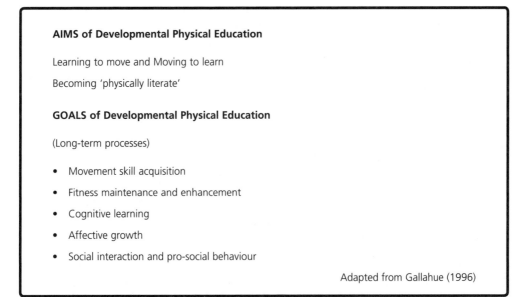

AIMS of Developmental Physical Education

Learning to move and Moving to learn

Becoming 'physically literate'

GOALS of Developmental Physical Education

(Long-term processes)

- Movement skill acquisition
- Fitness maintenance and enhancement
- Cognitive learning
- Affective growth
- Social interaction and pro-social behaviour

Adapted from Gallahue (1996)

Central to the notion of developmental physical education is the critical role of the teacher, who must make carefully considered, informed choices about the nature and level of interaction offered within teaching and learning episodes. Developmental physical educators must therefore be 'reflective practitioners' who are engaged in a constant self-appraisal, rigorous analysis of their teaching and the social context in which they work (Pollard, 2005). Graham, Holt-Hale and Parker (2004) further underline the need for the reflective physical educator to design and implement physical education curricula that match the needs of individual children within a specific context. The use of 'one size fits all' models of physical education provided by 'off the shelf' lesson plans clearly do not fit with this principle, and the teacher who believes in the role and value of primary physical education must be willing to constantly review and adapt approaches to maximize potential for learning. As a truly 'whole child' subject, it is imperative that those charged with delivering what is now commonly termed 'high quality physical education' understand the physical, social, emotional, affective and cognitive needs of the children in their classes.

This text provides a theoretical and practical grounding to developmental physical education and seeks to show how National Curriculum physical education in England (and similar curricula across the world) can be effectively delivered within a developmentally appropriate framework. What follows in the remaining chapters is therefore based on the following tenets which can be seen as a position statement for this book:

- The development of motor competence is at the heart of 'whole child learning' and neglecting to teach physical education ignores a crucial component of learning.
- Physical learning is inextricably linked to learning in other domains.
- Motor development is age *related* but not age *dependent*.
- Children's apparent ability in physical tasks is a result of the unique combination of hereditary (biological), environmental and task factors (to different extents for different children).
- A positive experience of physical education can contribute to the development of self-esteem and a positive self-concept, contributing to lifelong engagement in physical activity.
- Physical education is an opportunity to *bring learning to life* and should not be shackled by adult perceptions of 'letting of steam' or 'just having fun.'
- Curricular physical education is for ALL children, not just those who are deemed to be in need of a 'break' from the classroom or those who perform in school teams.
- The teaching of high quality physical education needs to be seen as a priority by teachers – without an investment of energy, enthusiasm and time, the quality of learning will suffer.

Summary

The time is now right for the role of physical education in the primary context to be emphasized, celebrated and repositioned to take up a central role in the life of every child. This text hopes to contribute to, at the very least, an enhanced enthusiasm, confidence and subject knowledge amongst educators working in these age phases. At best, it is hoped that those students and teachers who are willing and able to become truly reflective, developmental primary physical educators will feel empowered to make a difference in their own contexts and provide children with the quality of experience that is so richly needed and deserved.

This chapter has represented physical education as a vital learning conduit for all children and has introduced a range of themes that could be seen as justification for a raised status for the subject in schools. The teaching and learning of quality physical education experiences can clearly play a big role in reaching broad learning objectives in the primary school context. In some ways, however, the extent to which children enjoy physical education and movement for movement's sake may have been underplayed. The above arguments can be used by practitioners seeking to raise the status of the subject in school, although the uniqueness of physical learning aspects should not be devalued. Physical education is unique; physical education is valuable; and physical education is a fundamental right for every child.

The approach advocated in the following chapters is based on the premise that a 'body and movement curriculum' (or whatever we choose to call the subject area) is a birthright for all children, should lie at the heart of school provision, be fully inclusive to meet the needs of all and provide a stimulus for lifelong involvement in physical activity and healthy lifestyles.

Key Questions

1 What role does 'movement' play in the lives of children?

2 How can we draw upon children's seemingly natural exuberance for movement in the school context?

3 Can we position the curriculum to truly reflect the needs of the whole child?

4 To what extent has your own experience in physical education and sport been 'individually relevant'?

5 What is the status of physical education in the schools you have been in most recently?

Learning tasks

1 Write a short 'reflective' paragraph to summarize your own experiences of physical education in school. List positive and negative outcomes and experiences and begin to consider the implications for your own practice.

2 Consider and note your own 'rationale' or personal philosophy for primary physical education.

3 Consider a definition of a 'physically educated' person. Think about the actions, behaviours and knowledge that this person exhibits and reflect on your role as a physical educator within this process.

4 Reflect on your own strengths and areas for development in the subject. Identify what you need to know to help you become a high quality physical educator.

Links to The Framework of Professional Standards for Teachers

The content and focus of this chapter have direct relevance to the following Qualified Teacher Status standards. (QTS) (TDA, 2007) for those training to teach in primary schools: Q1, Q7, Q10, Q12, Q14, Q16, Q18.

Useful websites

www.afpe.org

The Association for Physical Education. Provides useful information and signposts for resources and membership.

www.dfes.gov.uk/pess

DfES. Physical education and school sport. Information pertaining to the current national strategy.

www.teachernet.gov.uk/pe

Teachernet. This site contains links to a wealth of information including curriculum materials and news items.

www.nc.uk.net

The current National Curriculum documentation, including aims and content of national curriculum physical education.

www.ofsted.gov.uk

OFSTED homepage. Subject inspection reports can be downloaded.

www.qca.org.uk/pess

Qualifications and Curriculum Authority (QCA) – A dedicated site for physical education and school sport, including case studies of how schools have improved quality, and downloadable resources.

The outcome statement of the 2005 World summit on physical education can be accessed via the home page for the International Congress for Sports Science and Physical Education **www.icsspe.org**

http://www.everychildmatters.gov.uk/

Details and background to the Every Child Matters agenda.

http://www.sportfocus.com/reguser/dynabizinfo/download.cfm?number=3037

The position statement from the 2005 UK physical education summit, which includes reference to the quality of primary physical education.

References and further reading

Andrews, J. (1979) *Essays on Physical Education and Sport*. Cheltenham: Stanley Thornes Ltd.

Arnold, P. J. (1979) *Meaning in Movement: Sport and Physical Education*. London: Heinemann.

BAALPE, CCPR, PEAUK and PE ITT Network (2005) *Declaration from the National Summit on Physical Education*. London, 24 January 2005, p. 4.

Available from: http://www.baalpe.org/pdfs/CCPR_summit/CCPR_dec.pdf [accessed on 12 June 2005].

Bailey, R. P. (1999) 'Physical Education: Action, Play and Movement', in J. Riley and R. Prentice (eds) *The Curriculum for 7–11 Year Olds*. London: Paul Chapman Publishing.

Bailey, R. and Pickup, I. (2007) 'Movement Learning', in R. Austin (ed.) *Letting the Outside In*. Stoke on Trent: Trentham Books Ltd.

Bailey, R., Doherty, J. and Pickup, I. (2007) 'Physical Development and Physical Education', in J. Riley (ed.) *Learning in the Early Years: A Guide for Teachers of Children 3–7* (2nd edn). London: Paul Chapman Publishing.

Bailey, R., Armour, K., Kirk, D., Jess, M., Pickup, I. and Sandford, R. (in press) The Educational Benefits Claimed for Physical Education and School Sport: An Academic Review, *Research Papers in Education*.

Barr, S. and Lewin, P. (1994) 'Learning Movement: Integrating Kinaesthetic Sense with Cognitive Skills', *Journal of Aesthetic Education*, **28**(1), 83–94.

Biddle, S. (1999) 'The Motivation of Pupils in Physical Education', in C.A. Hardy and M. Mawer (eds) *Learning and Teaching in Physical Education*. London: Routledge Falmer.

Bloom, B. S. (ed.) (1956) *Taxonomy of Educational Objectives: Book 1, Cognitive Domain*. New York: Longman.

Bruce, T. (1991) *Time to Play in Early Childhood Education*. London: Hodder and Stoughton.

Bruner, J. and Haste, H. (eds) (1987) *Making Sense: The Child's Construction of the World*. London: Methuen.

Davies, M. (2003) *Movement and Dance in Early Childhood* (2nd edn). London: Paul Chapman Publishing.

Dearden, R. F. (1968) *The Philosophy of Primary Education*. London: Routledge and Kegan Paul.

Dennison, P. E. and Dennison, G. E. (1989) *Brain Gym (Teacher's edition). Simple activities for whole brain learning*. Ventura, CA: Edu Kinesthetics.

Dewey, J. (1933) *How We Think; a restatement of the relation of reflective thinking to the educative process.* Boston, MA: Heath.

DfEE (1997) *National Literacy Strategy.* London: DfEE.

DfEE (1999) *National Numeracy Strategy.* London: DfEE.

(DfEE) and Qualification and Curriculum Authority (QCA) (1999) *Physical Education: The National Curriculum for England Key Stages 1–4.* London: QCA.

DfES (2003a) *Every Child Matters.* London: DfES.

DfES (2003b) *The National physical education and school sport professional development programme, primary resource pack, section 3.* London: DfES Publications.

DfES (2004) *Children Act.* London: HMSO.

DfES/DCMS (2003) *Learning Through PE and Sport – a guide to the Physical Education, School Sport and Club Links Strategy.* Annesley: DfES Publications.

Department of Health (2004) *At Least Five a Week: Evidence of impact of physical avctivity and its relationship to health, a report from the Chief Medical officer.* London: DoH.

Dewey, J. (1933) *How We Think: A restatement of the relation of reflective thinking to the educative process.* Boston, MA: Heath.

Evans, J., Rich, E., Allwood, R. and Davies, B. (2005) 'Fat fabrications', *British Journal of Teaching Physical Education*, **36**(4), 18–20.

Fisher, J. (2000) *Starting From the Child, Teaching and Learning from 3 to 8* (2nd edn). Buckingham: Open University Press.

Fox, K. (1988) 'The Self-esteem Complex and Youth Fitness', *Quest*, **40**, 230–46.

Fox, K. (2000) 'The Effects of Exercise on Self-Perceptions and Self-Esteem', in S. Biddle, K. Fox and S. Boutcher (eds) *Physical Activity and Psychological Well-being.* London: Routledge.

Gallahue, D. L. (1996) *Developmental Physical Education for Today's Children.* Duboque, IA: Brown & Benchmark.

Gallahue, D. L. and Donnelly, F. C. (2003) *Developmental Physical Education for all Children* (4th edn), Champaign, IL: Human Kinetics.

Gallahue, D. L. and Ozmun, J. (1998) *Understanding Motor Development: Infants, Children, Adolescents, Adults.* Duboque, IA: McGraw-Hill.

Gardner, H. (1993) *Frames of Mind: The Theory of Multiple Intelligences* (2nd edn). New York: Basic Books.

Graham, G., Ann Holt-Hale, S. and Parker, M. (2004) (6th edn) *Children Moving: A Reflective Approach to Teaching Physical Education*, Boston, MA: McGraw-Hill.

Hannaford, C. (1995) *Smart Moves: Why Learning is Not All in Your Head.* Arlington, VA: Great Ocean Publishers.

Harter, S. (1987) 'The Determinants and Mediational Role of Global Self-worth in Children', in N. Eisenberg (ed.) *Contemporary Topics in Developmental Psychology.* New York: Wiley.

Haydn-Davies, D. (2005) 'How does the concept of physical literacy affect what is and might be the practice of physical education?', *British Journal of Teaching Physical Education*, **36**(3), 45–8.

Independent Sports Review (ISR) (2005) *Raising the Bar: The final report of the Independent Sports review.* London: ISR.

International Obesity Task Force (2005) *EU Platform briefing paper.* London: IOTF.

Kimm, S.Y.S. and Obarzanek, E. (2002) 'Childhood Obesity: A New Pandemic of the New Millennium', *Pediatrics*, **110**, 1003–1007.

Malina, R. M. (1996) 'Tracking physical activity and physical fitness across the lifespan', *Research Quarterly for Exercise and Sport,* **67**(3), 48–57.

Morris, V. C. (1966) *Existentialism in Education*. London: Harper & Row, p. 116.

NASPE (1992) *Outcomes of Quality Physical Education Programs*. Reston, VA: AAHPERD.

Nichols, B. (1990) *Moving and Learning: The Elementary School Physical Education Experience*. St Louis. MI: Times Mirror/Mosby College Publishing.

Pollard, A. (2005) *Reflective Teaching: Evidence-informed Professional Practice* (2nd edn). London: Continuum.

QCA (2005) *Futures – meeting the challenge, a curriculum for the future: subjects consider the challenge*. London: QCA.

Sallis, J. and Owen, N. (1999) *Physical Activity and Behavioral Medicine*. Thousand Oaks, CA: Sage.

Siedentop, D., Hastie, P. A. and van der Mars, H. (2004) *Complete Guide to Sport Education*. Champaign, IL: Human Kinetics.

Smith, A. B. (1993) 'Early Childhood Educare: Seeking a Theoretical Framework in Vygotsky's Work', *International Journal of Early Years Education*, **1**(1).

Sonstroem, R. J. (1997) 'Physical Activity and Self-esteem', in W. P. Morgan (ed.) *Physical Activity and Mental Health*. Washington, DC: Taylor and Francis.

Speednet (2000) 'Primary School Physical Education – Speednet survey makes depressing reading', *British Journal of Physical Education*, **30**(30), 19–20.

Telama, R., Yang, X., Laakso, L. and Viikari, J. (1997) 'Physical Activity in Childhood and Adolescence as Predictor of Physical Activity in Young Adulthood', *American Journal of Preventive Medicine*, **13**, 317–22.

Training and Development Agency for Schools (TDA) (2007) *Draft Revised Professional Standards for Teachers in England*. London: TDA. Available from http://www.tda.gov.uk/upload/resources/pdf/d/draft_revised_standards_framework_jan_2007.pdf [accessed 5 March 2007].

UNESCO (1978) *Charter for Physical Education and Sport*. Paris: UNESCO.

Vygotsky, L. S. (1978) *Mind and Society: The Development of Higher Mental Process*. Cambridge, MA: Harvard University Press.

Whitehead, M. E. (2001) 'The Concept of Physical Literacy', *European Journal of Physical Education,* **6**, 127–38.

Whitehead, M. E. (2006) 'Developing the Concept of Physical Literacy', *ICSSPE Newsletter,* Summer.

Whitehead, M. E. with Murdoch, E. (2006) 'Physical Literacy and Physical Education – Conceptual Mapping', *Physical Education Matters*, **1**(1), Summer.

Wood, D., Bruner, J. and Ross, G. (1976) 'The Role of Tutoring in Problem Solving', *Journal of Child Psychology and Psychiatry*, **17**(2), 89–100.

An Introduction to Motor Development

Human development is a form of chronological unfairness, since late-comers are able to profit by the labors of their predecessors without paying the same price.

Alexander Herzen

Introduction

Chapter 1 made a case for a developmental approach to the teaching of physical education and gave a number of definitions of what this means, linked to broader educational theory. A simplistic interpretation might be to describe a developmental approach to teaching physical education as being that which takes full account of the individual child's physical needs. Within this there is an inbuilt premise that physical development is a lifelong process beginning at birth and only ceasing with death. In other words, throughout life all individuals will encounter motor skill development. The phases and stages of growth and physical development through which any individual will pass during a lifetime will each bring particular changes to how an individual copes with movement challenges, brought about by the unique interaction of an individual's personal biological make-up and the environments within which they are required to function.

A starting premise therefore might suggest that, for those charged with teaching children movement concepts and skills, and by implication, physical education, it is essential to possess knowledge about child development and growth. Teachers need to know when a child is ready to access new challenges and tasks that are appropriate to their individual and developing physical needs. Studying motor development accesses knowledge which describes processes of growth and physical development across a lifetime, and therefore – because lifelong motor development can be broken down into ages, stages and phases – a sound knowledge base can be achieved and used to inform practice. Knowledge of motor development can help the primary physical educator to plan appropriate tasks that are relevant to the phase of development demonstrated by individual children, and provides a sound base upon which to build learning experiences matched to specific, identifiable need.

Key points

- Motor development theory has been influenced by a range of concepts and perspectives over time and is an ever-evolving field of enquiry.
- Motor development describes the changes in the body's ability to move throughout the life cycle.
- Studying motor development helps the practitioner to be aware of individual children's unique needs, which in turn informs the planning, teaching and assessment cycle.
- A 'dynamic systems perspective' is favoured by many developmental physical educators as this describes how an individual's motor development is a unique product of hereditary, environmental and task factors.
- Efficient motor function is reliant on a variety of components and a well-taught developmental physical education curriculum will ensure that every child has access to activities which foster motor development.

Defining motor development

In essence, motor development describes processes of growth and physical development which occur across a lifetime and represent the continuous change in motor behaviour throughout the life cycle. The following represent a sample of definitions of the term 'motor development' each with its own particular slant and emphasis:

> Motor development is progressive change in one's motor behaviour brought about by interaction of the movement task with the biology of the individual and the conditions of the learning environment. (Gallahue and Donnelly, 2003)

Motor development is the sequential, continuous age-related process whereby movement behaviour changes. (Haywood and Getchell, 2001)

Kathleen Berger (2001) offers us a more general but complementary definition of human development which brings together such understanding with a scientific slant:

The study of human development is a science that seeks to understand how people change over time. Sometimes these changes are linear – gradual, steady, and predictable – but more often are not. (p. 31)

There is some common ground and general agreement about the principles in play here but essentially the message is that motor development is concerned with the changes to an individual's motor performance brought about by the interaction among the requirements of a task being confronted at any given time, the unique biology of the individual, and the particular conditions of the environment in which this is taking place. Put another way, every individual is different, will confront a given task in their own unique way and will adapt to the environment they are working in differently to others.

Motor development studies

The study of motor development involves the examination of the characteristics of motor behaviour as they change over time as a consequence of maturation and experience. A key purpose of studying human development theory, and what it tells us particularly about how children learn physical skills, is to develop a knowledge base for the effective teaching of physical education. The aim of equipping those charged with delivering appropriate, relevant, meaningful, exciting and enjoyable physical education depends on knowing what children's physical needs are at particular points of their physical development – taking into account both natural growth processes and the broader aims of education.

This contributes to what David Gallahue, Kathleen Heywood and Kathleen Berger, among others, describe as a *developmental approach* to the teaching of the subject, where the child is central and catered for in the learning process depending on specific physical needs at any given time. This is particularly crucial during primary school years and shifts thinking and planning away from age-group activity descriptions to a model based on each individual child. This notion supports Fisher's (2000) recommendation to 'start from the child' and fits with current attempts to personalize learning (DfES, 2004; Pollard and James, 2004) within the Every Child Matters (DfES, 2003) agenda.

A developmental physical education framework advocates an age-related rather than an age-dependent philosophy. It is the reason why it is essential that those training to teach physical education in primary schools (and those already doing so) are able to articulate a personal philosophy based on this premise.

Individual appropriateness is the key concept of developmental physical education based on the proposition that each child has his or her own unique timing and pattern of personal growth and development. It is therefore crucial that the activities children engage in as part of their physical education at school are geared to their stage of motor development and level of skill learning. Additionally, such movement learning provision should also take into account the individual child's state of motor and health-related fitness, and stages of social, cognitive and affective development.

Age-group appropriateness is of only secondary importance in the developmental physical education programme. It is essential to note that a developmental physical education curriculum is *not* based on chronological or year group categorization but *is* influenced by both. Children quite naturally diverge from expected age-group patterns of behaviour across their formative years – some may have confirmed special educational needs that require specific modifications to learning programmes, whereas others can be successfully accommodated within provision by careful attention to the concept of individual appropriateness. The key message here is therefore the much used claim that children are not miniature adults.

An introduction to the basic elements of motor development provides us with an understanding of the changes in movement competencies that occur throughout life. This enables the practitioner to:

- Compare and contrast motor development with other related fields of human movement study – like motor learning, exercise physiology and biomechanics.
- Demonstrate knowledge of the various forms of analysis that are used in motor development studies.
- Identify and describe with validity the major factors that influence motor development across the life span.
- Identify and describe a pool of knowledge about the anatomical and physiological factors that impact on motor development.
- Demonstrate a well founded familiarity with a variety of theoretical models of human development.
- Utilize for professional practice a theoretical framework that acknowledges the usefulness of ongoing study into the ever-evolving world of motor development theory.

The importance of examining the influential frameworks of **human development** that have impacted on theories of **motor development** studies exemplifies these points. Four frameworks introduced here are:

- **Phase-stage theory**: a descriptive theory based on the view that there are universal age periods characterized by typical behaviours which occur in phases or stages, last for certain lengths of time and are invariant.

- **Developmental task theory**: a predictive theory that contends that there are essential tasks that individuals must accomplish within a specified time frame if they are to function effectively and meet the demands placed on them by society.
- **Developmental milestone theory**: focuses on subtle strategic indicators of how far development has progressed and views development as an unfolding and intertwining of developmental processes, not as a neat transition from one stage to another.
- **Ecological theory** (also known as **contextual theory**): a theory that is both descriptive and explanatory and views development as a function of the environmental context and historical time frame in which one lives. The study of human ecology from a developmental perspective is a matter of studying the relationship of individuals to their environment and to one another.

A common thread for each framework is that the process of development is viewed as hierarchical, that is, the individual proceeds from general to specific, and from simple to complex, in gaining mastery and therefore an element of control over his or her environment. This is summarized in Table 2.1 which gives an overview of the different conceptual approaches adopted by significant human developmental theorists. Such studies have successfully informed the developing field of theoretical perspectives in motor development. Phase-stage, developmental milestone and developmental task theories make it clear that the human organism, through all aspects of its development, is moving from comparatively simple forms of existence to more complex and sophisticated levels of development. Until more recently these levels of development have been expressed primarily in terms of the cognitive and affective behaviours of the individual, with at best only indirect attention given to motor development. Ecological theories, however (particularly dynamic systems theory and behaviour setting theory), offer new perspectives on development and are particularly relevant to the study of motor behaviour.

Although the theoretical formulations of Erikson, Piaget, Havighurst and their ilk are of value, none adequately address motor development in any great detail. It is important to acknowledge that such theoretical viewpoints often focus only on specific aspects of development, for example cognitive or affective factors. In other words, developmentalists with a particular perspective tend to study certain behaviours or age spans. This can be seen with the 'maturationists', who focus on the infant period of growth and development, whereas the more descriptive developmentalists have a focus on later childhood and adolescence. Theorists who advocate an information-processing perspective focus specifically on age differences, whereas those studying from an ecological perspective are focused on the transitions from one skill to another, like crawling to walking to running.

New students of motor development must look beyond what they assume as happening across a life span and consider the more important processes that can be attributed to observed changes in motor behaviour. Knowing why you teach the way you teach is informed by an ability to interpret knowledge, to be able to sift through a range of theoretical standpoints and recognize the benefits and limitations of what each offers. In

Table 2.1 Conceptual frameworks for human development

Conceptual approach	Representative theorists	Research focus on
Phase-stage theory 'Universal age periods characterized by certain types of behaviour'	Sigmund Freud (1927) Erik Erikson (1963, 1980) Arnold Gessell (1928, 1954)	From birth through to childhood – psychosexual development Life span psychosocial development Maturational processes in the central nervous system – from birth to childhood
Developmental task theory 'Tasks to be achieved by a certain time'	Robert Havighurst (1953, 1972)	From infancy through to old age – the interaction of biology and society on developmental maturity
Developmental milestone theory 'Convenient guidelines for development to be gauged'	Jean Piaget (1969)	Cognitive development as an interactive process between biology and the environment – from infancy through to childhood
Ecological theory (dynamic systems branch) 'Studying the relationship of individuals to their environment and to one another'	Nicholas Bernstein (1967) Kugler, Kelso and Turvey (1982)	Life span development as a discontinuous, self-organizing, transactional process dictated by the individual and their environment
Ecological Theory (Behaviour Setting branch) 'Factors within the environment determining development'	Roger Barker (1978) Urie Bronfenbrenner (1979)	The individual's development as a function of their unique interpretation of specific environmental settings transacting with the sociological and historical milieu

practical terms, for teachers this is translated into setting appropriate tasks for children to work on, that they are ready for because they are at a particular stage of physical and cognitive development, delivered in an environment conducive to advancing learning, and taught in a style that facilitates individual learning.

Perspectives on motor development

Motor development is a relatively new field of study and research and as such there are evolving, ongoing and important issues under review, some of which remain unresolved. In essence, motor development is a product of its own history in as much as various theoretical perspectives have dominated thinking for a time, only to be replaced or further developed eventually by another perspective. Such new perspectives often help to advance our knowledge by introducing fresh ideas and new explanations for human behaviour. The importance of education professionals being aware of this and being able to interpret explanations accordingly to help inform what and how to provide for the individual learner's needs is essential in pursuing the aim of providing quality learning experiences. It follows that a depth of knowledge about what processes are at play in affecting motor behavioural change is part of this understanding and is therefore influential in determining the nature of activity provided to match those needs.

It is therefore essential to be able to keep knowledge updated, to understand the terminology used in the field, and appreciate the underpinning tenets that characterize all viewpoints of a developmental perspective; developmentalists, no matter their theoretical assumptions, view behaviour as a point on a continuum of change. It is a fact that the human body and its component systems are always changing – naturally through growth and development, and then the ageing process, each impacting on an individual's motor development throughout the life span. Developmentalists relate observed behaviour to the behaviour that preceded it and to the behaviour that will likely follow it.

Biological versus psychological perspectives

A basic view of how motor competency develops in humans would be to simply suggest that it is all part of growth and maturity, and will happen naturally. The combination of nutrition and activity will prompt physical growth and the unique biology of the individual will determine the particular characteristics through the infancy, childhood, adolescence and adulthood phases of life. A psychological perspective would suggest that alongside this is the need for the individual to adapt to the particular environment conditions (as characterized by Jean Piaget's phases of cognitive development), or the particular inherited traits that influence development from conception, and continue to have impact on development throughout life.

However, the field of motor development study has been influenced over time, with differing perspectives being prominent for periods, and others emerging as research and enquiry has unearthed further insight and knowledge about human development, and more pertinently, how this might inform motor behaviour throughout the life span. The following perspectives have all (over time and with different influencing factors in play) influenced motor development theory.

The **maturation perspective** advocates the notion that different systems (in particular the central nervous system) control or dictate motor development; the environment really doesn't affect one's developmental course. In other words, motor development is an internal or innate process; it also follows that the indicators of motor development happening in any one individual are signposted by qualitative and discontinuous events, such as the onset of crawling or walking.

The **descriptive perspective** was much influenced by use of many different standardized tests and norms for educational purposes. Motor developmentalists such as Anna Espenschade (see for example, Espenschade, 1947), Ruth Glassow (see for example, Glassow and Kruse, 1960) and G. Lawrence Rarick (see for example, Rarick and Dobbins, 1975) described children's performance in terms of quantitative scores on motor performance tests. For example, they described the average running speed and jumping and throwing distances of children at specific ages. Clearly there were limitations to the credibility of the results and what they could tell us about child development *per se*, not just being overtly descriptive but disregarding body shape, mass and size components of different children in the same age group.

The **behavioural perspective** is a branch of ecological theory that contends that the specific environmental conditions of one's 'life space' account for a large portion of individual variation. Different settings evoke different responses from individuals and hence lead to different patterns of development. An obvious example here would be the differences afforded to a child growing up in an urban or rural setting.

The **cognitive perspective** as characterized by Piaget's cognitive development theory, places primary emphasis on the acquisition of cognitive thought processes. Gleaned from careful observation of infants and children, his insight into the structures behind cognitive development, giving us developmental phases from birth to 11 years, has been hugely influential since the late 1960s. Piaget's theories recognize the importance of movement as key factors in the acquisition of increased cognitive structures, particularly for infants and pre-school years. Using chronological age as only a broad and general indicator of cognitive functioning, the observed behaviours of young children convinced Piaget that these represented *the* primary indicators of the individual child's ever-increasing cognitive complexity. His developmental phases (*sensorimotor* – birth to 2 years, *preoperational* – 2 to 7 years, *concrete operations* – 7 to 11 years, *formal operations* – 12 years and over) are an outcome of this research which has stood as a theoretical model for practitioner's over time.

The **information processing perspective** emerged during the 1960s and 1970s and is commonly associated with motor behaviour and development. It stresses the environment as the main driving force of motor development, and hinges its theory on the fact that humans are generally passive in their learning, waiting for a stimulus, from some external or environmental input, before responding. Researchers in this area have studied various areas of performance, such as attention, memory and the effects of feedback, across age levels. By studying the results firstly of young adults, then children and older adults, comparisons were possible and processes were identified that control movement and change over time. Within this framework, important links were also made to perceptual motor development in children, linked to some learning disabilities delaying perceptual motor development.

The **ecological perspective** stresses the interaction of all body systems and the inseparable nature of the individual, environment, and task. According to this perspective the consideration of the interaction of all elements (body type, motivation, temperature and equipment size) has to be taken into account to fully understand the emergence of a motor skill (such as 'kicking' as detailed by Roberton, 1989). In other words, all systems play a part in the resultant movement regardless of any one element playing a greater part than others because of their interdependence on one another. Because these different systems change throughout a life span, the conclusion to be drawn is that motor development is a life span process.

The **dynamic systems perspective** is a branch of ecological theory that views development as a nonlinear, discontinuous (enabling new movement patterns to replace old ones), self-organizing process composed of several factors – namely the task, the individual, and the environment – operating separately and in concert that actually determine the rate, sequence and extent of development. It is very appropriate for explaining the developmental changes that might trigger the reorganization of a movement to a less efficient pattern than previously performed, because positive changes do not necessarily occur in all systems over the entire span of adulthood. Lifestyle or disease or injury might strike different systems in different ways and have a range of impact.

It is important to remember that these various theoretical viewpoints often focus in their own particular way on only specific aspects of development; that is, developmentalists with a particular perspective tend to study certain behaviours or age spans – maturationists focus on infancy, whereas descriptive developmentalists focus on later childhood and adolescence. Motor development should be viewed as the progressive change in an individual's movement behaviour throughout a life cycle, marked with a continuous process of change to the systems over a life span. This perspective offers a non-reliance on stage-like or age dependency viewpoints – it does not allow for development to be domain specific, but acknowledges that change that is both positive and negative throughout life.

Models of motor development

Out of the previous section it is appropriate, therefore, that a theoretical model of motor development that integrates elements of each theoretical viewpoint, including a dynamic systems and behaviour setting perspective, is put forward in order to be able to describe and explain this important aspect of human development. This has been achieved with some success by David Gallahue (with colleagues) who has introduced a lifespan model, or 'hourglass' perspective, as shown in Figure 2.1.

The model is both explanatory and descriptive and suggests what typical phases and stages of development may be. It emphasizes the life span nature of motor development, and offers students a visual reference point that illustrates how inherited characteristics, the environment and the uniqueness of the individual impact on the tasks that promote movement skill development. By representation of both the processes and the products of motor development, we are presented with a constant reminder of the individuality of the learner.

Infant reflexes are identified as the first forms of human movement, followed by approximate periods of development categorized as phases. It is also illustrated that the sequence

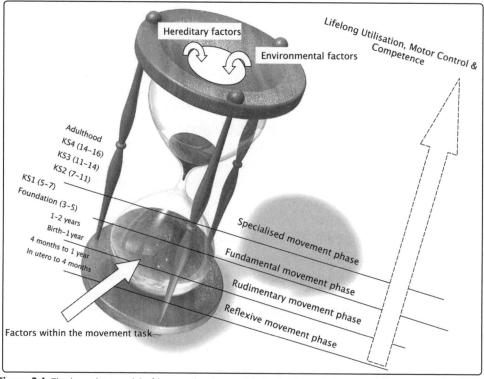

Figure 2.1 The hourglass model of human development (adapted from Gallahue and Ozmun, 2002)

of movement skill acquisition during the *rudimentary movement phase* is fixed but the rate is variable – dictated by *affordances* (which promote or encourage developmental change) and *rate limiters* or controllers (constraints that serve to impede or retard development) contained in any given task, the particular individual and the nature of the environment. All have a profound effect on the development of mature fundamental skills and the progression through to the specialized movement phase which relies on an underpinning maturity of fundamental skill development.

The hourglass model suggests that the primary goal of a person's motor development and movement education is to accept the challenge of change in the continuous process of gaining and maintaining motor control and competence throughout a lifetime. Overall the hourglass model is a helpful heuristic device for conceptualizing and explaining the process of motor development and reiterates the fact that understanding the process of motor development helps to explain how movement skill learning occurs, which is crucial to developmentally appropriate instruction – a key message for teaching.

In addition, the hourglass model affords us the opportunity to acknowledge each individual's unique timetable for development and the acquisition of abilities, specifically in this case, movement competence. Each individual's 'biological clock' is to an extent predictable, particularly when it comes to the sequence of movement skill acquisition during pre-school and infant periods. However, the hourglass model reminds us that the rate and extent to which this happens is determined on an individual basis, and is significantly influenced by what is expected of the specific movement task demands themselves.

The ability to move with freedom, comfort and with a sense of purpose are all attributes that we associate with the competent mover. If we add to this the benefits that these abilities bring, alongside a broader educational perspective, we can see the potential for impact of a well-taught physical education curriculum. However, it is clear that many children appear less coordinated or competent than others, or for whom a sequential and smooth transition between stages and phases of motor development appears difficult. Figure 2.2 shows a moving child and a range of components that contribute to what can be termed 'movement competence'.

In David Stewart's book *The Right to Movement* (1990) we are presented with a very useful insight into the key elements practitioners need to consider when dealing with children who are seemingly not developing physically at the same rate as their peers. With a standpoint that 'physical education is the development of a child's motor function', Stewart advocates at the same time the rights and entitlement to a full physical education programme for such children. His ideas examine the importance of each *component of efficient motor function* and what happens if any of these are removed, using a pyramid construct to illustrate his thoughts.

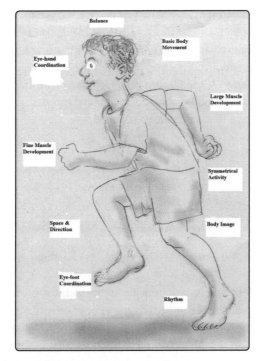

Figure 2.2 Components that contribute to movement competence

Components of developmental physical education

By identifying ten components of efficient motor function we gain an informed picture of the importance of providing the opportunities to nurture these developmental needs. These components are:

1 **Symmetrical activity** – the establishment of managing the difference between the right and left hand sides of the body; development of both sides of the body is necessary because this leads to a greater efficiency of movement and balance.

2 **Basic body movement** – training in basic body movement provides children with an ability to play games and take part in activities; through movement children learn further about their environment, their bodies and the body's relationship with space and direction.

3 **Large muscle development** – large muscle activities start children towards the development of their bodies in readiness for later life. The strengthening of the muscles around the pelvic and shoulder girdles in particular helps them to be able to carry out their daily tasks with vigour and alertness; the emotional stresses placed on children in school settings can be better met if they have a strong body.

4 **Fine muscle development** – during pre-school years children develop hand-muscle control in a haphazard and rather aimless manner – as a result many children are deficient in the area of fine muscle and hand dexterity. It is important for children to develop individual strength, finger coordination, and to begin their symmetrical training in the use of both hands. There are also necessary procedures to implement so as to enable children who have difficulty in tracking objects with their eyes to access learning – another important area for fine muscle development.

5 **Eye–hand coordination** – the combination of eyes and hands working together is necessary for the achievement of many tasks and experiences. Many children lack the ability visually to steer their hands through space to accomplish an appointed task.

6 **Eye–foot coordination** – children need to be able to control the movement and direction of their bodies by using their legs and feet to greatest advantage. Children need to be provided with experiences designed to correlate visual steering with movement of the feet.

7 **Body image** – children need to discover how their bodies move; they have to be able to sort out and distinguish one part of their body from another. Children begin to develop this awareness during infancy; so that this is further developed (and maximized to its highest degree) they need regular activities. If children develop a sound image of their bodies, they will have a base on which to build perceptual skills which will be required in future classroom activities and for life generally.

8 **Balance** – balance is the ability to sustain control of the body when using both sides simultaneously, individually or alternately. This involves transference of weight forwards, backwards and sideways. The ability to balance is essential in all locomotive tasks – if children have good balance their bodies can act in an integrated manner, freeing their minds to concentrate on related or abstract matters.

9 ***Rhythm*** – the development of rhythm helps children develop coordinated body management. It leads to an efficiency and ease of movement, characterized by flow and coordination of movement action.

10 ***Space and direction*** – as part of developing body image awareness children must be able to identify their body position relative to their surroundings. They must be able to plan and execute an efficient course of action when moving from one position to another. The children's awareness of space and direction helps them to read from left to right (in Europe and America at least) and to form letters in an organized way – likewise, for movement needs, the ability to move freely in limited space occupied by others necessitates spacial awareness and the ability to change direction, sometimes quickly and deftly.

By use of a construct that groups the ten components into a pyramid structure (shown in Figure 2.3), thereby showing a group of building bricks to represent the child's body, we are able to consider what happens if any of these bricks were removed. For example, if number 10 were removed, the space and direction component, children would experience problems with movement which would involve locomotive elements of any sort. If a further function were removed, say the eye–hand coordination element, an intensification of problems would ensue, resulting in children with major deficits to their motor function capabilities. Add a shortfall of, say large muscle development, and we are moving into the realms of

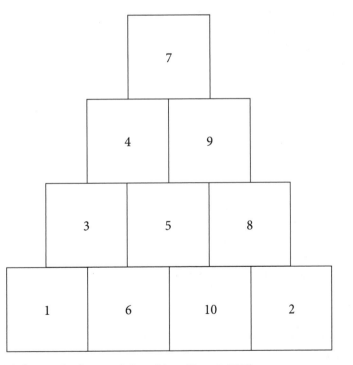

Figure 2.3 Pyramid of motor development (adapted from Stewart, 1990)

serious motor function deficiency. The knock-on effects to simply sitting in a classroom setting, let alone the skills required to manipulate a pencil or paint brush, illustrate the importance of servicing such needs with well planned and appropriate activity for the individual child, and reinforces the concept of a developmental curriculum that services the needs of all children.

Summary

In order to help each child achieve their full potential, the educator must ensure that the best possible provision for the learner is offered. Following the introductory review of theories and models of motor development above, we suggest here broad aims for a physical education curriculum, applicable from the early years through to secondary schooling:

Physical development provision

    to stimulate growth
    to enhance physical development
    to provide healthy exercise

Movement development provision

    to build on existing movement vocabulary
    to develop coordination and body tension
    to extend movement vocabulary

Movement skill acquisition

    to develop fundamental motor skills to the mature stage
    to introduce new motor skills
    to increase knowledge of dynamics of movement
    to develop coordination
    to teach accuracy in movement

Movement confidence development

    to teach movement observation skills
    to develop movement experimentation and expression
    to enhance self-expression
    to enhance self-confidence, self-image and self-esteem

General education

    to teach movement observation
    to teach appropriate vocabulary for discussing and explaining movement
    to stimulate thought processes
    to expect quality work from children

to encourage independence in and ownership of learning

to learn respect in cooperation and competition

to enhance positive attitudes towards health-related exercise

to provide experiences that teach children to plan, perform and evaluate their movement learning

to sustain feelings of enjoyment and well-being in physical activity

It is crucial, therefore that teachers ensure that content, activities and the range/variety of provision works towards these aims and takes into account the following features of high quality and developmental physical education, which should seek to:

Emphasize the acquisition of motor control and movement competency based on the unique developmental level of the individual.

Recognize and incorporate the many contributions that systematic, sensitive teaching can make to both the cognitive and affective development of the individual.

Encourage the uniqueness of the individual, based on the fundamental proposition that although motor development is age related, it is not age dependent.

In doing so, teachers will ensure, through making appropriately informed decisions about what, when and how to teach, that curriculum content is based primarily on the appropriateness of the activity for the individual and only secondarily on the appropriateness of the activity for a certain age group (Gallahue, 1996). For physical education to achieve what it commonly sets out to do, the structure, content and delivery must:

- focus specifically on the relationship between the particular requirements of a given or set task; on the unique individual biology of the individual; and on the conditions of the learning environment in which the learning is to take place;
- recognize that age-group appropriateness provides only general guidance for activity selection;
- focus on movement skill acquisition and fitness enhancement;
- insist on the individual appropriateness of developmental movement experiences;
- utilize learning mediums that are fun;
- emphasize moving and learning rather than sitting, waiting and watching;
- promote individual standards of success and achievement that minimize failure.

Key Questions

1 What do you understand by the term motor development?
2 How do the theories of and perspectives on motor development described above relate to your own practice as a primary physical educator?
3 How has your own experience in physical education matched personal learning needs (as brought about by hereditary, environmental and task factors)?

4 Does the physical education you see in primary schools meet the specific needs of individual children in each class?

5 What do you need to know (i.e. what specific knowledge, skills and understanding) in order to implement the principles introduced above?

Learning tasks

1 There is a school of thought that suggests children develop their motor skills automatically. If this were the case then instruction, teaching and practice of skills would be unnecessary. If one believes that motor skills develop automatically, physical education becomes an extra that can be eliminated to save resources in an increasingly accountable and value-for-money driven world. Where does this fit with your own view of the place of the subject in the overall education of children in the primary school?

2 Observe a group or class of children in Key Stage 2 physical education. Consider and describe the motor competencies that can be seen and identify children who are working at different levels of attainment. Have the tasks been designed with their specific needs in mind? How could the tasks be designed to be more individually relevant to each learner?

3 For one of the observed children, consider removing a variety of different components from the 'Pyramid of Motor Development.' What are the implications of doing so and what would happen if other components were to be removed?

Links to the Framework of Professional Standards for Teachers

The content and focus of this chapter have direct relevance to the following Qualified Teacher Status (QTS) standards (TDA, 2007) for those training to teach in primary schools: Q5, Q8, Q12, Q15, Q16, Q18b, Q19a.

Useful websites

http://www.aahperd.org/naspe/template.cfm?template=peappropriatepractice/index.html

For (US) guidance relating to developmentally appropriate practices in physical education.

http://www.tlrp.org/documents/personalised_learning.pdf

Teaching and learning research programme.

http://www.standards.dfes.gov.uk/personalisedlearning/

For information regarding personalized learning.

References and further reading

Bailey, R. and MacFayden, T. (2000) *Teaching Physical Education 5–11*. London: Continuum.

Berger, K. S. (2001) *The Developing Person Through the Life Span*. New York: Worth Publishers.

DfEE (2001) *Special Educational Needs and Disability Act*. London: HMSO.

DfES (2003) *Every Child Matters*. London: DfES.

DfES (2004) *A National Conversation about Personalised Learning*. Annesley: DfES. Available from: http://www.standards.dfes.gov.uk/personalisedlearning/downloads/personalisedlearning. Pdf [accessed on 20 July 2006].

Espenschade, A. (1947) 'Motor Development', *Review of Educational Research*, **17**(5), 354–61.

Fisher, J. (2000) *Starting from the Child*. Buckingham: Open University Press.

Gallahue, D. L. (1996) *Developmental Physical Education for Today's Children*. Dubuque, IW: Brown & Benchmark.

Gallahue, D. L. and Donnelly, F. C. (2003) *Developmental Physical Education for All Children*. Champaign IL: Human Kinetics.

Gallahue, D. L. and Ozmun, J. (2002) *Understanding Motor Development: Boston, MA: McGraw-Hill Infants, Children, Adolescents, Adults* (5th edn).

Glasgow, R. L. and Kruse, P. (1960) 'Motor Performance of Girls Aged 6–14 Years', *Research Quarterly*, **31**, 426–31.

Haywood, K. M. and Getchell, N. (2001) *Life Span Motor Development*. Champaign, IL: Human Kinetics.

Jess, M. (2004) *Basic Moves*. Edinburgh: The University of Edinburgh.

Last, G. (2004) *Personalising Learning: Adding Value to the Learning Journey through the Primary School*. London: DfES.

Maude, P. (2001) *Physical Children, Active Teaching*. Buckingham: Open University Press.

Pollard, A. and James, M. (eds) (2004) *Personalised Learning: A Commentary by the Teaching and Learning Research Programme*. Swindon Economic and Social Research Council (ESRC). Available from: http://www.tlrp.org/documents/personalised_learning.pdf [accessed on 12 July 2006].

Rarick, G. L. and Dobbins, A. (1975) 'Basic Components in the Motor Performance of Children Six to Nine Years of Age', *Medicine and Science in Sports*, **17**, 105–10.

Roberton, M. A. (1989) 'Motor Development: Recognizing our Roots, Charting our Future', *Quest*, **41**, 213–23.

Stewart, D. (1990) *The Right to Movement – Motor Development in Every School*. London: Falmer Press.

Training and Development Agency for Schools (TDA) (2007) *Draft Revised Professional Standards for Teachers in England*. London: TDA. Available from http://www.tda.gov.uk/upload/resources/pdf/d/draft_revised_standards_framework_jan_2007.pdf [accessed 5 March 2007].

The Growing, Developing and Moving Child

Chapter outline

Children should be allowed to dream a little longer, so that when a youngster declares he is much stronger than his father, then so be it.

Ken Fox

Introduction

This chapter builds on the theoretical perspectives of Chapter 2 and focuses on a variety of growth and development topics of infancy, early and later childhood. The central purpose of this chapter is to provide a profiled description of growth and development processes that typically occur during these age phases which will provide the primary educator with background from which to understand children's readiness to acquire and develop motor skills. The space in this particular text for detailed anatomical and physiological analysis of these processes is limited and we focus our efforts on suggesting practical implications for the practitioner to consider. We provide pointers for further reading at the end of the chapter for those who wish to study the biological perspective in more depth.

A consideration of the factors underpinning movement abilities enables the teacher to analyse movement and use enhanced knowledge and understanding to plan for the next stage of each child's learning in the physical domain. In particular, this chapter examines the factors that impact on growth and development and, in turn, how these phenomena have implications for learning in the physical domain. The reader is encouraged to consider why some children are apparently 'more able' than others at particular times and to consistently begin the planning process from a 'child-centred' perspective.

It is the stage of development – and not the age of the child – that is most crucial when planning and facilitating appropriate physical education lessons.

Key Points

- Children's growth and development progresses through identifiable stages and phases.
- This is affected by a range of prenatal, environmental, hereditary and task factors, creating a unique set of circumstances for each child.
- Childhood growth and development is a relatively steady progress, leading to a more rapid spurt at the onset of puberty.
- The earliest forms of infant involuntary movement have been linked by some to later, voluntary movements.
- Rudimentary movements can be categorized as locomotor, stability and manipulative skills and often seen as motor milestones through which children progress.
- Movements developed during childhood are often called fundamental movement skills and these are necessary for participation in a wide range of activities throughout the life span.
- Childhood self-concept development can be fostered by positive experiences in the physical domain.

The problem with chronological descriptions

Chapter 2 provided a range of theoretical frameworks through which practitioners can better understand motor development. There is widespread agreement that motor development is not age dependent, but that it is age related; in other words, although children will typically progress through definable stages, the exact time at which 'motor milestones' are reached will differ from child to child – sometimes markedly. This is best illustrated by considering the age at which an infant first begins to walk independently. This amazing feat can occur as early as nine or as late as fifteen months. The onset of locomotion is influenced by a range of biological, psychological and sociological factors and effectively illustrates the transactional model of motor development (See Figure 3.1).

A key point to note here is that children's 'abilities' in movement tasks are a result of a unique combination of hereditary, environmental and task factors (to different extents for different children). The 'early' walker may have developed muscular leg strength through being placed in a 'baby bouncer' and then offered positive feedback from significant others (e.g. a smile and a clap during early attempts to walk); the 'later' walker may be quite happy getting around on all fours, despite a physiological readiness to walk. The subsequent development of a range of skills is equally affected by this interaction between the task, the environment and individual factors.

Practitioners should be wary of attaching labels to primary aged children for this very reason; a common mistake is to assume that those demonstrating greatest 'ability' during childhood are the 'most able' performers or those with a 'natural' ability (Bailey and Morley, 2006). You can no doubt remember a child in your own class who was the best at sport or the fastest runner at sports day. Is this person still the most able? Did they go on to achieve great things? The answer to these questions could of course be yes, although it is clear in many cases that the ability shown owes most to levels of exposure (i.e. opportunities to practise) to particular activities.

The child who has been encouraged to throw and catch in the garden at home is likely to show greater ability in such tasks in physical education when compared to a child in the

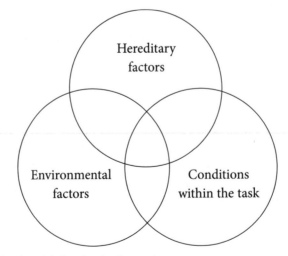

Figure 3.1 A transactional model of motor development

same class who has not had the same opportunities. This makes identification of talented children very difficult because the most talented children may not yet have been introduced to the very activities that are most suited to their physiological and psychological make-up. This provides further justification for ensuring that physical education teaching and learning remains inclusive and purposeful for all children and suggests that children should be introduced to a broad range of activities – particularly those which haven't yet been experienced outside school.

It is recognized that motor development is a *discontinuous* process; in other words we cannot predict exactly how motor development will progress from birth to death. It is also possible that rather than progress, an individual can regress across the life span and become less able in particular tasks. For example, child gymnasts rarely sustain their levels of performance into or throughout adulthood, partly owing to a loss in joint and muscle flexibility that occurs with age. You too can probably remember being able to perform particular physical skills as a child that would be difficult to perform now, either through lack of continued practice, lack of flexibility or 'specific conditioning', or lack of motivation.

This irregular pattern of motor development undermines attempts to represent physical education as a lifelong process, specifically when trying to describe progression within such models. However, approaching each learning episode from the transactional perspective illustrated in Figure 3.1 will help ensure that changes in body composition, psychological readiness and the demands of the task are well matched to the needs of the children. Furthermore, throughout well-taught physical education, children should become increasingly aware of their own bodies, including strengths and areas for development, and how these may change over time.

The individually unique combination of biological, environmental and task factors changes through time, particularly in relation to growth and development. The implications of this are clear, especially for those charged with delivering physical education in schools. Assessment in physical education cannot only happen at points of entry to and exits from a curriculum; it should be an ongoing, formative process to account for the ever-changing factors that contribute to this 'dynamic systems perspective'. Attempts to assess children's learning should therefore be cognizant of these changes and should help teachers to understand each child's specific learning needs.

A further difficulty of a chronological description of motor development is that it suggests that later attempts and performances are somehow *better* than early, more rudimentary attempts. Not only do such viewpoints belittle important early performances (and the incredible levels of effort and concentration that children commit to them), but they imply that children who have not yet achieved a degree of technical proficiency are in some way 'deficient'. A multitude of reasons can account for a wide range of technical competence in a variety of early curriculum activities. The amount of time spent practising (at home, in the playground and in lessons), levels of encouragement from family members, availability of appropriate equipment and space, as well as a child's anatomical and physiological make-up are contributory factors that result in a range of outcomes across a typical class, and in most cases even the most rudimentary of attempts at physical skills represent the child's 'best attempt'.

A chronological, sequenced view of motor development is problematic too in the context of 'inclusive' education where children with particular special education needs may be unable to match a 'textbook' model of a 'mature' or 'specialized' skill pattern. This does not of course mean that these children are unable to fulfil their physical potential, or indeed that they cannot become talented performers in their own right. In this regard, the developmental physical educator should remain true to the 'starting from the child' philosophy most often applied in early years settings and consider learning needs alongside learning potential of the children in his/her class.

Motor development, then, is not a clean-cut, continuous process. The models of skill development provided for discussion in Chapter 4 are themselves problematic, as they suggest that children will all progress from basic first attempts (often called the *initial* stage) to more organized and coherent patterns (often called the *elementary* stage) to a stage of greater maturity (often called the *mature* stage), ready for application to a specific sports or dance context (sometimes called the *specialized phase*). Just as age phases within curricula are artificially created, so too are such models of motor skill development. No one child is exactly the same as another, and the developmental physical educator should view such models as loose frameworks from which to plan, teach and assess each child's work.

Recognizing the limitations of these models should not prevent the physical educator from holding pictures of skill themes in his or her mind for comparison with a child's demonstrated work. Being able to identify what the child can currently achieve, and features for progression that could make the actions more controlled, fluent, powerful or accurate relies on some notion of what the actions *could look like* and is an important tool for the teacher concerned with providing effective feedback, feed-forward and scaffolding (see Chapter 5) to help the child reach his or her motor potential.

Accepting that each child's learning needs are positioned uniquely within a dynamic systems model necessitates that the primary school physical educator is aware of the range of growth and development features that typically occur before and during the primary age phases. This will help sharpen the observational skills of the teacher and his or her ability to consider what, where and how children learn in the physical domain. The following sections of this chapter aim to describe systems and processes that grow and develop over time and sequences these changes from conception through to later childhood.

Growth, maturity and development – what's the difference?

The terms growth, maturity and development are often used interchangeably, although they actually refer to different processes. *Growth* is a quantitative increase in size of the body or component parts of the body as a result of cellular processes (Malina and Bouchard, 1991), while *maturation* focuses on progress towards and rate of achieving full (i.e. adult) size (ibid.) *Development* implies a continuous process of change leading to a state of organized and specialized functional capacity (Haywood, 1993). *Development* is also used to describe behavioural changes that result from a child's interaction with his or her environment. As Bailey and McFadyen (2000, p. 75) suggest:

> development refers to the lifelong process of change by which individuals acquire competences in different areas. It is usually characterized by increased sophistication in organized and special-ized functioning as a result of both biological and environmental factors.

Throughout this chapter we will consider the range of growth, maturation and development processes that impact on motor development in the primary age phases, and pay particular attention to the following overlapping body functions, processes and systems:

- the skeletal system;
- the muscular system;
- the cardiovascular and respiratory systems;
- energy systems;
- perceptual-motor processes;
- concept of self.

Before providing a description of growth, maturation and development from conception to later childhood, we first look at general concepts and definitions of each of these systems and features.

Overview of the skeletal system

In physical education many intended learning outcomes are depicted by describing body shape, and changes to shape brought about by movement. Neither body shape nor movement would be possible without the skeletal system, made up of bones, cartilages, ligaments and tendons. The average adult skeleton is made up of 206 bones of differing sizes, shapes and functions, often described as components of the *axial skeleton* (i.e. the bones forming the upright axis of the body) and the *appendicular skeleton* (i.e. the bones of the upper and lower limbs and the structures through which they are attached to the rest of the body). Infants' skeletons are made up of more component parts and, over time, some of these parts fuse together to create larger bones.

Bones increase in size through the formation of new bone on the surface of cartilage or on older bone. A long bone, such as the femur (thigh bone), grows in length at either end in the region known as a 'growth plate'. These are made up of cartilage and are sometimes referred to as epiphyseal discs. Ossification is the process of bone formation, in which connective tissues such as cartilage, are turned to bone or bone-like tissue. Growth occurs when cartilage cells divide and increase in number at these growth plates, pushing older, larger cartilage cells towards the middle of a bone. Eventually, the older cells die and the space they occupied is replaced with bone. Although the potential length, width and shape of an adult's bones are determined genetically, nutrition and hormonal factors can contribute to either arrested growth or full achievement of genetic potential.

The body moves because contractile properties of muscles pull on the bones as levers. As a result, bones flex, extend, abduct, adduct and rotate around a variety of articulations; the movement possible at each joint relates to its structure and without these joints movement would be severely restricted. Because children's bones are not fully formed, the physical educator needs to understand bone growth and development at particular stages in order to plan appropriate physical tasks. There is some evidence that suggests moderate physical exercise can optimize childhood growth, leading some to claim that physical activity is necessary for normal growth (e.g. Micheli, 1984). However, there is also evidence that the growing bones of a child are susceptible to injury, particularly at the sites of growth plates, joints and muscle insertions (ibid.).

Overview of the muscular system

Movement would be impossible without contraction of the 500 or so skeletal muscles that are present in the body. Muscles, which form the largest tissue mass of the body, are commonly grouped into three types: those which are attached to bones and affect voluntary movement of the skeleton (*skeletal muscles*), involuntary (*smooth muscles*) which form the walls of organs, blood vessels, eyes, glands and skin, and *cardiac muscle* which provides the major propulsive force for sending blood through blood vessels.

Muscles are attached to the skeleton by *tendons* at sites called the *origin* (usually describing the attachment where least movement occurs) and the *insertion* (usually describing attachment to the bone where most movement occurs). Muscles work with and in opposition to other muscles in groups to help us accomplish specific movements.

Skeletal muscle is made up of muscle fibre, nerve tissue, blood and connective tissue. A muscle fibre is made up of between 100 to 1000 *myofibrils*, thread-like structures that contain contractile proteins. Each skeletal muscle cell is also connected to a nerve fibre branch stemming from a nerve cell. These *motor neurons* (extending from the spinal cord and meeting muscle cell at a *neuromuscular junction*) initiate the contraction process within muscles. Neurons are considered to be 'excitable tissue' as they respond to stimuli, convert this into a neural impulse and transmit this impulse along the axon to the muscles. The muscular system is, in this way, linked to the body's central and peripheral nervous systems.

A further consideration is type of skeletal muscle, which is generally described within three biochemical and performance-based classifications. These are *slow-twitch* fibres (sometimes called Type I), *intermediate* fibres (sometimes called Type IIa) and *fast-twitch* fibres (sometimes called Type IIb). Most muscle groups in the body contain a mixture of all fibre types, although the percentage of type in muscles is thought to be genetically determined. Sports science appears to offer conflicting views as to whether specific training can alter the fibre types, and it appears most likely that training can only help each type of fibre to function more effectively.

Muscles contract in a variety of ways, commonly described as either *isotonic* or *isometric* contraction. The former results in a shortening of the muscle, as in the flexion of the arm by contraction of the biceps, whereas the latter sees minimal shortening, but greatly increased tension. An example of an isometric contraction would be seen when trying to carry a load with an extended arm. The weight of the object would be pulling downward, but your hands and arms would be opposing the motion with equal force going upwards. The distinction between each type of muscle contraction is important for those considering weight-bearing activities in primary physical education (such as those seen in gymnastic activities, for example).

Overview of the cardiovascular and respiratory systems

Blood moves around the body to transport oxygen, carbon dioxide, nutrients, electrolytes, water, waste products and gases. In addition, blood plays an important role in maintaining homeostasis (the state of functional and compositional equilibrium in the body) and protecting the body against foreign bodies. The heart functions as a forceful pump to send blood to the lungs through pulmonary vessels and then to muscles in the body via systemic blood vessels. The right side of the heart receives deoxygenated blood from the body and pumps it via *pulmonary circulation* to the lungs, where carbon dioxide is exchanged for oxygen through a process of diffusion. The left side of the heart then pumps the oxygenated blood via *systemic circulation* to tissues of the body.

The respiratory system, through which oxygen enters the body and carbon dioxide leaves, works with the cardiovascular system to provide muscle cells with oxygen. Respiration is necessary because all living cells of the body require oxygen and produce carbon dioxide. Respiration includes ventilation (movement of air into and out of the lungs), gaseous exchange between the air in the lungs and the blood, transport of oxygen and carbon dioxide in the blood and gaseous exchange between the blood and muscle tissues. In addition, the cardiovascular and respiratory systems work together to regulate the pH of body fluids and without effective functioning the body's capacity to carry out everyday functions would be impaired.

Overview of energy systems

At the risk of stating the obvious, the body needs energy to complete normal functioning and physical activity. The body breaks up a substance called adenosine triphosphate (ATP), a high-energy molecule consisting of three phosphates attached to adenosine. This *cleaving* process, through which one phosphate is separated from ATP to form adenosine diphosphate (ADP), releases energy. This continual cycle sees ADP converted back into ATP and the process starts again. The body has three basic systems through which this can be achieved:

(i) ATP-CP: The ATP-CP system is the first of the *anaerobic* (i.e. without oxygen) energy systems. As ATP is used it can quickly be replaced through a chemical reaction with creatine phosphate: ATP is cleaved to produce energy and is then replenished by a reaction with creatine phosphate. The ATP-CP system is active at the beginning of all forms of activities but is especially important in high intensity exercises like weightlifting that require short bursts of energy. The source of fuel for the ATP-CP system is ATP and CP that is stored in the muscles and since only a small quantity can be stored this energy source is only effective for activities that last ten seconds or less.

(ii) The lactic acid system: This energy system, also operating without oxygen, is called *anaerobic glycolysis* but is commonly referred to as the lactic acid system because it produces lactic acid as a waste product. This system is important in moderately high intensity exercises that generally last less than two minutes and works in tandem with the other two energy systems. The source of fuel for this process of energy production is either glucose from the blood or stored glucose and is therefore generally effective for activities lasting two minutes or less.

(iii) The oxidative system: This system, commonly termed the aerobic system as it uses oxygen, picks up where the lactic acid system leaves off and is generally used after an activity has lasted longer than two minutes. The oxidative system can use protein, fats or carbohydrates as the source for energy but carbohydrates are the most efficient source for fuel. The use of protein, fats and carbohydrates as fuel is in contrast to both the anaerobic glycolysis system and the ATP-PC system which can only use glycogen or stored creatine phosphate.

Perceptual-motor processes

The perceptual-motor process involves the body receiving a variety of forms of stimulation through sensory receptors (visual, auditory, tactile, kinaesthetic) and transmitting this information to the brain. Sensory integration then occurs, whereby this new information is combined with previously stored memory, leading to motor interpretation (decision making) and movement activation, through which the observable movement act is executed. Following execution of the movement, feedback is provided through 'knowledge of results' and 'knowledge of performance', making use of various sensory modalities.

The quality of children's movement performance is significantly influenced by the accuracy of their perceptions, or ability to interpret information. The quality of movement depends on the accuracy of perception, the ability to interpret stimuli and to coordinate appropriate movement responses.

The terms eye–hand coordination and eye–foot coordination are used to express the dependency of efficient movement on the accuracy of one's sensory information. For example, the individual in the process of shooting a basketball free throw has numerous forms of sensory input that must be sorted out and expressed in the final act of shooting the ball: if the perceptions are accurate and if they are expressed in a coordinated sequence, the basket is made – if not the shot misses. All voluntary movement involves the use of one or more sensory modalities to a greater or lesser degree, depending on the movement act to be performed. As multisensory learners, children use their visual, auditory, tactile, and kineasthetic senses to learn about the spatial and temporal aspects of their expanding world.

Components of perceptual motor processes include:

1 Body awareness – knowledge of body parts, what they can do and how to make them move.
2 Spatial awareness – understanding of personal orientation in space (their own space and that shared by others).
3 Directional awareness – including an internal feel for direction (*laterality*) and knowing the name given for actual directions (*directionality*).
4 Temporal awareness – development of an internal time structure which enables coordinated, synchronized and rhythmical movements (frequently described as hand–eye and foot–eye coordination).

Concept of self

The term 'self-concept' has been used by many to describe an individual's awareness of personal characteristics, attributes and weaknesses and how these personal qualities are like and unlike those of others. There is thought to be a link between perceived competence, actual competence, self-confidence, self-esteem and self-concept, particularly when matched with perceived importance of specific activities. The teacher must therefore plan learning activities for children to enjoy, encourage them to value physical education highly, and anticipate a positive impact on global self-concept as a consequence of success. The extent to which this happens will depend largely on the appropriateness of tasks included within physical education.

It is clear that self-concept is an important part of affective development and that 'play' in all of its forms is a key vehicle through which children learn about themselves, their bodies and their potential for movement. Gallahue and Ozmun (1998) argue that a stable, positive self-concept is crucial to a child's ability to function effectively, whilst others contend that a positive self-concept is linked to enjoyment and motivation (Sonstroem, 1997). Children's self-concept is greatly influenced by social conditions, in particular, verbal and non-verbal communications from others.

From conception to later childhood

However we choose to provide descriptions of typical growth and development across the childhood age phases, we cannot avoid using socially created age-based boundaries. With regard to formal curricula (such as the current NCPE), age phases provide a convenient structure within which to plan for continuity and progression, although they can sometimes hide the true needs of a child because learning needs are not only determined by age.

For the purposes of this chapter, however, the following age classifications are used to help structure a description of typical features of growth and development. These should be seen as approximate age groups.

- *Prenatal* – from conception to birth
- *Neonatal* – from birth to four weeks
- *Infancy* – from four weeks to two years
- *Early infancy* – from four weeks to one year
- *Later infancy* – from one year to two years
- *Early childhood* – from two to six years old
- *Later childhood* – from six to eleven years old.

Prenatal growth and development

Growth begins at the moment of conception (the union of the ovum and sperm) and follows a relatively ordered and precise sequence during the prenatal period. Conception determines each human's genetic make-up, influencing later growth and development. The prenatal period lasts on average 40 weeks and growth during this time is characterized by three distinct phases – the fertilized egg, or *zygote* (first two weeks after fertilization), the *embryo* (second to eight weeks) and the *foetus* (ninth to fortieth week).

Features of each of the three stages are shown in Table 3.1.

A key feature of prenatal development is the differentiation of embryonic cells at the end of the zygotic period and beginning of the embryonic period. At the end of the first month, three distinct layers of cell are present, each of which mark the beginnings of system development. The *ectoderm* is the layer of cells from which the nervous system and sense organs develop; the *mesoderm* is the starting point for the skeletal, muscular and circulatory systems; the *endoderm* eventually becomes the digestive and glandular systems.

The embryonic period is a time of vulnerability and the embryo is susceptible to a range of genetic and environmental factors that could result in disrupted growth and development, which are introduced below.

Hereditary factors can have a marked impact on later development. The developing embryo consists of 46 chromosomes (23 pairs) which in turn are made up of an estimated 20,000 genes. It is the genes that determine a variety of structural characteristics such as potential body size, structure, hair and eye colour, and gender. A variety of genetic factors are thought to alter the process of development, with the most widely known chromosomal alteration manifesting itself as 'Down's Syndrome'.

Children with Down's Syndrome have one extra chromosome, owing to 'trisomy #21' (or three number 21 chromosomes) and the rate of occurrence appears to be correlated with maternal age. There appears to be no preventive 'cure' for Down's Syndrome, although some studies suggest that supplementation of diet during pregnancy with folic acid will reduce risk (Lucock, 2000). Children with Down's Syndrome generally experience slow rates of growth, potential for respiratory difficulties, language and communication difficulty and slow rates of motor development. Genetic disorders can also result in other 'birth defects', the most well known of which include clubfoot, sickle cell anaemia and spina bifida, each of which have specific implications for the child's experiences in physical activity.

Table 3.1 The three stages of prenatal development (Adapted from Malina, Bouchard and Bar-Or, 2004)

Prenatal period	Characteristics
Zygotic period 0–2 weeks	Rapid cell division and formation of the blastocyst which implants itself in uterus wall. Several cellular layers begin to form and the embryo becomes clearly differentiated. Further development hinges on successful implantation in the uterus wall.
Embryonic period 2–8 weeks	Rapid growth through increase in number of cells. Differentiation of embryonic stem cells into specific cell types and eventually into tissues, organs and systems. A period of organ and system formation at the end of which the basic anatomical and physiological features are established. These features continue to change in size and proportion during the foetal period and postnatally until adulthood is reached. This is the most critical stage for development of bodily systems and a time when environmental factors or conditions can have a detrimental impact on these processes. Skeletal development occurs at *primary ossification centres* at the foetal age of two months.
Foetal period 9–40 weeks	No new anatomical features appear, but tissues, organs and systems develop rapidly in terms of size, mass, proportion and functional development.

Nutritional and chemical ingestion by the mother during the prenatal period will affect the unborn child. The degree of risk varies depending on scale and type of ingestion, and could adversely impact on birth weight (used as an indicator of newborn infant survival) or cause 'abnormal' development. A poor supply of nutrients from the placenta through osmosis to the foetus is a systemic cause of malnutrition (*placental malnutrition*), whereas *foetal malnutrition* is most commonly caused by an inability of the foetus to metabolize the nutrients that are being passed to it. Poor dietary intake by the mother (*maternal malnutrition*) is also a problem in many parts of the world, and therefore an awareness of the problems associated with *under nourishment* (i.e. not enough nutrients or calorific intake) and *malnourishment* (i.e. eating the wrong food) is important for those concerned with prenatal development.

The unborn child may also be exposed to prescribed, over the counter or illicit drugs. Such chemicals may interfere with cell differentiation or impact on the flow of oxygen and nutrients through the placenta. The ability of the foetus's liver to balance waste products in the blood can be affected, most commonly leading to jaundice, which if left untreated in the newborn infant, can lead to brain damage.

The treatment of 'everyday' conditions (such as headaches, acne, hypertension, diabetes, allergies and water retention), as well as common pregnancy-related conditions, must be cognizant of potential risk factors. Outside the control of a doctor, unborn infants may also be exposed to illicit drugs, alcohol and tobacco. Each of these chemical compounds has been shown to contribute to low infant birth weight, possible birth defects and postnatal growth problems (Roche, 1999; Streissguth *et al.*, 1993).

A number of medical conditions suffered by a mother of an unborn child are also thought to contribute to developmental difficulties. Sexually transmitted diseases, maternal infections, hormonal and chemical imbalances, incompatibility of blood type between mother and foetus, and emotional stress can all lead to recognizable conditions and infant infections, as well as motor, sensory and cognitive disability.

Environmental factors are also thought to have some impact on prenatal development, although it has proved difficult for the scientific community to establish causality. Chemical pollutants such as lead and mercury, as well as exposure to radiation are commonly believed to increase risk of developmental problems, and some suggest that other pollutants such as acid rain and less common chemical compounds can increase risk of birth defects.

A final range of factors to consider at this stage includes what happens at the point of entry to the world – birth. **Birth process factors** include the use of drugs to sedate and relieve pain, the position of presentation of the infant, and the use of forceps or other mechanical instruments to withdraw the baby from the birth canal. Problems can arise within each of these processes and could result in permanent disability to either the baby or mother.

Most mothers in the developed world are now able to make an informed choice about behaviours during pregnancy and how they would like to plan the birth process itself. Within a transactional perspective, these decisions are not made in a biological vacuum, but are influenced and shaped by a range of sociological, economic and psychological motivations. In all cases, however, the subsequent growth, development, and maturation of the infant is affected by factors outside his or her own control and the implications for the physical educator are clear: understanding the factors that influence motor development will help to the practitioner to 'start from the child' and plan tasks that are differentiated to meet the needs of each child – whatever these needs may be.

Infancy growth, development and movement

The growth and development processes during the first two years of life are truly incredible; infants progress from tiny, helpless, relatively sedentary dependants to bigger, upright and expressive explorers. During infancy, physical growth has a definite link to motor development, typified by the role of the infant's relatively large head in affecting early attempts to maintain equilibrium. The bones of infants are therefore softer and have higher water content compared to adults. Bones harden and children are increasingly able to manipulate their body with greater surety – inevitably increasing their range of experimentation and exploration.

Weight and length

Birth weight varies owing largely to the factors described above. Low birth weight babies and premature babies generally catch up with their counterparts if nutritional intake is optimal, although babies born with weights at the extremes of what is normally expected are thought to be equally susceptible to obesity in later life.

At birth, around 400 ossification centres exist, and a further 400 appear after birth (Haywood, 1993). Bone growth after birth follows a relatively predictable and rapid pattern. The newborn infant is already approximately one-third of his or her final height and by the second birthday approximately half of adult height (Bee and Boyd, 2004). Growth curves typically indicate rapid gains in weight and body length throughout infancy, with the first six months being a time for 'filling out'. At approximately two years of age, the rate of growth (height and weight) slows slightly until the next spurt during adolescence.

Body proportions

In addition to bone and tissue growth, the proportions of the body are important considerations. In an infant, the head houses a brain which is close to adult size and as consequence will take up a larger proportion of the overall height of the body. The hand, wrist, ankle and feet all have fewer bones at birth than at adult maturity; for example, the adult wrist is made up of nine separate bones, whilst a one-year wrist has only three.

Muscular system

At birth, muscle mass accounts for approximately one quarter of body weight, and virtually all muscle fibres are present. Muscle growth during infancy occurs predominately as a result of *hypertrophy* (increase in muscle cell size) and in response to the growing skeletal structure to which the muscles are attached. At birth, it is thought that up to 20 per cent of muscle fibres are yet to differentiate into fast or slow twitch, although those claiming that early infant activities can impact on the mature proportion of these fibres are yet to provide sufficient supporting evidence.

Brain development and the nervous system

The brain triples in weight in the first two years of life, owing largely to the rapid rate of *synaptogenesis*, the process of creating connections or synapses between neurons (Nowakowski, 1987). It is thought that the brain creates more neural pathways than are ultimately required and that a 'pruning' process takes place to eliminate redundant pathways, starting at around 18 months. As a consequence, a one-year-old infant has a greater density of synapses than an adult and there seems to be growing agreement that neural complexity not retained in the early years is not reprogrammed later. The implications of this for early years practitioners and parents is that early stimulation in a rich, multisensory environment is vital for the optimum development of brain organization.

A second neurological process occurring during infancy is that of *myelination*, the creation of fatty sheaths around the axons of nerve fibres. These sheaths provide insulation from other neurons and assist conductivity of the nerves. The process of myelination of spinal nerves begins two to three weeks after birth and continues for to three years. The pattern of myelination is thought to impact on motor development, particularly in relation to the onset of voluntary movement and the suppression of random, postural and reflexive movements exhibited in the newborn infant (see 'Infant movement' below). It is possible, for example, that a 'late crawler' (or even 'non-crawler') is unable to crawl due to incomplete myelination, rather than lack of muscular strength or poor perceptual-motor integration.

Cardiovascular and respiratory systems

The transition from life in the womb (a well-insulated aqueous environment) to life outside the womb is a dramatic experience for the newborn child (Malina, Bouchard and Bar-Or, 2004). The infant is faced with the challenge of breathing for itself, and with coping with circulatory changes in heart and blood vessels brought about by the commencement of ventilation and changes in blood pressure resulting from cutting the umbilical cord. The birth process works to expel lung fluid and, with the onset of respiration, alveoli expand to allow gaseous exchange to commence. The number of alveoli increases postnatally, matched with a progressive increase in lung volume between birth and reaching adult maturity. The development of the heart, blood vessels and the lungs is affected then by several adjustments at birth, after which the systems are mature enough to allow efficient functioning. Throughout postnatal growth, heart mass and volume grow proportionally to body weight, whereas the lung volumes grow proportionally to height.

Perceptual development

From the moment of birth, infants begin to learn how to interact with their new environment and receive information from a variety of visual, auditory, olfactory, gustatory, tactile and kinaesthetic sources. Newborn children attach little or no meaning to this range of stimuli, but over time begin to make sense of them as the stimuli take on meaning and can be integrated with previously stored information.

Key features of infant perceptual development include rapid development of visual perception, auditory, olfactory and gustatory perception. Although the eye is anatomically complete at birth, it is not fully developed and the early weeks and months following birth see rapid development of visual acuity (degree of detail seen), accommodation (the ability of each lens to bring the retinal image into focus), peripheral vision, binocularity (both eyes working together on a stationary object (fixation), or on a moving object (tracking), colour vision, form and depth perception. Visual perception is thought to have reached sophisticated levels by the age of six months.

Whilst visual perception is often thought to be the most important of the senses with regards to motor development, the integration of several sources of information is also considered to be highly significant. *Intersensory integration* is thought to be important in infant learning (Bahrick and Lickliter, 2000), and in a number of studies, infants have demonstrated the ability to link simultaneous information from a variety of senses.

Concept of self

Most theorists now agree that the newborn infant has some sense of 'separateness' from the parent (Bee and Boyd, 2004), and that early interaction with others, objects and the environment help the infant to begin to understand his or her own role in the world. A self-concept established in infancy is also dependent upon nurturing from parents or carers who exhibit appropriate responses to the infant's attempts to interact with the world. Self-awareness in infancy has been the subject of significant experimental study, most notably using mirrors to gauge onset of self-recognition, commonly agreed to be around 15 to 24 months.

Infant movement

Newborn infants demonstrate a number of random, involuntary, reflexive actions, some related to survival (seeking food and protection) and others theoretically linked to the onset of later, voluntary movements (primitive postural reflexes and rhythmical stereotypies). 'Rhythmical stereotypies' are movements performed repeatedly by infants for their own sake (Gallahue and Ozmun, 1998) and provide evidence that human motor development is a self-organizing system that seeks increased control (Thelen, Kelso and Fogel, 1987).

For the first four months of infancy, the majority of movement is reflexive, as the infant reacts to changes in pressure, sight, sound and touch. These infant reflexes and rhythmical stereotypies are summarized in Table 3.2.

Infant reflexes are thought to be controlled by lower brain centres, whereas the onset of voluntary locomotion is a function of the cerebral cortex, or higher brain centres. The appearance and disappearance of infant reflexes is used by some as a measure of 'normal' development and for diagnosis of central nervous system disorders. This application of the maturational viewpoint has been contested by some theorists who suggest that the disap-

Table 3.2 Selected infant reflexes and rhythmical stereotypies (Adapted from Gallahue and Ozmun, 1998)

Reflexes	Brief description	Approximate onset and disappearance
Primitive reflexes		
Moro and startle	These are elicited when a supine infant is shocked by a tap on the tummy, the head being allowed to drop back, or by a sudden loud noise. In the *moro reflex*, arms extend and then flex; in the *startle reflex*, the action is immediate flexion.	Birth to 6 months
Search and sucking	Infants head turns towards perceived source of food as the area around mouth is stimulated (*search reflex*); stimulation of the lips, gums, tongue and hard palate will prompt the *sucking reflex*.	Birth to 1 year (search); birth to 3 months (sucking) but voluntary response persists
Hand–mouth	Scratching base of palm causes chin muscles to contract and lift (*palmar-mental* reflex).	Birth to 1 month (?)
Palmar grasping	Hand closes tightly around an object which is stimulating the palm.	Birth to 4 months
Babinski	Stroking sole of foot causes extension of toes.	Birth to 4 months
Plantar grasping	Contraction of the toes – follows from above.	4 to 12 months
Asymmetrical and symmetrical tonic neck	Supine infant's head turned to one side results in arms and legs assuming an '*en garde*' fencing-like position (asymmetrical); symmetrical reflex is elicited in supported sitting position – extension of head and neck results in extension of arms and flexions of leg…if head and neck are flexed, opposite occurs.	3 to 6 months approximately, but not all infants display the reflex

Reflexes	Brief description	Approximate onset and disappearance
Postural reflexes		
Labyrinthine and optical righting	Infant held in upright position is tilted forwards, backwards or sideways – the response sees child moving head in opposite direction of movement of trunk to maintain head position (*labyrinthine*). Becomes the *optical righting* reflex where eyes are seen to follow the lead of the head.	2 to 6 months (*labyrinthine*), 6 months to 1 year (*optical*)
Pull-up	Upright sitting infant holding hands with adult will, when tipped backwards, flex arms to remain upright.	3 months to 1 year
Parachute and propping	Protective movements of the limbs in the direction of a displacing force. Similar to startle reflex and relies on vision.	4 months (forwards and backwards), 6 months (sideways) or 10 months (backwards) until infant begins to walk
Crawling	Prone infant uses upper and lower limbs to stimulate an 'army crawl'-type action when pressure applied to sole of foot.	Birth to 3 or 4 months (voluntary crawling appears around 6 or 7 months)
Primary stepping	Infant uses legs to 'walk' when held erect with body weight on flat surface.	First 6 weeks to 5 months
Swimming	Rhythmical extension and flexion of arms and legs when placed in prone position in or over water.	2 weeks to 4 months
Rhythmical stereotypies		
Legs and feet	Rhythmical kicking when in prone or supine positions.	4 weeks to 32 months (maximum)
Torso	For example, arching of back and extension of arms and legs rather like an 'airplane' from a prone position.	Unspecified
Arms, hands and fingers	Waving, banging and rhythmical clapping actions.	Unspecified – 42 weeks (maximum)
Head and face	'No' and 'Yes' actions.	

pearance of reflexes is due to disuse and that stimulation of locomotor reflexes can enhance infants' acquisition of voluntary movement (Zelazo, 1983). Such an explanation of infant motor development would fit with a dynamic systems theory which would suggest that neuromaturation is only one of several rate limiters influencing the emergence of voluntary movements.

As reflexive movements disappear, more complex, voluntary actions begin to form in the movement vocabulary of the infant. These are often called motor milestones to show the landmark status of acquisition of new skills such as standing unaided and walking.

The descriptive study of infant motor development was pioneered by Mary Shirley (1931) and Nancy Bayley (1935) and has been informed by others such as Louise Ames (1937) and Arnold Gessell (1945) who, despite minor differences, promoted a *maturational* perspective.

It appears that the sequence of motor development in infancy is predictable, although the rate at which this occurs differs from child to child based on the unique interaction between the individual, the task and the environment. This dynamic systems perspective has been favoured in recent years and protagonists argue that the achievement of 'milestones' is a consequence of the development of many systems, not just the nervous system.

In Chapter 2 we introduced Gallahue's 'hourglass model' of motor development and this suggests that such motor milestones are the foundation on which later, fundamental movement abilities are built. These *rudimentary movement abilities* can be classified with regard to stability, locomotion and manipulation and are summarized in Table 3.3.

The rudimentary movements listed in Table 3.3 enable the infant to interact with the environment and with others in an increasingly complex fashion. The shift during this time is from self-gratification and involuntary movement to independent *movement for a purpose*. Gradually, the infant gains control over the major muscle groups of the body – at first those in the trunk and neck and later in the arms, legs and fingers – and begins to skilfully interact with the environment in a range of imaginative, creative and increasingly skilful ways.

The development of more complex movement skills begins during infancy as first rudimentary movements enable the child to interact more widely with the environment, and then fundamental movements develop to enable a greater range and variety of movement responses. Most theorists agree that the early and later childhood phases represent the key time for developing increasingly mature movement patterns (between ages two to six) and applying these to more complex sequences (ages six to eleven). The next section of this chapter profiles growth and development through early and later childhood and considers the implications of these for the physical educator.

Early childhood growth, development and movement

On entering this period, the child is generally required to interact with a more complex world and with greater numbers of people. The young child typically becomes increasingly confident and independent as he or she attends toddler groups or pre-school settings. This period is normally characterized by a move out of nappies and is often caricatured as a time for 'terrible twos', or temper tantrums. However, what follows throughout childhood represents an '*exciting time for gaining control of the body, for increasing strength, speed, power, coordination and balance, for discovering what the body can do and for learning new skills*' (Maude, 2001, p. 6)

Table 3.3 Rudimentary movement abilities in infancy (Adapted from Gallahue and Ozmun, 1998)

Rudimentary movement ability	Example	Approximate age of onset
Stability tasks	Turns to one side	Birth
	Turns to both sides	1 week
	Held with support	First month
	Chin held up off surface	Second month
	Lifts head and chest	Second month
	Attempts to roll over (supine to prone)	Third month
	Success in rolling over (supine to prone)	Sixth month
	Prone to supine roll	Eighth month
	Sits with support	Third month
	Sits with self-support	Sixth month
	Sits alone	Eighth month
	Stands with support	Sixth month
	Supports with hands held	Tenth month
	Pulls to supported stand	Eleventh month
	Stands alone	Twelfth month
Horizontal locomotion	'Army crawl'	Sixth or seventh month
	Crawling (legs and arms used in opposition)	Ninth month
	'Walking' on all fours	Eleventh month
	Walks with support	Sixth month
Upright gait	Walks with hands held	Tenth month
	Walking when led	Eleventh month
	Walking alone (hands high)	Twelfth month
	Walking alone (hands low)	Thirteenth month
	Ineffective reach	First–third month
Reaching	Definite, corralling reach	Fourth month
	Controlled reach	Sixth month
Grasping	Reflexive grasp	Birth
	Voluntary grasp	Third month
	Two-hand palmar grasp	Third month
	One-hand palmar grasp	Fifth month
	Pincer grasp	Ninth month
	Controlled grasping	Fourteenth month
Releasing	Eats without assistance	Eighteenth month
	Basic release	Twelfth–fourteenth month
	Controlled release	Eighteenth month

The early childhood period is characterized by steady increases in height and weight, although *growth rate* decelerates compared to that experienced during the first two years of life. Ossification is dynamic and bone growth continues at a steady rate, with hardening of the bones in hands and wrists generally occurring in advance of those in the ankles and feet. By the age of four, the child is approximately double his or her birth length and the weight gained between the ages of two and five is less than that gained in the first year. Gender differences in growth are minimal, although boys tend to be slightly taller and heavier than girls and both exhibit a gradual decrease in subcutaneous ('under the skin') body fat.

During this time, there is a considerable change in body proportions. The child's bones lengthen and the head is no longer the largest component of the body. The chest becomes larger than the abdomen, and the stomach protrudes less, positively impacting on the child's ability to maintain balance in a variety of increasingly challenging contexts. During early childhood, young bodies begin to resemble more closely the proportions exhibited in older, school-aged children.

The parts of the brain that control movement are not yet fully myelinated – this happens towards the end of this period (Todd *et al.*, 1995), so full achievement of mature patterns of movement is not always possible until that time. By the age of three, the brain is approximately 75 per cent of adult weight. Young children are developing a growing sense of 'self and space,' although confusion often persists with regards to awareness of body, directional, temporal and spatial awareness. Anyone who has asked a large group of three-year-old children to form one circle or to 'find a space' in the hall will recognize this! Visual development is still progressing during this period; parts of the retina are not fully developed until the age of six and young children tend to be far-sighted, having greatest difficulty seeing objects that are close to them. Auditory perception during this time can be affected by ear infections, commonly occurring due to the short and flat shape of the still growing inner ear.

During early childhood, a sense of autonomy and initiative are being developed, although the youngest children in this age group tend to appear egocentric (i.e. can only see things from their point of view). Young children become curious about the world around them and need to express this through active, exploratory behaviour. As children successfully begin to show initiative and develop autonomy, timid and cautious actions shown by two-year-olds normally give way to confident (sometimes over-confident) actions demonstrated by four- and five-year-old children.

The development of a positive self-concept comes with appropriate experiences and positive reinforcement for effort and achievements. At the end of the early childhood period, children are generally expected to begin to conform to social expectations in readiness for 'school'. The transition from a 'play-based' experience to a more formal learning structure is challenging for many children, leading some writers to consider the extent to which 'child culture' is at odds with 'school culture' (Bailey, Doherty and Pickup, 2007).

Early childhood movement

Movement helps young children to engage actively with experiences, to construct their own views of the world (Bruner and Haste, 1987), and to take an active, inventive role to reconstruct tasks through their own understanding (Smith, 1993). Such a steady period of growth represents an ideal time for developing motor competence and children can rapidly develop fundamental movement skills during this time. Gross motor control develops more quickly than fine motor control and the most skilful actions tend to be those which use the large muscle groups and whole body (e.g. jumping and running). Children in this age group typically run with ease, walk upstairs using one foot per step, may pedal and steer a 'trike' or a bicycle with stabilizers, tiptoe, walk along a line, jump and throw overarm in an increasingly mature way (see Chapter 4).

Later childhood growth, development and movement

This age phase is typified by steady but slow increases in height and weight and greater organization of the sensory and motor systems. A 'head to toe' (*cephalocaudal*) and centre to periphery (*proximodistal*) pattern of development tends to continue so that the larger muscles of the body are considerably more developed than the fine muscles at the start of the six to eleven age phase.

Later childhood tends to be a time of body lengthening and filling out as children move towards adolescence and the onset of puberty. The later childhood years are characterized by a slow rate of growth, particularly between the ages of 8 and 11 or 12, and this appears to correlate with marked improvements in coordination, balance and agility. Size of the head remains almost the same as in early childhood, with positive implications for motor ability in general and balancing activities in particular.

Gender differences in growth remain minimal and few differences in physique or body weight are seen until the onset of puberty. Girls do appear to mature physiologically at a faster rate than boys, leading to an earlier onset of puberty. Girls typically experience a growth spurt between the ages of 10 and 13 years of age, developing a broader pelvis and hip girdle compared to boys. This may impact positively on ability to balance in some gymnastic activities, owing to a raised centre of gravity. During this period, limb growth tends to exceed growth of the trunk and boys tend to exhibit greater limb length and height than girls in this period.

Gender differences in muscular strength begin to be noticed for the first time; nine-year-old boys are broader across their shoulders than their female counterparts and have *slightly* greater muscle development in the upper trunk area. This may account for greater distance achieved in throwing activities by boys, although there are no anatomical reasons why girls cannot be equally proficient in the throwing action. Because of these minimal physical differences, boys and girls can safely take part in the same activities. This is reflected within organized sport clubs and their national governing body regulations which tend to allow mixed participation (even in contact sports such as rugby union) until the age of 12.

Children during this age phase tend to have low endurance levels and tire easily, although respond well to appropriate aerobic training. Children have to take in more air per unit of body weight than adults, generally breathe faster than adults during exercise and take shorter and shallower breaths (their lungs are smaller). As a consequence children need to divert more physical energy to the process of breathing (which in effect means increased muscular work for their body systems).

As a result of the extra expiration required, the child loses more body fluid. In cold weather (and when children are working in unheated indoor work areas) the cold and or dry air constricts everything – blood vessels and all the air passages of the respiratory system. This means that children will have problems getting enough oxygen to help them through aerobic exercise. These conditions are particularly problematic for asthmatic children and there is an increased risk of an asthma attack. Chronic asthma sufferers should not therefore engage in exercise requiring high levels of aerobic output under such conditions. Some children only suffer from exercise-induced asthma – these children should use an inhaler before and during the taught session where necessary.

Perceptual abilities become increasingly refined during later childhood and an increasingly complex range of tasks can be performed. 'Handedness' is established during this period, reaction times gradually improve and the mechanism for visual perception is fully established. Enhanced sensory–motor integration sees improvements in hand–eye and foot–eye coordination and when these are applied in appropriate learning activities further improvements can be made. Where children are not afforded appropriate opportunities to integrate all sensory modalities, perceptual motor development will not proceed at an optimum level and future development of motor skills may be delayed.

In most cases, children generally appear eager to learn and to please teachers and parents, but need reassurance and guidance. By the end of the later childhood period, boys and girls tend begin to show separate interests, have an increasing sense of fairness, are willing and able to assume positions of authority, yet often demonstrate inconsistent levels of maturity. Childhood self-concept becomes firmly established during this time and enduring attitudes, perceptions and dispositions towards physical education, activity and sport may already have been shaped.

Later childhood movement

The **start** of the later childhood period (around the age of seven) is a time when children have the potential to achieve 'mature' patterns in fundamental movement skills. The **end** of the period (around the age of 11) *should* mark a transition from this position of potential to one of realization – expressed through the application of fundamental skills and the accomplishment of *specialized* skills within more challenging and relevant contexts. Maturity in a range of fundamental skills holds the key for immediate and lifelong participation in more recognizable sports, dance and recreational pursuits and should be the focus of observation and assessment at the point of transition from Key Stage 1 to 2. Towards the end of Key Stage 2, the majority of children will be able to demonstrate greater linkage of increasingly complex patterns of movements and actions – in readiness for developing skills in sports and other activities ('skills' and the teaching and learning of them are discussed in detail in Chapter 4 of this book).

In later childhood, children begin to exhibit an increasingly wide ability range; those who have begun extracurricular and community sports activities will have had greater opportunity to practise, refine and apply their skills and some children will receive greater support and encouragement from family members than others. The influence of parents, carers, siblings and friendship groups in this period is an increasingly important factor in fostering a positive attitude to physical exercise, activity and health.

Some children will have discovered a particular activity that captures their imagination and this, whatever it may be, often fills any spare time that the child has. Most practitioners will have taught children in this age phase who appear to be highly driven within their chosen sporting pursuits, and who hold dreams of becoming sporting heroes themselves. In some sports and dance activities, an early specialism (e.g. in swimming and gymnastics and some dance activities) is sought by organizers, although it is pleasing to see the acceptance of a 'multi-skills' approach by many national governing bodies. There is no doubt that the 'typical' class in later childhood will present a wide range of motor abilities, dispositions to particular activities and levels of motivation.

Factors affecting childhood growth and development

Whilst hereditary factors determine the limits of our growth, a range of other factors can influence the extent to which this potential is reached. Central to this is the extent to which the growing child receives optimum (or even adequate) nutrition during this time. The first four years of life are, in particular, a key period when malnutrition or under-nutrition can lead to complications in growth and development. Deficiencies in particular vitamins and minerals can lead to specific conditions (such as a lack of Vitamin D leading to rickets), whilst a high intake of fat-rich foods during childhood increases the risk of childhood obesity and the associated health problems. In addition, children's growth and development can be adversely effected by illness and injury, particularly injuries that cause damage to growth plates in long bones.

Implications for primary physical education

Foundation Stage and Key Stage 1

Opportunities for 'gross motor play' are very important and physical learning environment should be carefully designed to meet children's needs in this regard, through provision of sufficient space, dedicated areas for movement and use of appropriate size and weight of equipment. Educators must also seek to capitalize on the imaginative zeal with which young children approach their play-based learning through the use of cross-curricular links to drama and role play, art and dance. Children's desire to explore can be utilized through problem solving and exploratory tasks design, and practitioners should consider teaching styles that encourage the young learner to seek solutions to problems themselves.

The focus for physical learning should lie within the range of fundamental movement skills and movement concepts (see Chapter 4), allied to an appropriate choice of teaching and learning strategy and style. Initial skill learning should focus on bilateral actions – walking, running and hopping – before more complex actions such as skipping and galloping are introduced. Coordination of multiple actions with speed and agility will be too demanding for most children and such tasks are best saved until later childhood. Children should be allowed to take regular short rest periods and be provided with access to water during activities, particularly when the activity is aerobic in nature.

The initially egocentric children in this age group should also be encouraged to share their work with others by 'showing and telling' and developing their work with partners and in small groups. Teachers should take into consideration the need for young children to develop their ability to get dressed and undressed and to tie shoelaces. The establishment of an effective routine for changing, going to the toilet and moving from classroom to physical education space is crucial during this time. However, it may be advisable for early years settings to suggest a more flexible approach to 'kit' during early physical learning experiences; young children 'move' across the curriculum and during break times and the distinction between classroom-based learning and physical education-based learning is not as strong at this stage as it is later in the primary years.

Equipment used should be colourful and rich in texture to create a multisensory learning environment which will aid perceptual development. Resources should be light in weight and suited to the size of the young children – adult versions of bats, balls and rackets should definitely not be used. The use of inappropriately large equipment can place strain on the soft and malleable bones and connective tissues of the child and can lead to injury. All children should receive ample positive feedback and be encouraged to give activities a try; making mistakes should be seen as a vital component of the learning process and children should feel confident that all attempts will be valued.

Key Stage 2 and transition to secondary school

In Key Stage 2 most children will welcome opportunities to refine fundamental movement skills and to begin transition to specialized skills in a range of more recognizable activity contexts. An increased emphasis can be placed on skill outcome (such as accuracy, form and level of attainment) as well as effort, although children still require positive affirmation, ample constructive feedback and the knowledge that they are taking part in a secure and safe environment. Children in later childhood benefit from opportunities to develop upper body strength and strength to body weight ratio, highlighting the importance of weight-bearing activities and inverted balances in the gymnastic activity context.

Exploration and guided discovery teaching styles can still be used during later childhood, although this may move more towards problem-based learning where small groups and larger teams of children are challenged to work out solutions for themselves. Some children in later childhood will also become increasingly frustrated with physical education that doesn't challenge them at an appropriate level and teachers must do everything they can to build on what children can already do. For those children who take part in regular out-of-school learning in sports clubs, school physical education must complement and extend their wider learning.

The increasingly large groups used provide an excellent context within which children can take on a variety of leadership roles, and for group discussions concerning fair play and winning and losing. Increasingly competitive activities can be introduced when skill levels and perceptual-motor development of children is sufficient to allow full participation and unhindered learning. This may mean that mixed ability groups are taught through increasingly differentiated tasks.

Summary

Motor development can be viewed within a framework that consists of a number of ages, phases and stages, as have been described in this chapter and Chapter 2. Table 3.4 illustrates the approximate points of transition through which the majority of children will progress.

If we were to add another column to Table 3.4, indicating the typical skills acquired during these different periods, then we would see that there is never a period throughout one's life which is not affected by some change to a person's motor competency. This might be for a number of interrelated reasons, but would also acknowledge that change occurs at whatever stage of development an individual is at. In the early and later childhood periods, the educator has a unique opportunity to provide meaningful learning experiences in the physical domain that could have a lasting impact on the child as he or she moves into adolescence and adulthood.

Table 3.4 Ages, phases and stages of motor development

Approximate age	Movement phase	Stage of motor development
Birth to 4 months 4 months to 1 year	Reflexive Movement phase	Information encoding stage Information decoding stage
Birth to 1 year 1 to 2 years	Rudimentary Movement phase	Reflex inhibition stage Precontrol stage
2 to 3 years 4 to 5 years 6 to 7 years	Fundamental Movement phase	Initial stage Elementary stage Mature stage
7 to 10 years 11 to 13 years 14 years and up	Specialized Movement phase	Transitional stage Application stage Lifelong utilization stage

Key Questions

1 What are the key growth and development processes that impact on a child's motor development?
2 How are early reflexive movements and rhythmical stereotypies linked to later voluntary movements?
3 How does physical education impact on self-concept development during childhood?
4 If we want to 'start from the child', what information do we need to know about the child in order to plan effectively?

Learning tasks

1 Create a visual representation to show the timeline of child motor development from conception to later childhood. Focus on the development of movement skills.
2 Carry out a case study of an individual child in one of the identified age phases. Describe and analyse their movement skills and consider the range of factors that have contributed to the observed behaviours.
3 Identify potential barriers that may prevent children successfully achieving a mature pattern in all fundamental skills. How can the primary physical educator help overcome these?

Links to the Framework of Professional Standards for Teachers

The content and focus of this chapter have direct relevance to the following Qualified Teacher Status (QTS) standards (TDA, 2007) for those training to teach in primary schools: Q5, Q8, Q10, Q12, Q13, Q15, Q16, Q18b.

Useful websites

http://www.surestart.gov.uk/resources/childcareworkers/birthtothreematters/

Birth to three matters is a framework to support children in their earliest years.

http://www.esds.ac.uk/longitudinal/access/ncds/

National Child Development Study

Includes searchable data from respondents on child development from birth to early adolescence.

http://pediatrics.about.com/od/growthanddevelopment/

Readily accessible information regarding childhood growth and development.

http://www.medschl.cam.ac.uk/paediatrics/pages/growthstudy.htm

Maternal and Early Childhood Growth and Development Study

http://www.who.int/nutrition/topics/childgrowth/en/index.html

World Health Organization site with information relating to childhood growth and development.

References and further reading

Allen, K. E. and Marotz, L. (1989) *Developmental Profiles: Birth to Six*. Albany, New York: Delmar.

Bahrick, L. and Lickliter, R. (2000) 'Intersensory Redundancy Guides Attentional Selectivity and Perceptual Learning in Infancy', *Developmental Psychology*, **36**, 190–201.

Bailey, R., Doherty, J. and Pickup, I. (2007) 'Physical Development and Physical Education', in J. Riley (ed.) *Learning in the Early Years: A Guide for Teachers of Children 3–7* (2nd edn). London: Paul Chapman Publishing.

Bailey, R. and Morley, D. (2006) 'Towards a Model of Talent Development in Physical Education', *Sport, Education and Society*, **11**(3), 211–30.

Bailey, R. and McFadyen, T. (2000) *Teaching Physical Education 5–11*. London: Continuum.

Bee, H. and Boyd, D. (2004) *The Developing Child*. Boston, MA: Pearson Education Inc.

Biddle, S. (1999) 'The Motivation of Pupils in Physical Education', in C. A. Hardy and M. Mawer (eds) *Learning and Teaching in Physical Education*. London: Routledge Falmer.

Bruner, J. and Haste, H. (eds) (1987) *Making Sense: The child's construction of the World*. London: Methuen.

Cratty, B. J. (1986) *Perceptual Motor Development in Infants and Children* (3rd edn). Englewood Cliffs, NJ: Prentice-Hall.

Doherty, J. and Bailey, R. (2003) *Supporting Physical Development and Physical Education in the Early Years*. Buckingham: Open University Press.

Evans, J. and Penney, D. (1996) 'The Role of the Teacher in Physical Education: Towards a Pedagogy of Risk', *British Journal of Teaching PE*, **27**(4), 28–35.

Fox, K. (1992) 'Physical Education and Self-esteem', in N. Armstrong (ed.) *New Directions in Physical Education: Toward a National Curriculum*, Volume 2. Champaign, IL: Human Kinetics.

Gallahue, D. L. and Ozmun, J. (1998) *Understanding Motor Development – Infants, Children, Adolescents, Adults*. Dubuque, IW: McGraw-Hill.

Haubenstricker, J. and Seefeldt, V. (1986) 'Acquisition of Motor Skills during Childhood', in V. Seefeldt, (ed.) *Physical Activity and Well-Being*. Reston, VA: AAHPERD.

Haywood, K. M. (1993) *Life Span Motor Development* (2nd edn). Champaign, IL: Human Kinetics.

Haywood, K. M. and Getchell, N. (2001) *Life Span Motor Development* (3rd edn). Champaign, IL: Human Kinetics.

Kalverboer, A., Hopkins, B. and Geuze, R. (eds) (1993) *Motor Development in Early and Later Childhood: Longitudinal Approaches*. Cambridge: Cambridge University Press.

Lucock, M. (2000) 'Folic Acid: Nutritional Biochemistry, Molecular Biology, and Role in Disease Processes', *Molecular Genetics and Metabolism*, **71**(1–2), 121–38.

Malina, R. M. and Bouchard, C. (1991) *Growth, Maturation and Physical Activity*. Champaign, IL: Human Kinetics.

Malina, R. M., Bouchard, C. and Bar-Or, O. (2004) *Growth, Maturation and Physical Activity* (2nd edn). Champaign, IL: Human Kinetics.

Maude, P. (2001) *Physical Children, Active Learning*. Buckingham: Open University Press.

Micheli, L. (1984) *Pediatric and Adolescent Sports Medicine*. Philadelphia: W.B. Saunders.

Nowakowski, R. S. (1987) 'Basic Concepts of CNS Development', *Child Development*, **58**, 568–95.

PEAUK (2003) *Observing Children Moving* (CD-ROM). Reading: Tacklesport Ltd.

Roche, A. F. (1999) 'Postnatal Physical Growth Assessment', *Clinical Pediatrics and Endocrinology*, (**8/12**), 1–2.

Sharman, C., Cross, W. and Vennis, D. (2004) *Observing Children* (3rd edn). London: Continuum.

Sheriden, M. (1995) *From Birth to Five Years – Children's Developmental Progress*. London: Routledge.

Smith, A. B. (1993) 'Early Childhood Educare: Seeking a Theoretical Framework in Vygotsky's Work', *International Journal of Early Years Education*, **1**(1).

Sonstroem, R. J. (1997) 'Physical Activity and Self-esteem', in W. P. Morgan (ed.) *Physical Activity and Mental Health*. Washington, DC: Taylor and Francis.

Streissguth, A. P., Bookstein, F. L., Sampson, P. D. and Barr, M. (1993) *The Enduring Effects of Prenatal Alcohol Exposure on Child Development: Birth Through Seven Years, a Partial Least Squares Solution*. Ann Arbor, MI: University of Michigan Press.

Thelen, E., Kelso, J. A. S. and Fogel, A. (1987) 'Self-organising Systems and Infant Motor Development', *Developmental Review*, **7**, 39–65.

Todd, R. D., Swarzenski, B., Rossi, P. G. and Visconti, P. (1995) 'Structural and Functional Development of the Human Brain', in D. Chiccheti and D. Cohen (eds) *Developmental psychopathology, Vol. 1: Theory and Methods*, New York: Wiley, pp. 161–94.

Training and Development Agency for Schools (TDA) (2007) *Draft Revised Professional Standards for Teachers in England*. London: TDA. Available from http://www.tda.gov.uk/upload/resources/pdf/d/draft_revised_standards_framework_jan_2007.pdf [accessed 5 March 2007].

Zelazo, P. R. (1983) 'The Development of Walking: New Findings and Old Assumptions', *Journal of Motor Behaviour*, **15**, 99–137.

Skill Themes and Movement Concepts

He who would learn to fly one day must first learn to stand and walk and run and climb and dance; one cannot fly into flying.

Friedrich Nietzsche

Introduction

This chapter introduces and explores a range of physical skills that can be developed, extended, practised, refined and applied within primary physical education. The list of skills provided and discussed is not exhaustive, but seeks to provide practitioners with a basis of motor actions that can be viewed as transferable across activity areas, applied and developed in different contexts, and that can contribute to the developing physical literacy of each child. This chapter refers to a variety of conceptualizations and definitions of 'skill themes'. The reader is encouraged to consider the links between skills and their transfer-ability across different activity areas and to be creative when asking children to develop and apply these skills within lessons.

Key points

- A broad base of skills enables children and young people to access physical activity and its multitude of forms throughout the life span.
- The development of motor competence across specific skill themes is age related but not age dependent and no two children will be the same.
- There is never only one way in which to execute a skill – the 'correct response' is necessitated by the immediate social and environmental context.
- Skill themes can be learned through appropriate provision of opportunities to practise, some timely feedback and instruction and, crucially, through making mistakes.

Physical skill development

The development of physical skills and techniques is *the* distinctive objective of physical education. No other subject within the curriculum sets out to foster the development of fine and gross motor skills associated with a broad and balanced range of activities. Whilst the development of social, cognitive and affective skills is a legitimate additional objective of physical education, the physical domain provides the unique focus absent in other curriculum subjects. The learning of physical skills is a desirable aim of the subject for a variety of reasons.

The learning and development of a range of physical skills:

- enables ongoing engagement in a range of different activities that require participants to have a 'skills set' so as to take part;
- allows children to join in with others positively in social- and play-based contexts beyond the curriculum;
- enhances the development of physical self-esteem and therefore contributes to global self-esteem, self-confidence and intrinsic motivation to take part;
- fosters links between mind and body and is thought to stimulate cognition and promote wider educational benefit;
- is an inherently enjoyable activity or at least should be when facilitated in an appropriate way.

Critically, if lifelong participation in physical activity is a goal of school-based physical education, then a 'proficiency gap' (Jess, Dewar and Fraser, 2004), whereby many young people are excluded from certain activities because they do not have the skills or confidence with which to choose to take part, needs to be addressed. This is seen by some as a reason to re-examine the nature and content of physical education so that the subject can make more of an impact on young people in the twenty-first century (ibid.) Current adult activity levels, together with concerns about rising obesity amongst young people, would suggest that many people do not feel empowered, able or motivated to access the multitude of sporting and recreational activity options available in the community.

Skill themes, fundamental movements and movement concepts

It is important for the primary practitioner to understand the various terms used to describe aspects of skill development. A variety of words have been used interchangeably in teaching, sports coaching and 'training' texts. For example, Knapp (1963) produced three different definitions of skill as being either:

1 basic movements such as walking, hopping, curling, stretching … and other acts of this kind in their more elementary stages;
2 an act in which the aim is the production of some pattern of movement which is considered to be technically sound;
3 an act or a whole collection of actions in which there is a clearly defined goal or set of goals … and involves interpreting the needs of the situation and making the right decision… (Knapp, 1963, pp. 2–3).

Knapp's description appears at first to be sensible. On closer consideration, however, wouldn't it be fair to say that the 'basic' skill of walking (for a 13-month-old child at least) involves interpreting the needs of the situation, an element of decision making, and is generally done for a defined goal?

Gross and fine skills

Traditional classifications have included the terms *gross* and *fine* motor skills. These terms refer to the scale of movement and the relative size of muscle groups used to instigate them. Gross motor skills are therefore large body actions that require contraction of muscle groups of the arms, legs, trunk and shoulders to effect. Fine motor skills are smaller movements, usually requiring degrees of control and accuracy (such as holding a pencil to write with). Both fine and gross motor skills are of concern to the primary school teacher, particularly during the early years of schooling where broad physical development forms a vital learning area of the Foundation Stage curriculum (DfEE/QCA, 2000). It should also be acknowledged that there is a clear link between the development of fine motor skills and an ability to maintain equilibrium over the whole body and we should not underestimate the importance of the use of the whole body in even the most slight, imperceptible actions.

The way in which a young child sits when learning to hold an instrument such as a pencil, a pair of scissors, or to model clay, is an important factor in ensuring that balance of the whole body is maintained, allowing for small, accurate actions in the hands. In this example and others, the clear-cut distinction between fine and gross skills is somewhat misleading and we encourage practitioners to view all skills (both large and small in scale) as whole body actions. One helpful way of explaining this is provided by two processes that determine the onset of movement in the young child – namely, *cephalo-caudal* and *proximo-distal* development.

Cephalo-caudal development refers to the onset of bodily control, starting from the head at birth and developing subsequently throughout the body towards the feet at a later point. The reasons for this are perhaps obvious – the use of ankles and feet to increase speed, height and efficiency in locomotion, or to manipulate objects with dexterity and variety is not an immediate priority for the newborn infant. *Proximo-distal* development refers to development of motor control from the centre of the body outwards. In this way, control over the shoulders and torso is achieved to aid sitting and standing before fine control is achieved over the wrists, hands and fingers.

In either view of the above descriptions of the onset of motor control, children will appear to sit somewhere along a developmental continuum. Whilst it is possible to suggest that certain elements of control will emerge at or around particular ages (see Chapter 3), such classifications tend to be socially created to help parents and carers to make judgements about a child's development and to identify any concerns. It is advisable, however, to view the onset of motor control and the subsequent development of ability in specific skills as child-specific and related to the unique set of variables impacting on that child. In this way, any movements and skills shown by children can be viewed and celebrated as major achievements.

Open and closed skills

The *open* and *closed* skill terminology is frequently used and is one that many trainee teachers will be familiar with, particularly those who have studied physical education or sports studies at GCSE or 'A' Level. This distinction relates to the context within which the skill is performed. For example, a closed skill will generally be the same each time a performance is attempted, as conditions surrounding the performer are uniform. In athletics, for example, the sprint start will be practised over and over again to the same technical definition. An open skill is more widely influenced by the environment and, whilst certain techniques will be similar each time, a performer's response is geared towards a multitude of factors (such as proximity of an opponent, state and stage of the match, weather conditions and so on).

We would argue that the majority of skills that are relevant to the primary physical education curriculum are in fact open skills; the unique positioning of the individual in relation to environmental and task factors at any stage will mean that skills and desired outcomes are varied in design and execution. Furthermore, the sprint start for the 100m and other 'closed' skills, is never *exactly* the same; the emotions and feelings, anxieties and pressures felt by the performer will differ each time owing to competition, pre-match preparation, fitness levels, weather conditions, crowd noise and so on.

Self-paced and externally-paced skills

Self-paced skills are those where the mover initiates the action – he or she decides how and when the action will take place. Externally-paced skills are those where the mover reacts to cues within the environment, or in some cases an opponent. A tennis serve is an example of a self-paced skill, whereas rallying in tennis is an example of an externally-paced skill. In primary physical education, fundamental skill development should occur within self-paced activities at first, with an evolving use of external-pacing as competence grows. For example, children playing a cooperative net game may catch the ball every time it comes to them and then strike the ball from their own hand to return. This may evolve to a game where the ball is being struck in response to the speed and direction of a partner's stroke, shifting the emphasis from self-pacing to externally-pacing and thus making the task more demanding.

Discrete, serial and continuous movement

Discrete skills have a definite start and finish and are usually very quick – seldom requiring more than a second to complete. Continuous skills have a more subjective starting and end point (eg. walking, running and swimming). Serial skills are a sequence of discrete skills performed together (e.g. a dance routine, a gymnastics sequence). These skills may require many seconds to complete, and may appear to be continuous, although they might have a discrete beginning and ending.

Movement patterns and skill themes

Malina, Bouchard and Bar-Or, (2004) make a distinction between *movement patterns* and *skills*. Patterns, they suggest, are basic movements that can be performed at a variety of proficiency levels. The term *skill* is used to emphasize accuracy, precision and economy of performance and development of skill is seen as more specialized, building on the general concept of the movement patterns (ibid., p. 196). Gallahue and Donnelly (2003) also suggest that patterns are an organized series of related movements that are too restricted to be classified as fundamental movements or indeed sports skills, whilst a *fundamental skill* is specifically defined as 'an organized series of basic movements that involve the combination of movement patterns of two or more body segments' (p. 52). Where stability, locomotor and manipulative skills are linked together by the child, *movement phrases* are formed.

The development of movement ability can be traced from the *reflexive* movement stage of the newborn infant, through to *rudimentary movements*, to *fundamental* and *specialized* movements in childhood and beyond. David Gallahue's 'hourglass model', described in Chapters 2 and 3, effectively shows how broad age phases can be linked to movement development, whilst acknowledging the difference of every child within the dynamic systems model. Fundamental movements, when considered as a broad range of skills in this model can be clearly seen to underpin later development of more specialized, applied actions.

The term 'fundamental' has also recently been adopted by a variety of exponents of a 'Long Term Athlete Development' (LTAD) approach to athletic training (Bayli, 1990, 2001, 2004). Bayli's work on LTAD stresses the importance of high training to competition ratios (i.e. lots of opportunities to practise), a focus on the process rather than outcome (i.e. the quality of the teaching and learning) and experiences centred on the development of basic movement competence to underpin later athletic specialization. In most of the sports-based applications of Bayli's work, a stage of athlete development termed 'FUNdamental' is included, usually within periods of early and later childhood.

Whilst the primary physical educator will be concerned with wider educational objectives than solely developing the 'athlete', it is heartening to know that the majority of national sports governing bodies have now designed programmes to fit more closely with this notion. The development of a broad base of skills to enable later specialized participation in a range of activities in specific sports contexts is one which has immediate relevance to practice in Key Stages 1 and 2. The language of the NCPE advocates a progressive development and refinement of skills over time and the application of skills and ideas to increasingly complex scenarios.

Categories of skill themes

Theorists agree that there are three broad categories of skill themes: those that involve the body travelling in space, those using control to manipulate objects and those which see the body striving to maintain balance. Categorizations describe these three categories as locomotor, stability and manipulation, and explain a clear developmental pathway from reflexive and then rudimentary movements that begin in the infancy period. For consistency, the earliest forms of movement can also be categorized within the same broad groups as more complex actions seen in the fundamental stage. The ability of a young child to crawl, stand and begin to walk provides the child with an early experience of locomotion and stability, usually mixed with a desire to reach out and grasp an object (often something that they aren't actually allowed to touch!).

Whilst different exponents of developmental physical education may call categories of skills by slightly different terms, we believe the definitions below accurately describe what these are. The three broad categories of skill themes used throughout this chapter follow.

1 *Stability skills* form the basis from which all other movements occur. Stability skills enable the body to maintain equilibrium, either statically (such as in a 'held' balance in gymnastic activities) or whilst moving (such as in dodging an opponent in tag rugby). Because all of these skills involve some degree of transference of weight, they are necessary for the execution of virtually all locomotor and manipulation skills. Additionally, many stability skills involve movement around either the horizontal or vertical axis of the body. Examples of stability skills include:

- bending
- stretching
- spinning
- sinking and falling
- twisting
- turning
- pivoting
- swinging
- inverted supports
- body rolling
- landing and stopping
- dodging
- balancing

2 *Locomotor skills* are used to transport the body in a vertical or horizontal plane from one point to another. The child uses these skills to move the body through space in a variety of contexts, sometimes to achieve a particular goal (e.g. to set a personal best time for a run), or for aesthetic purposes (e.g. in performing a short dance motif). Before locomotion can occur, a degree of stability is needed to remain upright (in the case of walking). Examples of locomotor skills are:

- walking
- running
- jumping
- hopping
- galloping
- sliding/side-slip
- skipping
- leaping
- climbing

3 *Manipulative skills* are used to impart to or receive force from an object, sometimes called *ballistic* (giving force) and *reception* skills. In physical education, these tend to be gross motor skills, using large movements to send, receive and travel with objects and implements. Fine motor manipulation is also a concern, especially in the Foundation Stage, where gripping a pencil, tying shoelaces and cutting with scissors are all skills to be mastered within 'physical development'. Whilst sending, receiving and 'travelling with' skills are the most commonly given examples of manipulation, force is also imparted to objects in other ways. Exchanging batons in a sprint relay, pushing off the blocks in a sprint start, planting hands on a box top to achieve stability and spring in a vault are also manipulative components of movement phrases. Examples of manipulative skills are:

- throwing (underarm and overarm)
- catching
- kicking (static and moving)
- trapping (with body or implement)
- striking (static and moving ball)
- volleying (hands, body, feet, implement)
- bouncing
- dribbling (hands, feet, implement)
- ball rolling
- punting (i.e. kicking a held ball from the hands)

Selected specialized sport-related movement skills
Football skills
Basketball skills
Netball skills
Gymnastic skills
Athletics skills
Dance skills
Striking skills
Swimming skills
Racket skills
etc.

Selected fundamental movement skills

Stability	Locomotion	Manipulation
1. Axial	**1. Basic**	**1. Sending or propelling**
bending	walking	object rolling
stretching	jogging	throwing
twisting	running	kicking
turning	leaping	punting
swinging	hopping	striking
	jumping	volleying
		bouncing
2. Static and dynamic (moving) actions	**2. Combinations**	**2. Receiving**
upright balances	climbing	trapping
inverted (or upside-down) balances	galloping	catching
rolling	sliding	
rocking	skipping	
starting		
stopping		
dodging		

Figure 4.1 The relationship between fundamental and specialized skills

Three stages of development

Within the *fundamental movement phase* of motor development it is generally acknowledged that three broad stages of development can be modelled to aid observation and analysis. This said, it must be reiterated here that these models are simply an aid for comparison and description; the majority of children will exhibit traits across two stages and may not demonstrate an 'exact fit'. For the child identified as an *initial* or *early mover*, the question for the teacher is how to facilitate performance towards an *elementary* and then *mature* stage. Eventually, pupils will be working at levels of competence that are increasingly mature and applicable within specialized contexts – a time when progressive transition from the fundamental movement phase to the *specialized movement phase* occurs.

Stage 1 – The initial, immature or early mover stage

In this stage, young children (typically two to three years old) make early, purposeful attempts at a fundamental skill. The movements tend to look uncoordinated and lack coordination of the muscle groups. Judging of distances between objects, direction of propulsion and requirements of force are crude, and the attempt may look inhibited or over-exaggerated. Children in this stage respond well to encouragement and praise and will show quick improvement when tasks are presented within informal, play-based activities using a variety of equipment and apparatus.

Stage 2 – The intermediate, transitional or elementary mover stage

During this stage, the child appears to become more skilful. Coordination, accuracy of movement and control are increasingly evident, although the fluency of movement remains a little 'awkward'. Gallahue and Donnelly (2003) suggest that many adults have not progressed from this stage in a variety of fundamental movement skills owing to insufficient instruction, limited opportunities for practice and poor feedback. The transition from this stage to the next is crucial if young people and adults are to be empowered with choice of lifelong physical activity and should be a primary goal of physical education, particularly in Key Stage 1 of the NCPE.

Stage 3 – The mature or later mover stage

This stage of development is generally categorized by increased coordination, fluency, efficiency, accuracy and economy of action. The child looks less clumsy and is able to integrate a number of skills into flowing sequences. The child at this stage of development is also one who is usually getting stronger and whose skeleto-muscular system can enable greater force to be generated through movement; the result is therefore faster, increasingly dynamic and varied actions. In the right circumstances, the majority of children are able to achieve a mature pattern of movement around the age of transition from Key Stage 1 to Key Stage 2. If this is achieved, an increasingly complex range of tasks can be performed and the skills can be applied in a number of challenging contexts.

Where mature patterns of fundamental skills are successfully achieved, children's participation in recognizable sports-based activities becomes a realistic goal. This also coincides with broad age phases where children are increasingly aware of sport and many will have begun to take part in community sports and dance clubs. The goal, then, is for all children to move towards a *specialized movement skill phase*, which allows children to apply skills in a range of contexts, continue to become increasingly skilful through further opportunities to practise, and make informed decisions about ongoing, lifelong participation.

With regards to the NCPE, it is tempting to simplify progression between the stages of fundamental skill development towards specialized movement and lifelong participation and to link the stages to an age-group categorization of what physical education should look like at each Key Stage. It is important, however, to remain true to developmental physical education, as most children will not fit the ideal type that this would suggest. Some children will be ready for specialized application long before others, due simply to increased opportunities to practise and parental encouragement. Some children will appear more advanced in some skills compared to their own performance in others, and some will remain unenthused and unlikely to want to progress in activities that have not been presented in an appropriate way. Each child's rate and characteristics of skill development will be unique to the individual and will remain so throughout life. The primary physical educator must therefore consider:

1 The importance of using non-judgemental language when describing early attempts at an initial stage of development. A child attempting an overarm throw for the first time will undoubtedly be an expert 'early thrower'.
2 That theoretical models of particular stages of development (such as Gallahue's Initial, Elementary and Mature model) are, by definition, over-simplified and will normally not 'fit' *every* child's actions. Individual idiosyncrasies are evident in all the best performers in the world, and there is no absolutely right way to perform a skill.
3 Actions of particular body segments within any one skill may be at different stages of development. For example, in an overarm throw, the leg position and stance may be seen to be 'mature' whilst the arm action is 'elementary.'
4 Children will not develop in every skill theme at the same pace and may show mature patterns in some skills earlier than in others.

Developmental sequences in fundamental skills

Theorists have attempted to show how skills mature in different ways. The maturation of a skill theme from an early, simple attempt through various steps or stages to a more mature pattern was first described in detail by Seefeldt and Haubenstricker (1982, cited in Haywood, 1993). An alternative model for skill analysis uses body segments to describe what a child's actions will look like when attempting specific actions. In this case, the description is about the body segment rather than stage of development. In both cases, the description of what the performer looks like is essentially subjective and arbitrary. Whichever approach is used for qualitative skill analysis, the outcome of assessment must be greater knowledge of children's learning needs in the physical domain.

It is unlikely that many primary physical educators will find time to video individual children and perform a detailed skill analysis using a more objective, perhaps biome-chanical, approach. This is very labour intensive and primary practitioners will need to find ways in which specific observations can be recorded quickly to maximum effect. An informed observation of pupils' work in physical education will aid assessment *of* and *for* learning and enable the teacher to plan future learning tasks with confidence. The key questions to be addressed by the teacher are:

- What level of proficiency is being shown by the child?
- How do I know (what is the evidence?) … and how can I describe the actions I see?
- What would the next individually relevant level of proficiency for this child look like?
- How can I help bring about learning and improvement in performance so that the child can achieve this?
- What tasks can I facilitate to help this progression?
- What can I do and say to help this progression?
- How do I know when the child has met the specified learning objectives?

It would be impossible in a book of this nature to examine in detail every fundamental movement skill, discuss the emergence of mature patterns and suggest activities that would help develop such skills. Instead, we give three examples of fundamental skills (one from each of locomotor, stability and manipulation) and show how observation and assessment of physical actions can be used to raise the quality of teaching and learning.

Example 1: Running

Running is arguably the locomotor skill most commonly used in team sports and individual athletic events and is an excellent way of maintaining and increasing cardiovascular fitness and health. It is surprising therefore, that this skill is rarely *taught*, and development of the mature pattern of running is generally left to biological chance. Whilst performance in speed-based events will ultimately depend not only on technique but also genetically determined proportions of fast and slow twitch muscle fibres (see Chapter 3), it is clear that many children and young people have little awareness of their own bodies during running and the changes that they can make to their actions to run faster, slower and further.

Table 4.1 examines the running pattern at three arbitrary stages of development (initial, elementary and mature) and describes the movements typically seen in arms and legs.

The descriptions provided in Table 4.1 are approximations to an idealized account of three stages. Children may look exactly like one particular stage or exhibit traits for all three. Similarly, a child may demonstrate a mature pattern of arm action alongside an elementary pattern of leg action. The model presented is a simple one that provides a basis for initial observations and comparison and should help the teacher to ascertain immediate learning needs.

Activities to promote a mature running pattern

Initial activities should make use of questioning by the teacher to illicit a variety of movement experiences. Early runners should be asked to run with a variety of *force*

Table 4.1 Descriptive stages of running (with reference to leg and arm actions)

	Leg action	Arm action
Initial	• Short and limited swing • Stiff, uneven stride • No or limited 'flight' phase • Incomplete extension of rear support leg on push off • Some outward rotation of leg from hip	• Stiff, short swing (but opposite arms and legs used) • Variable degrees of elbow flexion • Horizontal swing/rotation • Elbows extend when arms swing back
Elementary	• Increased stride length • Increased flight phase • Support leg extended more fully at take off	• Increased arm swing • Arm swing becomes more vertical
Mature	• Stride length at maximum • Leg stride fast • Support leg shows complete extension • Recovery thigh parallel to ground and heel tucked close to bum as thigh swings forward • Legs working in 'straight lines'	• Arm action vertical in opposition to leg action • Arms bent at approximately 90 degrees • Arms working in 'straight lines' with little rotation of trunk

(e.g. softly, heavily), *time* (e.g. quickly, slowly), *flow* (e.g. smoothly, jerkily), at a range of *levels* (e.g. tall, low to ground), in a variety of *directions* (e.g. forwards, diagonally, change direction), in relation to *objects* (e.g. around the hall, across the space, along the line) and with and without *others* (e.g. by self, following or leading a partner, side by side). The focus on such features of movement will enable the children to consider the 'best' way of running quickly or slowly, or different techniques that can be applied for different purposes. Such variations can also be linked together to create greater complexity of task and applied within conditions of particular games such as those that involve chasing and dodging, or which link travelling with sending and receiving.

Key teaching points to promote a mature running pattern
Teachers should be aware of key movement vocabulary and 'teaching points' when helping to develop running skills in children. Key teaching points include:

• keep your head up and look forward;
• lean slightly forward;
• run with knees high and heels flicking bottom (emphasizes full range of motion);
• relax the shoulders and let your jaw go floppy as you run;
• bend your elbows (approximately 90 degrees);
• faster arms result in faster feet;
• heel to ground first (for slower sustained running) and then push trough balls of feet;
• run on balls of feet for faster sprinting.

Example 2: Body rolling

Primary aged children are able to use their bodies to roll in a variety of ways. The 'type' of roll relates to direction and body shape during the roll around the body's axis. Efficient rolling actions are directly transferable from the gymnastic context to diving, trampolining and swimming (the tumble turn) but elements of body control in inverted and rolling positions are also evident in many sporting activities. Whilst some schools have shied away from teaching body rolling (particularly the forward roll) in recent years, it is clear that children enjoy the feeling of being upside down and are quickly able to develop a repertoire of rolling skills when afforded the opportunity to do so. The development of body rolling is described in Table 4.2 in the context of the forward roll.

Activities to promote a mature rolling pattern

Initial activities should make use of questioning by the teacher to illicit a variety of rolling responses. Early rollers should be asked to roll with a variety of *force* (e.g. rolling quietly, loudly), *time* (e.g. quickly, slowly, in slow motion), *flow* (e.g. smoothly, jerkily), at a range of *levels* (e.g. from high to low or in a medium position), in a variety of *directions* (e.g. forwards, backwards, sideways), in relation to *objects* (e.g. around the mat, along the soft bench, through the hoop) and with *others* (e.g. at the same time as your partner, away from your partner). Such variations can also be linked together to create greater complexity of task and applied within conditions of guided discovery activities and more formal approaches to teaching and learning. Once the mature pattern has been achieved, children can be challenged to link their rolling actions to other movements and to vary the rolls they achieve (e.g. consecutive forward rolls, backward roll to a squat, rolls along a line or bench).

Key teaching points to promote a mature rolling pattern

Teachers should be aware of key movement vocabulary and 'teaching points' when helping to develop body rolling skills in children. Key teaching points include:

- remain tucked in a small ball;
- as little of your head touching the surface as possible – push through hands to take weight;
- tuck chin to chest;
- roll slowly to show control – can every part of your spine touch the mat in sequence?;
- extend arms forward at end of roll to help maintain momentum and get to standing position.

Example 3: Overarm throwing

The overarm throw is used commonly in a number of adult games and has been studied widely by motor developmentalists. Children demonstrate a range of throwing skills, depending on the object being thrown and desired outcome (accuracy or distance), and

Table 4.2 Descriptive stages of forward roll development

	Body position	Head, arms and legs
Initial	• Body curled in a 'loose C' position • Uncurls to an 'L shape' at end of roll	• Head makes contact with surface • Arms uncoordinated
Elementary	• Body curled in a 'tight C' position at start of roll, but uncurls to an 'L shape' at end of roll • Ineffective in executing symmetrical movements	• Head leads action, but top of head still touches surface • Hands and arms contribute to action, although little push off at start • May have uneven push off with arms and feet
Mature	• Body weight supported on hands at start of roll • Body stays in a 'tight C' shape throughout (hips and knees flexed throughout the roll) • Momentum means that child is returned to starting position on feet again	• Head leads action • Back of head touches surface lightly • Arms aid in push off and both legs used • Arms extend forwards to maintain momentum as lower back takes the weight

the overarm throw eventually has greatest application in many striking and fielding games contexts.

Activities to promote a mature throwing pattern

Initial activities should make use of questioning by the teacher to illicit a variety of throwing responses. Early throwers should be asked to throw with a variety of *force* (e.g. throwing softly, forcefully), *time* (e.g. quickly, slowly, in slow motion), *flow* (e.g. using as little movement as possible or as much movement as possible), at a range of *levels* (e.g. from high to low or in a medium position), in a variety of *directions* (e.g. forwards, backwards, sideways), with a variety of *objects and in relation to other objects* (e.g. a tennis ball, a football, at a target, over a net) and with *others* (e.g. to a partner). Such variations can also be linked together to create greater complexity of task and applied within conditions of guided discovery activities and more formal approaches to teaching and learning. Once the mature pattern has been achieved, children can be challenged to link their throwing actions to other movements and to vary the distances and degrees of accuracy they achieve. This may include fielding techniques in striking and fielding games or individual challenge events in athletic activities. Refinement of throwing technique will be necessary for different implements (sizes and weights) and for different athletic events. Throwing the javelin for example has many parallels with the overarm throw, although 'putting the shot' requires significant adjustments. In all throwing 'events' however, a common theme is the generation of tension within the whole body to create maximum propulsive force on release. In all cases this is achieved by bringing the arm through 'fast and last'.

Table 4.3 Descriptive stages of overarm throwing development

	Arm action	Trunk	other
Initial	• Action is from elbow and is more of a push than a throw • Arm extends forwards and downwards	• Body is facing direction of throw • Very rigid – little or no trunk rotation during throw	• Fingers splayed at release • Feet are stationary, although some shuffling actions in preparation
Elementary	• Arm swung upwards in preparation and elbow flexed • Arm swung forwards during execution	• Some rotation towards throwing side during preparation • Upper body bends forwards as arm throws	• Ball held behind head • Forward shift of body weight • Steps forwards with leg on same side as throwing arm
Mature	• Arm swung backwards in preparation • Opposite arm raised for balance and aim • Throwing elbow moves forwards as arm throws • Forearm rotates – thumb points down	• Trunk markedly rotates towards throwing side during preparation phase • Throwing shoulder drops slightly • Body sideways on to direction of throw	• Rotation through hips, legs and spine • Weight initially on rear foot and weight shifts – often marked with a step with opposite foot

Key teaching points to promote a mature throwing pattern

Teachers should be aware of key movement vocabulary and 'teaching points' when helping to develop throwing skills in children. Key teaching points include:

- use opposite arm and leg;
- position shoulder towards the target, to encourage a side-on action
- non-throwing arm used to point at the target and help balance;
- throwing arm up and ball near to ear;
- elbow leads on forward swing;
- rear foot follows through;
- arms comes through 'fast and last'.

Using an observational checklist

It is possible to make use of an 'observational checklist' to conduct a detailed assessment of specific fundamental skills. Such a checklist would be used to record judgement of skill 'stage' against a preconceived model of what this *should* look like. Checklists can focus on body segments or the sequential nature of the skill – for example, by breaking the skill down into preparation, execution and recovery phases. The example provided here (see Figure 4.2) is based on segmental analysis of the running locomotor skill and is designed to enable real time recording by a skilled observer.

It is advisable that observations are made from more than one angle – a view from the front, behind and both sides will enable a more complete assessment to be made. Teachers

Observational Checklist For Running					
Class:		Date:		Age Phase/Key Stage:	Observer:

Name	Leg action	Trunk action	Arm action	Overall	Comment
I = Initial pattern; E = Elementary pattern; M = Mature pattern; S = Specialized/sports application					

Figure 4.2 Example observational checklist for fundamental movement skills

should also be aware that movements observed towards the end of the lesson may be influenced by levels of fatigue – something that is known to adversely impact on performance.

The number of children for whom assessments can be recorded in this way will depend on amount of time available, the skill being assessed, the experience and speed of the observer and the lesson format. We suggest that teachers should avoid lessons that are planned for the sole purpose of assessment – this is often counter-productive to children's learning. Instead, skilled observation must be planned for within particular parts of each lesson, making use of colleagues where possible and focused on a sample of children each time. It is also important not to jump to conclusions too readily. Where a child demonstrates technique that is far from 'mature' but is effective with regard to intended outcome (for example a child may be the fastest runner despite looking 'awkward'), this should be noted; some of the world's best performers have shown unconventional yet very efficient technique (champion runners Michael Johnson and Paula Radcliffe, for example) and it would be a big mistake to assume that children whose techniques are unconventional should be 'coached' out of what comes naturally.

We also encourage teachers to produce their own formats for observation and assessment. These should always be linked clearly to the lesson's stated learning intentions and enable a specific focus on acquisition and development of skill. In addition, children in Key Stage 2 will be able to make use of similar recording sheets in their own self- and peer-assessment tasks and provide an excellent focus for evaluating and improving their own and others' work. When combined with self-check cards and posters describing and showing what skills look like (by, for example, making use of an elite performer's technique) such an approach to skill development becomes very powerful.

A key outcome of skill assessment should be the enhanced ability of the teacher to plan the next relevant stage of learning and to design tasks with particular learning needs in mind. A focus on the assessment of fundamental skill development at the transition from early to later childhood (or from Key Stage 1 to 2) is particularly informative regarding design of subsequent units of work. It should also be noted that alternative formats for observational assessment should be used for broader learning objectives in social, affective and cognitive domains and that the format suggested above should not be the sole method of physical education assessment in play.

Planning the next physical learning activity

The analysis of skill should be used to inform subsequent planning; deciding that a group of children is working at a 'mature' level is all well and good, although effectively meaningless without a focus on *how* and through *what* activities these children can be helped to become 'specialized' movers. The focus should be on creating tasks that are designed to illicit increasingly skilful, mature and refined responses, rather than simply asking children to replicate a demonstrated model of action. The tasks that can be designed to illicit such responses are infinite in number and variety and specific examples of activities can be seen within some of the recommended reading at the end of this chapter. The reader is also encouraged to consider the generic planning and teaching guidelines discussed in Chapter 5 of this text, particularly with reference to choice of teaching style.

Movement concepts

In addition to clarifying what skill themes are, Graham, Holt-Hale and Parker (2004) added a layer of modification to the performance of skills. *Movement concepts*, they argue, describe *how* skill themes are performed. The use of a rich and varied movement vocabulary to describe movement encourages children to consider where, how and with whom the skills will be carried out. Movement concepts are therefore ways in which a skill can be changed, expounded or progressed according to the requirements of a context. This has a clear implication for the use of language across the curriculum and suggests that movements experienced in physical education can enrich vocabulary by using a range of verbs and adjectives to help children to explore their own and others' actions.

The notion of movement concepts can be traced to influential work on movement analysis carried out in the dance context, most famously by Rudolph Laban (1948, 1966, 1980). His analysis of skills classifies movement into broad concepts, each concept suggesting a range of movement which may be explored (Smith-Autard, 1996). Davies (2003, p. 3) describes the body as 'the instrument of action' and explains how colour and form can be given to the 'playing' of the instrument through changing the dynamic quality, space within which the body moves and relationships between people and objects. Figure 4.3 summarizes Laban's analysis of movement within four interrelated sections. Each section has direct relevance to the moving child who will explore body actions in response to a range of stimuli and apply skills within various contexts.

Body actions		Qualities of movement	
Bending – stretching – twisting		Time:	
Transference of weight – stepping		Sudden	
Travelling		Sustained	
Turning		Quick	
Jumping (five types)		Slow	
Gesture		Weight:	
Stillness		Firm	
Body shapes		Light	
Symmetrical		Relaxed	
Asymmetrical		Flow:	
Body parts – isolated and emphasized		Free	
		Bound	
		Combinations	
Space		**Relationships**	
Size of movement		Relationships with objects	
Size of space		Relationships with people	
Extension in space		Alone in a group	
Levels:		In pairs:	
High		Copying – mirroring	
Low		Leading – following	
Medium		Unison – canon	
Shape in space:		Meeting – parting	
Curved		Question – answer	
Straight		Group work:	
Directions in space:		Numerical variation	
Three-dimensional		Group shape	
Planed		Inter-group relationship	
Diagonals		Spatial relationships:	
		Over	
		Under	
		Around	

Figure 4.3 A summary of Laban's analysis of movement (adapted from Smith-Autard, 1996)

Teaching and learning of skill themes

Whilst ensuring that children are given opportunities and support to develop a range of physical attributes and skills, we must also be wary of the merits and pitfalls of a 'technical' approach to the development of movement skills. If we are to plan tasks that are meaningful, purposeful, individually relevant and motivational (in keeping with the principles of developmental physical education offered in Chapter 1) the way in which teaching and learning episodes are 'framed' and facilitated is critical.

There is a common misconception amongst practitioners about the most effective way to facilitate the development of children's movement abilities and motor skills. This is in part linked to differences between teaching and coaching and indeed physical education and sport, although we would argue that 'sports coaching' *per se* has, for too long in some cases, utilized a technical (e.g. 'this is *the* way to hit a ball, catch, execute a dance step') rather than a skill (e.g. 'what is the best way to hit the ball in this situation?') approach.

If one observes televised sport or professional performers, it is easy to see that there is not just one way to catch or kick a ball, to execute a dive or to choreograph actions in dance. There are of course common key factors of skills that enable the successful achievement of objectives, but it would be absurd to suggest to children that there is only one way in which a skill should be performed.

The engagement of the learner in problem solving and planning of their own performance not only links learning of skills to broader educational objectives such as analysing, synthesizing and communicating knowledge, but helps to develop more able and creative performers at an elite level. The ability of athletes in all disciplines to think under pressure and to make decisions to change outcomes of highly competitive situations is a trait seen amongst the world's best performers.

The aim of developing skilful performers through carefully planned and progressive lessons raises questions about teaching behaviours, teaching and learning strategies and the use of particular teaching styles. It would seem appropriate that a developmental approach to teaching physical education should make use of a range of methods to ensure that learning is pitched at an appropriate level and in a relevant context for every child.

For some, the use of direct teaching approaches may be right on occasions, although for us, problem solving and exploratory activities hold most appeal. These approaches are discussed more fully in Chapter 5; for now, we ask that primary physical educators do not view 'subject knowledge' as a series of technical teaching points (sometimes called 'key factors') with which knowledge is imparted by the teacher to the learner. Instead, we encourage reflective practitioners to consider and seek to develop more relevant 'pedagogy content knowledge' (Shulman, 1986) which enables the teacher to understand how particular topics, problems or issues are organized, represented and adapted to meet the diverse interests and abilities of learners. This not only helps to meet the aims of developmental physical education in seeking to personalize the learning experience, but helps the teacher to consider the individual, task and environmental factors at large.

The choice of teaching and learning strategy utilized in primary physical education should also be cognizant of broader theories of how children learn. In Chapter 1 we touched on the work of Lev Vygotsky, and his work and theories are particularly informative when considering constructivist learning approaches. Social learning theories acknowledge the critical role played by teachers in the learning process. This notion has sometimes been overlooked by advocates of child-centred education (Blenkin and Kelly, 1987), where observation of busy, happy and well-behaved children seemingly engaged in a movement task may be wrongly construed as 'learning'.

We should not lose sight, however, of the role of the teacher in skilfully intervening to help move the children from the present level of attainment towards potential achievement.

This juncture between what the child can do *now* and what the child could achieve *in the future* (short, medium and long term) should remain at the forefront of the teacher's mind in the ongoing planning, teaching and assessment cycle.

Social learning theory also informs us of the relevance and role of 'collaborative' and 'active learning', whereby children's communication and interaction with each other is a vital part of the learning process. In accepting this, we should do everything we can to ensure that primary physical education is *not* characterized by the following indicators of poor practice:

- children waiting in queues for a 'turn';
- children working in silence at the bequest of the teacher who is keen simply to 'control' behaviour;
- children simply copying the teacher or doing what they are told to do;
- teacher giving instructions but not asking questions;
- a lack of resources to scaffold learning;
- busy, happy and well-behaved children who are learning absolutely nothing.

The picture painted here is hopefully not one that is seen in today's schools. On a more subtle level, though, we regularly see a lack of transference of teaching strategies from the classroom to the physical education environment. For example, children work in groups at tables rather than in individual rows in the classroom, yet in the school hall children work as individuals or in lines. In the classroom, resources (pencils or tools, for example) are positioned for each group to access, normally in the centre of each table, yet in the hall we often only see one pile of mats or one bag of balls in the corner. The developmental and reflective physical educator should make connections between what they do in the classroom to what they do in physical education; how children learn doesn't change even though the physical education 'classroom' brings a different requirement for organization on a bigger scale.

Summary

The fostering of fundamental movement skills and movement concepts during the primary years is seen as a crucial step for children to be proficient and to have a real choice of future adult activities. Fundamental skills should form the physical learning focus in early years and Key Stage 1 settings and should continue to be a part of learning and refinement for older children. Teachers must familiarize themselves with appropriate vocabulary and language to use during teaching episodes and have a common idea of a number of teaching points around which feedback and feed-forward can be planned. An approach to skill development that is open-ended and allows children the chance to make mistakes and solve problems is welcomed.

Key questions

1 What are fundamental movement skills and how can these be used as a focus for physical skill learning?
2 What are the key skill themes to be explored during the primary years?
3 How can observation and assessment of fundamental skills assist in the planning process?
4 What do I need to know as a teacher of fundamental and specialized movement skills?

Learning tasks

1 Observe a group of children in a physical education lesson. Focus on the range and type of skills that are being demonstrated. Create a list of the skills under three broad headings – stability, locomotor and manipulation.
2 Design an observational checklist for use during a subsequent physical education lesson. Use the checklist to decide the level of skill being demonstrated by the group of children. What activities would you plan for these children in the following lesson? What specific movement vocabulary and feedback can you plan to use with the children during the next lesson. If possible, seek an opportunity to put your ideas into teaching practice.

Links to the Framework of Professional Standards for Teachers

The content and focus of this chapter have direct relevance to the following Qualified Teacher Status (QTS) standards (TDA, 2007) for those training to teach in primary schools: Q11b, Q12, Q18, Q19, Q21, Q22, Q23, Q24.

Useful websites

http://www.scu.edu.au/schools/edu/projects/migi/secure/teacher2/FMS.HTM
An Australian University (Southern Cross) site dedicated to Fundamental Movement skills:
New South Wales Department of education and training.
http://www.curriculumsupport.education.nsw.gov.au/primary/pdhpe/gamessport/fms001.htm
Information on teaching fundamental movement skills.
http://www.earlyyearsfundamentals.co.uk/
Fundamental movement ideas from the British Gymnastics Association

References and further reading

Bartlett, R. (1997) *Introduction to Sports Biomechanics*. London: E&FN Spon.
Bayli, I. (1990) *Quadrennial and Double Quadrennial Planning of Athletic Training*. Victoria BC: Canadian Coaches Association.

Bayli, I. (2001) *Sport System Building and Long-term Athlete Development in British Columbia*. Canada: SportsMed BC.

Bayli, I. (2002) 'Long Term Athlete Development: The Systems and Solutions', *Faster Higher Stronger*, 6–9.

Bayli, I. and Hamilton A. (2004) *Long-Term Athlete Development: Trainability in Childhood and Adolescence. Windows of Opportunity. Optimal Trainability*. Victoria: National Coaching Institute British Columbia & Advanced Training and Performance Ltd.

Blenkin, G. and Kelly, A. (1987) *The Primary Curriculum: A Process Approach to Curriculum Planning* (2nd edn). London: Paul Chapman Publishing.

Davies, M. (2003) *Movement and Dance in Early Childhood* (2nd edn). London: Paul Chapman Publishing.

DfEE/QCA (2000) *Curriculum Guidance for the Foundation Stage*. London: QCA.

Gallahue, D. L. (1996) *Developmental Physical Education for Today's Children*. Dubuque, IW: Brown & Benchmark.

Gallahue, D. L. and Donnelly, F. C. (2003) *Developmental Physical Education for Today's Children*. Champaign, IL: Human Kinetics.

Gallahue, D. L. and Ozmun, J. (1998) *Understanding Motor Development – Infants, Children, Adolescents, Adults*. Dubuque, IW: McGraw-Hill.

Graham, G., A. Holt-Hale, S. and Parker, M. (2004) *Children Moving: A Reflective Approach to Teaching Physical Education* (6th edn). Boston, MA: McGraw Hill.

Haywood, K. M. (1993) *Life Span Motor Development* (2nd edn). Champaign, IL: Human Kinetics.

Jess, M., Dewar, K. and Fraser, G. (2004) Basic Moves: Developing a Foundation for Lifelong Physical Activity, *British Journal of Teaching Physical Education*, Summer, 24–7.

Knapp, B. (1963) *Skill in Sport: The Attainment of Proficiency*. London: Routledge and Kegan Paul.

Knudson, D. V. and Morrison, C. S. (1997) *Qualitative Analysis of Human Movement*. Leeds: Human Kinetics.

Laban, R. (1948) *Modern Educational Dance*. London: MacDonald and Evans.

Laban, R. (1966) *Choreutics*. London: MacDonald and Evans.

Laban, R. (1980) *The Mastery of Movement* (4th edn). London: MacDonald and Evans.

Magill, R. A. (1993) *Motor Learning: Concepts and Applications*. IW: Brown and Benchmark.

Malina, R. M., Bouchard, C. and Bar-Or, O. (2004) *Growth, Maturation and Physical Activity*. Champaign, IL: Human Kinetics.

PEAUK (2003) *Observing Children Moving*. Reading: PEA/TackleSport.

Seefeldt, V. and Haubenstricker, J. (1982) 'Patterns, Phases or Stages: An Analytical Model for the Study of Developmental Movement', in J. A. S. Kelso and J. E. Clark (eds) *The Development of Movement Control and Coordination*. New York: Wiley, pp. 309–18.

Sharp, B. (1992) *Acquiring Skill in Sport*. Eastbourne: Sports Dynamics.

Shulman, L. S. (1986) 'Those Who Understand: Knowledge Growth in Teaching', *Educational Researcher*, **15**(2), 4–14.

Smith-Autard, J. M. (1996) *Dance Composition* (3rd edn). London: A & C Black.

Training and Development Agency for Schools (TDA) (2007) *Draft Revised Professional Standards for Teachers in England*. London: TDA. Available from http://www.tda.gov.uk/upload/resources/pdf/d/draft_revised_standards_framework_jan_2007.pdf [accessed 5 March 2007].

Teaching Curriculum Physical Education

5

Chapter outline

As a teacher I possess tremendous power to make a child's life miserable or joyous. I can be a tool of torture or an instrument of inspiration.

Haim Ginott

Introduction

The focus of this chapter is on teaching and learning strategies required to fully utilize the activity areas detailed in the current PE National Curriculum (DfEE/QCA, 1999). The chapter builds on knowledge of physical, perceptual-motor, cognitive, social and affective aspects of child development covered in earlier chapters and aims to sharpen the reader's focus on the planning, teaching and assessment cycle. Generic principles of this process are discussed and these are subsequently applied to specific activity examples in Chapter 6. We have not, however, provided schemes of work to be followed. Sample planning frameworks are included to provide a starting point for the planning process; we believe that a primary teacher wishing to deliver the subject effectively for all children is in the best position to plan his/her own sequences of lessons and should not teach from 'off the shelf' plans.

Key Points

- The teaching of high quality physical education is not possible without knowledge of what children can already do (gained through observation and assessment) and planning to meet specific learning outcomes.
- The reflective practitioner will constantly seek to adapt and improve lesson content to maximize learning potential and pupil achievement.
- The teacher must consider his/her teaching style, strategies and behaviours to maximize the opportunity to impact on the learning episode.

Curriculum documentation and implications for physical education

The 1988 Education Reform Act (DfEE, 1988) first introduced a National Curriculum for state maintained schools in England and Wales which stipulated the subjects to be taught to all children in primary and secondary classrooms (i.e. between the ages of 5–16, across four 'Key Stages'). English, mathematics and science were identified as the 'core subjects', whilst technology, history, geography, modern languages, music, art and physical education were the 'foundation subjects'. The Act also introduced a series of national tests at ages 7, 11, 14 and 16; provided schools with an opportunity to become self-governing; and introduced a new inspection regime.

The National Curriculum, and hence the physical education component of this, has since evolved against a backcloth of seemingly endless initiative, policy and curriculum innovation. The existing NCPE documentation (DfES/QCA, 1999) attempted to enhance clarity and coherence in teaching and learning (QCA, 1999; Casbon, 1999) and introduced strands of learning to be pursued throughout each activity area.

At the time, a stated rationale for introducing the 'four strands' was to 'clarify requirements and establish a more effective framework for planning, performing and evaluating' (QCA, 1999, p. 10). Whilst the nature and content of curricular physical education has been called in to question (see, for example, Penney, 1999), it appears sensible to agree with Young's (1998) advice to design curricula that are reliable frameworks for helping young people to make sense of their worlds, rather than as relics of former traditions and historically embedded practices.

At the time of writing this text, 'QCA Futures: Meeting the Challenge' (see http://www.qca.org.uk/10969.html) aims to promote broad debate about the future of learning. The Qualifications and Curriculum Authority claim to want to ensure that curriculum development responds to changing demands and is informed by the latest and best thinking. The current context for physical educators is also influenced by additional education policy and government intervention, most notably in the form of the Children Act (DfES, 2004), the associated *Every Child Matters* (DfES, 2003a) Green Paper and the *Excellence and Enjoyment* document (DfES, 2003b) which outlines a vision for the future of primary education.

Within the context of educational policy change and what has been seen by some practitioners as 'initiative overload', it seems improbable that the content of the NCPE will prevail in its current format in years to come. It would, however, be remiss not to include specific reference to the activity content of this document, as without knowledge of what we are currently expected to deliver, it would be impossible to suggest change, to innovate or to interpret guidance materials in a developmental way. The flexibility offered to the primary physical educator by the current NCPE should be embraced and effectively utilized by all those seeking to provide developmentally appropriate learning episodes.

Whatever the requirements of the centrally produced curriculum of the day, we should always bear in mind our duty to 'protect the spirit of enquiry, to keep it from becoming blasé due to overexcitement, wooden from routine ... or dissipated through random exercise on trivial things' (Dewey, 1933, p. 34). It is unlikely that this can be achieved without an immersion into thoughtful reflection on and in action by the teacher and by giving due consideration to the planning, teaching and assessment cycle that this chapter has as a focus.

Current National Curriculum expectations

NCPE currently provides two foci for teaching and learning. Underpinning the curriculum lie 'four aspects' of physical education knowledge and understanding which should permeate learning and teaching episodes across all Key Stages (see Figure 5.1) and within all six activity areas. In primary age phases, the acquisition and development of skills will normally be an objective in all lessons as children will be experiencing and refining skills, in some cases, for the first time. Learning intentions from within the other 'aspects', however, should not be neglected and, through careful planning, the teacher must also look to provide opportunities for children to discuss, evaluate, solve problems, suggest ways to improve, and develop a personal awareness of health and fitness.

There is an acknowledged need for lesson content to include as much physical activity as possible, particularly at a time where, for some children, physical education may provide the only regular opportunity for exercise. Tasks should therefore be designed for maximum participation and minimum time 'off-task'. However, there is a dual need to ensure that tasks also include opportunities for pupils to communicate and discuss aspects of their work with the teacher and each other. At times, this may involve pupils checking each other's work against specific criteria on a task card, videoing performances and analysing immediately on the screen of the camera, or discussing changes that their group should make to a movement sequence. Denying pupils the chance to engage in such meaningful dialogue at the expense of providing maximum activity would be a mistake and potentially detrimental to the amount and quality of *learning* that will subsequently take place.

The 'breadth of study' provided within the NCPE is currently symbolized through teaching and learning within six 'activity' areas. These are:

1 Dance activities (Key Stages 1 and 2)
2 Games activities (Key Stages 1 and 2)

Acquiring and developing skills	Selecting and applying skills, tactics and compositional ideas
Evaluating and improving performance	Knowledge and understanding of fitness and health

Figure 5.1 The four 'aspects' of National Curriculum physical education knowledge, skills and understanding

3 Gymnastic activities (Key Stages1 and 2)
4 Swimming activities and water safety (Key Stage 1 *or* Key Stage 2)
5 Athletic activities (Key Stage 2)
6 Outdoor and adventurous activities (Key Stage 2).

The six activity areas outlined in the 'breadth of study' should be viewed as loose frameworks for the development and application of skill themes and not as formal, adult versions of 'sports'. For example, the versions of games being played in Year 6 will begin to look a little like mini versions of adult games, assuming that children's skills match the expectations provided by particular rules, pitch dimensions, team structures and so on. 'Traditional' or formal genres of dance (e.g. ballet, tap, jazz) should not necessarily dominate the curriculum at the expense of creative opportunities for children to make and practise their own dances; gymnastic award schemes centred on a bank of specific techniques should not remove the opportunity for children to work collaboratively to plan and refine their own sequences on the floor and a range of apparatus. The principle of individual relevance should be at the forefront of teachers' minds when considering specific lesson content and in the subject leaders' thoughts when mapping planning across the curriculum (see Chapter 8).

Interpreting curriculum requirements

It is entirely possible (if not a little extreme) to teach each of the six activity areas in a swimming pool, although in light of the need to provide a range of opportunities and experiences for children this may not be entirely desirable. It should also be noted that the names of specific sports (such as hockey, football, rugby, netball, cricket and rounders) or particular forms of dance do not actually appear within curriculum documentation and should therefore not appear on school-based plans or units of work. Instead, specific movement terms and themes are introduced for the teacher to develop progressively over a period of time.

From a developmental perspective, it is suggested that some primary aged children will be ready to apply their physical skills, knowledge and understanding, spatial and conceptual awareness to relatively demanding contexts, whilst for other children in the same class, such tasks could be construed as inappropriate, poorly planned and over-demanding challenges. The concern here is therefore to consider how teachers can begin to plan tasks to meet the needs of the class and have a positive effect on motivation and enjoyment for all.

This 'timeline of readiness' is age related but not age dependent and it is impossible, therefore, to say that suddenly, on entering a new age grouping or Key Stage, lesson content, teaching style and activity foci should automatically change. This reinforces the clear but often overlooked need to differentiate physical education activities in order to meet the needs of all children, a strategy that will be examined in detail later in this chapter. For now, we examine a number of key issues that must be addressed by the teacher when planning to bring about effective learning.

Planning to bring about learning

Central to the planning process is the question 'what do we want the children to learn?' Whether the teacher is a subject leader mapping the whole school curriculum, a class teacher working in collaboration with others to design termly or half-termly plans, or a trainee teacher planning in detail for one lesson, the question must be answered. In determining objectives for the pupils' learning, two further questions need to be addressed, namely 'what do the children *already* know?' and 'what will the children be able to learn in the future?'

These questions reiterate the need for teachers to develop a detailed view of children's abilities and attributes, knowledge, skills and understanding within physical education. Communication with other teachers, learning support assistants, parents and community sports coaches, will enable a mosaic of information to be collated over time; this constantly evolving picture of a child's abilities in the subject must inform specific planning for subsequent learning and, consequently, a full engagement with the planning, teaching and assessment cycle is unavoidable for any developmental physical educator.

The teacher should not view the setting of curricula learning objectives in a mutually exclusive way. The development of physical skills is facilitated by the ability to work within pairs or small groups and to listen and follow instructions; the ability to evaluate and improve one's own and peers' performances is aided by effective communication skills and so on. Whilst the acquisition and development of physical skills is the unique aspect of the physical education curriculum that must be planned for by the teacher, the wider concern for 'learning' and for fostering skills relevant to the aim of improving the quality of life for each child must also permeate the planning process.

Learning episode 5.1: What can children already do?

Niah has been learning to swim from the age of 2 and, now aged 6, is confident in the water, is developing a range of strokes and is building her stamina to swim unaided. She has always enjoyed water-based play in the pool and especially likes to glide, float, hop, jump, twist, turn and roll in the water. Last week she enjoyed doing handstands in the water and travelling under a bridge shape that her brother made with his legs. In physical education, Niah's class have just started a unit of work in gymnastic activities entitled 'travelling and balancing'. The teacher soon sees that Niah and some of her friends are able to travel in a variety of ways and is especially impressed to see children travelling around, under and through a variety of shapes made by their partner.

The Qualifications and Curriculum Authority consider primary physical education to show weaknesses that have a direct bearing on the quality of learning. In the 2004/5 annual report on achievement and assessment (QCA, 2005, pp. 5–7), it was found that some primary teachers lack confidence in the subject, do not carry out assessment to support learning, and are too concerned with class management at the expense of achievement and challenge. In addition, a narrow focus on 'acquiring and developing skills' was noted, reinforcing Ofsted's (2004) view that:

> pupils' ability to describe the strengths and weaknesses in their own performances remains underdeveloped. For example, one Year 5 pupil could explain that, when striking a ball, he had to step sideways, keep a firm wrist and racket head, but he was less confident explaining why the ball might travel in the wrong direction or drop into the net. (Extract from subject report viewed at http://live.ofsted.gov.uk/publications/annualreport0405/4.1.10.html)

Such comments have direct implications for the teacher when choosing specific teaching strategies to support learning and to enable pupils to make sufficient progress. How can we plan to help children to evaluate and improve performances, as well as to develop competence in a range of motor skills? There is obviously not just one answer to this question and a range of teaching behaviours, styles and strategies are available for the practitioner to choose from. This is made even broader when, in most primary schools, other adults are available to support learning in curriculum time *and* digital technology is readily available to support teaching and learning.

What are we learning today?

It is worth considering here what we mean by *learning objectives*. According to Pollard (2005):

> Objectives express what we intend that the pupils learn in terms of skills, knowledge and understanding. They are the essential planning tool of the teacher, as without clear, concise objectives linked to specific activities, the teacher has little basis on which to define the purpose of the task clearly for the pupils, or assess pupils' progress. (p. 210)

In general terms, lesson objectives are an expression of *what* we want all the children to learn and/or *how* we want them to learn it; this is subtly different to expected pupil outcomes that will be demonstrations, through actions, words and behaviours, of what pupils of all abilities have learned.

It is useful to consider the framing of learning objectives as statements that can be shared with the children. In this way, WALT ('we are learning to ...') and WILF ('what I am looking for is …') statements can indicate both the learning outcomes and pupil outcomes that have been planned for. For example, a Year 2 gymnastic activities lesson planned within the theme of 'shape' may include the following shared objectives:

WALT: (i) We are learning to make a variety of different shapes with our bodies on the floor and on apparatus.
 (ii) We are learning to think about how we can improve our shapes.

WILF: (i) I am looking for you to show me clear shapes, control when moving from one shape to the other, and shapes that show real contrast on the floor and apparatus.
 (ii) I would like you to be able to tell me or your partner something that you could do next time to improve your shapes.

Learning episode 5.2: Sharing learning objectives with the children

'Otters' class (Year 4) are getting changed for their second physical education lesson of the week. The class teacher has decided that the children will be able to progress and achieve more effectively by following the same activity area during each lesson across the full summer term, giving 12 lessons to refine and apply athletic skills, knowledge and understanding.

As the children are changing, the teacher uses the interactive whiteboard to remind children what they achieved earlier in the week. The whole class is shown video of them taking part in 'fast' and 'slow' running activities. As the children change (and try to beat their existing class record of 4 minutes 39 seconds) they are asked to watch their running games and to remember how they changed their actions to run at maximum speed.

Once everyone is ready, the teacher asks what they have remembered and then says (whilst pointing to the written objectives on the board): 'today, we are going to use our fast running skills to work in small teams in a variety of new races and challenges. When we are running, I would like you to show me your high knees, fast feet and relaxed shoulders … AND I want you to help improve your team-mates' techniques by being their coach.' The children are keen to get to the school field and quickly line up ready for the transition from the classroom.

The principle of WILF described above has been used effectively to demonstrate, as part of the National Physical Education, School Sport and Club Links (PESSCL) strategy (DfES/DCMS, 2003), pupil outcomes of high quality experiences in the subject. The ten pupil outcomes have been identified as:

1 A commitment to physical education and sport.
2 An understanding of what they are trying to achieve and how to go about doing it.
3 A knowledge of healthy and active lifestyles.
4 A confidence to get involved in physical education and sport.
5 The demonstration of skills and control in all activity areas.

6   Willing participation in competitive, creative and challenge-type activities.

7   Thinking and making appropriate decisions for themselves.

8   A demonstrable desire to improve and achieve.

9   Appropriate stamina, suppleness and strength to maintain energy, activity levels and concentration.

10   A keenness to take part in and talk about what they are doing and a clear sense of enjoyment shown through actions.

(Adapted from DfES/QCA, 2005)

For the beginning, or pre-service teacher, thorough planning of lessons or parts of lessons in physical education will give some degree of peace of mind and confidence. Concerns relating to class and behaviour management, health and safety and the contextual changes from classroom to physical education space can all be alleviated by planning in detail. However, planning should also be seen as a framework from which the teacher *is* allowed to deviate through being responsive to children's needs during the lesson.

A lesson plan and its associated objectives should not be a strait-jacket for children's learning and the most effective teachers will regularly go 'off plan' to allow children to progress at an optimum level. This of course requires sound subject knowledge so that the teacher can (whilst fully engaged in the teaching and learning process) alter or abandon activities to maximize learning potential and provide specific feedback to improve pupils' attainment.

Planning considerations

It is unlikely that a trainee or 'beginning teacher' will need to embark on a long-term planning process or curriculum mapping exercise, and this chapter focuses mainly on the planning of a sequence of individual lessons, often called a unit of work or a medium-term plan (the long-term planning process is discussed further in Chapter 8 within the likely remit of the subject leader).

It is advisable that a trainee in the early stages of 'Qualifying to Teach' is afforded opportunities to plan at a smaller scale and teach alongside an experienced teacher in the first instance. Early teaching experiences within physical education must also include sufficient time to observe children's work and to make reflective comments concerning children's learning in the subject. This may be something that the trainee teacher needs to seek out personally by taking a proactive approach to the school-based training process. Planning an activity for a small group, or a specific component of the lesson such as a warm up for the whole class, will be demanding for the beginning teacher and an attempt at sequencing a number of lessons in the full role of class teacher should only be attempted at an appropriate stage of the ITT process – even then with subject-specific mentoring from suitably experienced colleagues.

Before embarking on any planning exercise, there is a range of contextual information that the teacher must consider. An attempt to answer the questions below will help in the early stages and can be viewed as 'pre-planning considerations.'

- How is the NCPE normally implemented in my school? (i.e. What does the school policy say? What programmes of study are taught?)
- What have the children learned in physical education before/most recently?
- What individual needs have already been identified?
- Is evidence of prior learning available?
- Can I make links to other subjects in the curriculum to reinforce understanding?
- Are the children motivated to take part in physical education?
- Do the children take part in school or community physical activities?
- Where will the lessons take place and what constraints will there be in using this space?
- Who uses the space before and after me?
- What time (before school, break and lunch) can I invest to prepare the space?
- What are the health and safety policies in my school and what risks does the change in environment from classroom to hall/playground/pool or field bring?
- What is the school accident and injury policy?
- What will the children wear and where do they get changed?
- What teaching and learning strategies and styles do I wish to adopt, and why?
- What equipment is available in the school?
- Who else in the school can offer me advice?
- What other resources will I need to develop to support pupils' learning?
- Will I have other adults working with me?
- Do I need to develop my own subject knowledge in this activity area and where will I find out this information?

Concern about children's safety

The physical education learning environment provides specific challenges for the practitioner concerned with the well-being and safety of the children. The typical indoor 'classroom' is more readily controlled by the adult to ensure that 'rules' are adhered to. A larger, more flexible and varied space, either in the hall, playground, pool or field, has immediate implications for class management. However, an understanding of the difference between *appropriate challenge* and *real hazard* needs to be developed to ensure that over-concern does not limit opportunity for children to experience a degree of appropriate challenge.

We currently live in a world where 'risk anxiety' prevails and many teachers and schools appear fearful of the increasingly litigious society in which they work. This is problematic for physical educators who should seek to fully and safely utilize space, different levels and environments for educational gain. Children appear to welcome and look for opportunities to take risks (Stephenson, 2003) in their daily lives and many writers believe that risk taking is something that is a necessity for development of thinking, problem solving and being creative (Costa, 1991). To help manage the safe use of space in physical education, it is useful to explore the relationship between the people taking part, the environment in which the activity is taking place, and the organizational structure of the activity. The British Association for Advisers and Lecturers in Physical Education (BAALPE) has for some time been the focal point for provision of nationally recognized best practice guidelines. At the time of writing, we advise all practitioners to consult with the *2004 Safe Practice in Physical Education and School Sport* handbook (BAALPE, 2004) and ensure that their schools update their own copy of this publication as new versions are published in the future.

Learning episode 5.3: A safe and challenging environment

A Year 2 class teacher has expressed concerns about safety in curriculum gymnastic activities. As a result, she is unsure how to use large apparatus and where to place mats.

Her class of children are becoming increasingly skilful and appear ready to develop their work with an emphasis on variety and versatility of actions. Recognizing this, she seeks support and guidance from the subject leader who reviews the school physical education health and safety policy with both Year 2 teachers, who share the same concerns. The subject leader explains that, in accordance with current recommendations, mats should be placed where low level landings are expected, or where they wish to see rolling and some inverted balances.

The teachers come up with a range of ideas for apparatus layouts and create resource cards that will show children how a variety of low and high level apparatus can be linked and placed in the school hall. Having shared these ideas with colleagues at a staff meeting, and rehearsed the layouts with each other in the hall, they utilize their cards in the following week's lesson. The children appear more engaged in the whole planning, performing and evaluating process and appear confident and safe in their actions on all apparatus. The teachers become increasingly confident in planning gymnastic activities and are asked by the headteacher to facilitate a whole staff in-service meeting at the start of the following term.

To effectively manage 'challenge' in contexts away from the classroom, the teacher must accept that time should be invested in thinking through the events that are likely to happen in the context of teaching physical education. Spending time getting 'hands on' so as to become familiar with the apparatus in the hall, preparing resources to support learning, or discussing the specific role of the learning support assistant, is time well spent and forms a vital ingredient in any risk assessment procedure on or off site. The risk assessment process can follow a template-type approach and each school setting will have its own procedures and guidance. Further information regarding risk assessment is contained in Chapter 8 of this book within the likely role of the subject leader.

> Teaching physical education – and, in particular developmental physical education – cannot be done well without an investment in time for thought, reflection and preparation on the part of the teacher. This investment is time well spent and is necessary for pupils to achieve to their full potential.

Maximizing links across the curriculum

In 2003, the DfES, through its 'Excellence and Enjoyment' strategy document, encouraged schools to 'take ownership of the curriculum, shaping it and making it their own. Teachers have much more freedom than they often realise to design the timetable and decide what and how they teach' (DfES, 2003b, p. 3). This freedom to decide what and how to teach should perhaps encourage teachers to explore and blur the boundaries that have been created through the design and traditional implementation of a subject-based curriculum.

Cross-curricular work has been shown to enhance motivation amongst pupils and bring learning across the curriculum to life. The teaching and learning of concepts that pervade the subject curriculum is a challenging notion for teachers to take on board, especially at a time when pupil achievement in English and mathematics is often the focus for assessment and reporting in the primary age phases and beyond.

Medium-term planning

Medium-term plans generally show the outline content of a series of lessons, usually over a period of weeks such as a half term. In primary physical education this has traditionally consisted of about six consecutive lessons, yet limiting learning to a discrete period of time such as this is a little problematic. In many schools, two lessons of physical education per week are used to teach two different activity areas, resulting in a long time-lag between learning episodes (i.e. a full week). In addition, where learning time in physical education is lost at particular times of the year (the hall becoming unavailable due to school nativity play rehearsals in December, for example), the six-week unit often becomes reduced to five or less lessons.

Some schools have begun to 'block' units of work so that both lessons in the same week are used to teach the same activity area. This enables work to be revisited more quickly and has so far impacted positively on pupil confidence and progress (QCA, 2005). This means that a 12-lesson unit of work can be planned across a six-week half term, giving greater scope for concentrated attention to specific learning intentions. Timetabling could also be used to strengthen subject links. Dance activities, for example, could follow a literacy lesson where poetry and verse discussed and written could be used as the stimulus for movement in physical education.

Whatever the length of the planning period, a medium-term approach is helpful for the teacher and assists in the sequencing and progression of activities towards a relevant learning objective. However, medium-term planning can be problematic where a teacher is unable or unwilling to deviate from the original plan to allow for individual needs and pace of learning. For the class teacher, writing a medium-term plan is a good way to begin to visualize what learning and progression is possible within the time constraints of a discrete period of time. A medium-term plan is a framework within which to work on a weekly basis, but teachers should also feel confident to change and augment original plans. It would be very unusual for any teacher not to have to alter the content of plans on a lesson by lesson basis – hence the additional need for short-term lesson plans that will give a detailed account of specific content. In some cases, the original medium-term plan will look very different to the lessons actually delivered. Where this happens, beginning teachers should not worry – it is simply a sign of reflective practice in action. It would be a greater problem if the original plan was adhered to just for the sake of staying within the pre-written script. The ability to change teaching content 'real time' as lessons unfold is also recognized as a trait of experienced teachers.

In projecting children's learning in physical education across a number of lessons, the teacher must ask three key questions:

1 *What have the children already learned in this activity area or skill theme?* This question will be relatively easy to answer if the class teacher has taught the same activity to the same class earlier in the year. Where an activity area was last taught by a colleague, assessment and records from the corresponding unit of work should be sought, and/or time built into lesson one to make a baseline assessment of children's abilities. Of course, the class teacher will have a wealth of relevant knowledge about the children's wider learning and will also be able to incorporate cross-curricular elements into the plan to draw on children's strengths and interests.

2 *What do I think is a reasonable outcome for the majority of pupils after the prescribed number of lessons?* Consultation with curriculum documentation will give the teacher an idea for exploration, perhaps starting from specific movement vocabulary, a particular skill theme or linked themes, or a level of expected performance. The theme of the sequenced lessons can then be stated together with a projected outcome.

3 *What activities should I plan for to help achieve this outcome?* In answering this question, individual relevance must be at the forefront of the teacher's mind, used in conjunction with activity-specific knowledge to create an optimum context for children's learning. When planning at a medium-term level, teachers will not need to write in detail for each specific activity. Instead, the medium-term

plan will indicate the type of activity during each phase of the lesson; further detail will be added to the framework at the short-term planning stage.

Once the learning outcome of the medium-term unit has been identified, the sequence of lessons can be written in a number of ways. One approach is to write the outline of the final lesson first so that this fits neatly with the projected learning outcome of the unit. Once this has been mapped, a return to lesson one of the sequence will ensure that prior learning is reflected in task design. The teacher can then work from the first to last lessons, ensuring that children are provided with opportunities during each lesson to:

- consolidate earlier learning;
- practise and refine existing skills;
- learn and begin to develop new skills:
- evaluate and improve their work;
- be observed and assessed;
- work towards specific learning intentions.

Each lesson should therefore build on the last – hence the need for short-term planning to reflect amendments to the original medium-term plans where pupil progression and achievement differ from the medium-term projection. At medium-term level, the teacher should plan for a coherence in activities that ensures each lesson is not an isolated one-off learning experience, but a coherent continuous cycle that enables progression and continuity. Different phases of each projected lesson provide opportunity for this progression and continuity to be carried forward. For example, 'warm ups' can be similar from week to week, but build on an increasing skill and knowledge base as this grows over time. Warm ups should link to themes introduced during previous lessons, and the main body of lessons should provide opportunities for the addition of new ideas and skills and the refinement of existing ones. We have included an example medium-term planning template as Appendix 1 at the end of this book which can be 'tweaked' for teachers' own use and for compliance with locally designed school-based templates that are already in place.

Short-term planning

Whereas medium-term planning is a projection of children's learning *before* the teaching cycle has started, a short-term plan is generally written *during* the medium-term teaching cycle. Assessments and observations made are used to inform the next stage of the plan–teach–assess cycle and new knowledge and understanding of children's developing abilities is used to tailor learning to meet specific needs. A short-term lesson plan will consist of two sections. The first section could be viewed as 'background' contextual information, to include:

- Date
- Lesson duration
- Lesson venue
- Age Phase/Year group
- Number of children
- NCPE Activity and NCPE reference
- Prior learning and place in sequence
- Links to other physical education work/ transferability of skills and understanding
- Cross-curricular linkage
- Learning intention(s) (ideally shown with reference to the four 'aspects')
- Assessment criteria
- Specific individual provision
- Use of teaching assistant or other adults
- Use of ICT to support learning
- Link to QtT standards (for trainee teachers).

The second section of the lesson plan should be seen as a guiding 'map' of the lesson and the teacher should feel confident and happy with any format used. Some teachers prefer to use written descriptions to describe children's activities and teacher's activities, although we would suggest that the environment and context in which physical education is taught necessitate a more detailed structure, particularly for the beginning teacher. The template included as Appendix 2 at the end of this book is an example that includes specific reference points for high quality delivery. The tabular format is flexible (the lines in-between sections are deliberately 'dotted' to suggest flexibility of lesson phases) and teachers are encouraged to write succinctly, making use of abbreviations and bullet points.

It is important for teachers to be comfortable with the planning format used and we encourage the use of a structured 'table' for physical education lesson planning; the physical education environment is different to the classroom used for almost all other subjects and this shift in context, together with an increased requirement to use large-scale equipment and apparatus with vigorously active children places increased focus on depth of planning.

The structure of the individual lesson will vary from activity to activity, or depend on learning intentions and teaching strategies used. For example, a games activity lesson could be sequenced in several ways:

warm up → skills practice → skills application → cool down

warm up → small sided games → skills practice → small sided game → cool down

warm up → exploration → guided discovery → instruction → application → cool down

Whichever approach is used it is important for the various phases of the lesson to be clearly linked by common themes, language and purpose and for each activity to contribute towards the achievement of overarching learning intentions.

Warming up and cooling down

It is commonly accepted practice that warm ups and cool downs should form part of lessons in physical education. From a physiological perspective, warm ups prepare children for more vigorous activity by raising temperature, elevating heart rate and increasing blood flow to the muscles. This assumes, however, that children arrive at physical education from a restful state; in practice, physical education is often taught immediately after a break which has included some physical activity in the playground and required children to move from the classroom to a different venue.

From a scientific perspective, some doubt now exists as to whether 'traditional' warm ups involving static stretching of muscle groups are actually beneficial. It is clear though that warm ups are necessary in order to establish a purposeful and enjoyable start to the lesson and should be used to engage children immediately in learning. A focus on the names of particular muscle groups and body systems also has tremendous cross-curricular potential and is a valuable time for addressing knowledge and understanding of fitness and health. We would encourage trainees and teachers to think of warm ups as a time for 'warming up for learning' as well as preparing the body for more strenuous activity. Warm ups should include:

- a simple, known activity to enable an immediate start and acclimatization to the working space;
- aerobic activity to gradually increase blood flow and heart rate;
- an introduction of activities that prepare the muscle groups and joints that will be used more vigorously later in the lesson;
- an introduction of skill themes and language to be developed/applied later in the lesson;
- an opportunity for children's understanding to be reinforced and checked through questioning, generally with a link from the previous lesson;
- activities that the children find fun and motivational, whilst enabling the teacher to maintain a purposeful working environment.

In the primary school, the physical education lesson does not start and end in the physical education space. Changing time and the transition from classroom to hall or field can be used as part of *warming up to learn*. On arrival at the physical education space, *immediate* activity is important – something that can be achieved only if the space is ready and resources are fully prepared in advance. The teacher must liaise with others to ensure this is the case – there is no worse start to a lesson than asking 30 eager children to sit and wait whilst the piano and dining tables are moved!

If warm ups become 'warming up for learning', then cooling down should also address both physiological and educational objectives. A period of more gentle activity helps the heart and body return to a resting state and helps muscle groups to relax following periods of intense contraction. As muscles are warm at this stage, this period of time is also the most effective for improving muscle flexibility through appropriate stretching activities. Finally, this part of a lesson represents an opportunity for children to reflect on their own learning in physical education and to provide others with feedback. This is an ideal time for plenary discussion, review and recap, discussion relating to success against pre-planned learning objectives and for providing group feedback and feed-forward.

Structuring the lesson

The structure of an individual lesson (in other words the way in which different sections or phases link together) will depend on a range of factors, not least the activity content and teaching strategies being used. It is imperative that each section of the lesson is linked to what has happened before and what will happen next; that the teacher and pupils do not view each section as a separate, isolated activity; and that it is clear where and how pupils' learning will be facilitated. Traditionally, an approach used has seen children's activities progress from simple to more complex, from slower to faster actions, and from individual to group work. We would suggest, however, that teachers should not be constrained by any historically embedded approach to planning and encourage practitioners to innovate through application of a variety of methods. If children's learning is always at the heart of the planning process then the teacher cannot go too far wrong.

Each individual lesson should allow children to learn new skills or enhance existing ones through improved technical quality and improved application within a relevant context. In many circumstances, we would encourage the use of problem-solving and decision-making type activities early in the lesson as this is often the time when children are most easily engaged and ready to learn. The often heard question 'can we play a game yet?' can be effectively answered with a 'yes of course, straight away!' response where children have the necessary knowledge skills and understanding to work effectively within an immediate 'application' activity.

Each lesson plan should indicate likely progressions of specific skills, especially where 'acquire and develop skills' is a stated learning intention within the plan. This will help the teacher to visualize specific 'teaching points' for focus with the children to help improve the quality of skill learning through provision of appropriate feedback and use of questioning.

Each component part of an individual lesson should show a clear link to the stated learning intentions. It should be clear to the reader what the learning intentions are and how the children will be asked to go about achieving them. In addition, there will be a clear 'audit' trail between learning intention, activity content and assessment criteria. In other words, it should be made explicit how, where, what and by whom assessment is being utilized to support the learning process.

Differentiation of task

In keeping with the developmental principles running through this text, we suggest that high quality *developmental* physical education is, by definition, designed to meet the needs of every child. If this is so, then differentiation of task will be a central teaching strategy used to achieve this. Differentiation can be used to different degrees. In other words, children can do what is basically the same task as each other with a slight difference (using a balloon instead of a ball in early catching experiences for example), *or* the tasks can be entirely different (but designed to help meet the same learning intention). The common factor in planning differentiated tasks is that the learning intention is shared by all children, although the level of attainment expected may differ from group to group.

Differentiation by outcome can be used so that children *perform at their own level* within a common task experienced by all. In response to a question such as 'show me how many different ways you can travel in space', there is clearly no right or wrong answer; some children will imaginatively perform several locomotor skills using different levels, speeds and directions, whilst others will demonstrate a limited range of response. This method presumes that children are self-adjusting and will only ever perform at their own level. There is scope to use this approach in warm up activities and in some activities where mixed ability groups will share the same apparatus (in gymnastic activities, for example). However, a more focused consideration of individual learning needs will necessitate **differentiation by task,** in other words specific adjustments to activities for specific reasons.

Adjustments can be made to a wide range of task parameters, commonly shortened to the acronym 'STTEP' which is illustrated in Figure 5.2. This will help you to think of things that could be changed within tasks to meet specific learning needs, although it does not include more subtle adjustments such as vocabulary, learning resources used to scaffold learning, or planned-for use of support staff to facilitate learning.

S	Space	Making the space bigger or smaller or a different shape. In games activities, for example, a bigger space for small sided invasion games reduces pressure on attackers and creates more space through which to attack.
T	Time	Some skills can be performed slowly or quickly (or other factors changed to increase time pressure), making the tasks more or less demanding. Faster paced skills are not always more difficult – performing a gymnastic sequence as slowly as possible will create greater challenges for accuracy and control.
T	Task	The specific requirements of each task can be altered completely. Children of different abilities can be asked to perform specific tasks to help meet the same learning intentions.
E	Equipment	Equipment can be used to increase or lessen performance demands. A small, hard ball in striking and fielding games will be harder to hit than a larger, softer and slower-moving ball, for example.
P	People	Greater numbers of children involved in a task tend to make the group task more complex. A class dance becomes a challenging choreographic exercise with all children involved.

Figure 5.2 The 'STTEP' principal of differentiation

Another way of seeing 'differentiation' is as a strategy through which children of all learning needs can be included in physical education learning. *Inclusion* is most commonly discussed in relation to special educational needs and specific disabilities, although considering individual differences within a transactional model would suggest that every child requires some level of individual provision. The list offered below is an attempt to show how all children, at some stage of their schooling, may be construed as having a need for specific provision:

- girls
- boys
- ethnic minorities
- religious groups
- pupils who are unfit
- pupils who are overweight and obese
- gifted and talented pupils in PE and sport
- children who wear glasses
- gifted and talented pupils in other curriculum areas
- pupils who lack confidence
- new arrivals
- pupils with English as an Additional Language
- pupils with Special Educational Needs
- travellers
- looked-after children.

If we accept that *every child* brings a unique set of factors and circumstances to the physical education learning experience, then the need to provide carefully differentiated and inclusive tasks would appear to be obvious. On a broader scale, we should also aim to identify barriers that may serve to exclude some children in school from physical education and extracurricular activities and work with colleagues to ensure that provision is fully inclusive.

Equipment and resources

In planning tasks to meet the learning needs of children, a broad range of facilities, equipment and resources can be used. Modern-day equipment suppliers offer a plethora of lightweight, colourful, varied, exciting and richly textured resources that will appeal to multisensory learners. Whilst the range of available equipment will be governed by budgetary allocation, all teachers should be aware that the type, range, degree of choice and application of equipment and resources can significantly improve pupil learning in physical education. The use of materials in dance activities for example (ribbons, flags, papier-mâché, masks, etc.), can help bring learning to life and need not cost too much. Considerations at the planning stage should include not only *what* (and how much) equipment, resources and apparatus will be used, but *how*, *where* and with *whom*. Both teachers and pupils may find it helpful to map out positioning of equipment in advance of the lesson to ensure that space is used effectively and to prepare for the teaching and learning episode.

Teachers should also find parallels to their classroom-based work when thinking about *where* to place equipment. For example, the typical primary classroom is organized around groups of tables, each with its own pot of pencils and learning materials. In physical education, each group should have an accessible, close by and appropriate allocation of equipment to negate the occurrence of long queues and to help continuity between tasks. For this reason, a number of equipment 'bases' should be positioned strategically around the outer edge of the work space in advance of the lesson.

Observation and assessment

Assessment is an essential part of any teaching and learning episode. The process of assessment allows the teacher to study the rate and level of children's learning and engages the teacher in analysis, evaluation and appreciation – hallmarks of the 'reflective practitioner'. Crucially, assessment informs future planning, and encourages the teacher to continually question lesson content, to aim for continuity, to consider likely progressions, plan for task differentiation and set meaningful targets. At an individual level, effective assessment will also help to identify areas of specific need, recognize children with developmental difficulties and highlight those who may be 'gifted and talented'. Assessment during the learning process also provides opportunities for the teacher to provide constructive feedback, to reinforce positive behaviours and actions and provide effective and personalized reporting to parents and colleagues.

Because children's work in physical education is visible, insightful and skilful, observation is a key tool to aid the developmental physical educator's assessment procedures. Each lesson plan should include reference to the criteria being used for assessment, which in turn should be explicitly linked to the intended learning outcome(s). Where these are skill specific, an observational checklist as introduced in Chapter 4 could be used by the teacher, learning support assistant or the pupils themselves. For broader learning intentions, a less detailed, but highly focused tracking chart for a group of children in the class could be used to record subjective assessment of pupil progress. A simple example of this is provided here (Figure 5.3).

The observation, assessment and recording process should also link clearly to 'level descriptors' which help to describe children's attainment at a particular time. These are currently referenced strongly to the four aspects of the NCPE and should be seen as a tool

Profile Group Assessment Record for Primary Physical Education

Date:

Lesson plan reference/National Curriculum reference:

Place in sequence/prior learning:

Class learning intentions (L.I.):

1.

2.

3.

4.

Name of child	L.I. 1	L.I. 2	L.I. 3	Individual L.I.	Comment

Symbols used to denote: Notes/points to aid future planning:

   Learning intention fully met   △

   Learning intention partly met   ∧

   Learning intention not met   /

Figure 5.3 Tracking chart to record subjective assessment of pupil progress

to help explain progress and achievement to pupils, colleagues and parents. The plethora of assessment information in play on a daily basis is sometimes difficult to rationalize and an effective way of tracking pupil learning in physical education is to produce 'pupil learning diaries' or 'portfolios' of work. These can eventually include pupils' self-evaluations, peer assessments, video clips and still images, together with teacher commentary regarding achievement, and are useful documents to use at points of transition. The mosaic of information contained in such a portfolio will help the teacher describe a child's progress and ensuing learning needs at any given time during the short-, medium- or long-term learning cycle.

Using other adults to support physical education teaching and learning

One of the most significant changes experienced in schools in recent years has been the growth in the number of adults other than teachers working in schools. The use of learning support assistants (LSAs) in primary physical education allows the class teacher to manage and coordinate work to maximize learning time. In some cases, the LSA can be directed to work with individual children or groups of children to address individual learning needs; at other times the LSA can support the wider teaching and learning process through observing, assessing and applying resources to scaffold pupils' learning.

Our recent observations in schools would suggest that LSAs are an under-used resource in primary physical education, commonly being used to help organize children into groups, to retie shoelaces and to take children to the toilet! It is the class teacher's responsibility to effectively manage the LSA's work and it will be necessary to:

- share learning intentions with the LSA prior to the lesson (ideally involving the LSA in the planning process);
- provide specific guidance relating to teaching points, movement vocabulary and teaching strategies;
- plan tasks within lessons for the LSA to be responsible for (such as observing and assessing).

The role of the LSA in primary physical education is clearly very important, especially when there is a wide range of ability and learning needs. It will be necessary for the teacher to establish effective lines of communication at busy times of the day to ensure that the LSA is fully engaged in the learning process. LSAs should also be included in professional development opportunities in the subject area and should be made aware of the modules that are currently available for 'adults other than teachers' (AOTTs) through the prevailing Physical Education School Sport and Club Links strategy (DfES/DCMS, 2003) (discussed more broadly in Chapter 7).

Using technology to support physical education teaching and learning

The place of Information and Communications Technology (ICT) within the National Curriculum is clearly stated: 'Pupils should be given opportunities to apply and develop their ICT capability through the use of ICT tools to support their learning in all subjects' (DfES/QCA, 1999, p. 38). Although not currently compulsory in physical education at Key Stages 1 and 2, ICT can clearly make an important contribution to physical education teaching and learning. ICT should not be used in physical education teaching and learning without the underlying aim of *bringing about learning*. The use of technology should support children's learning so that children learn more at a faster rate than would otherwise be possible. Three broad principles apply to the use of ICT in physical education:

1 The use of ICT in physical education teaching must draw upon acknowledged good practice and comply with whole school policies.

2 The use of ICT in physical education must be directly related to the teaching and learning objectives within short-, medium- and long-term plans.

3 The use of ICT in physical education should allow the teacher and/ or the pupil to achieve something that could not be achieved (or achieved as effectively/efficiently/quickly) without the use of ICT.

(Adapted from TTA, 1999, p. 3)

There is a wide range of software and hardware available for the teacher to use in today's schools. In physical education, most appeal seems to be with capturing visual images of pupils' work and using still photography or video footage to assist in the 'evaluate and improve' aspects of teaching and learning. Other uses for ICT can be to support the teacher's own assessment and record keeping and for sharing events through school and partnership intranet communities. The primary physical educator should make use of available resources but not be sidetracked from the business of teaching and learning; in other words, the use of ICT in physical education should enhance existing good practice and help raise the quality of children's learning experiences.

Teacher behaviour, style and strategies

Within the 'dynamic systems perspective' advocated throughout this chapter, the teacher plays an important role in planning, organizing and resourcing lessons, specifically deciding the detail of movement tasks. In addition to this, each teacher plays a slightly different role in the way in which he or she impacts on the learning experience through their own attitudes, behaviours, styles and strategies. This range of factors can include enthusiasm, presentation (e.g. wearing appropriate physical education kit), body language and verbal communication, voice projection, choice of teaching style and broader teaching and learning strategies. Whilst each teacher will bring a unique individual set of qualities and competencies to the teaching role, there are a number of planned-for decisions that can be made deliberately to maximize learning potential.

Whilst learning can take place independent of any intent by a teacher to bring this about through experimentation, copying and 'play', the skilful teacher can plan to draw on these traits in children who have 'learned to learn'. Rink (2006) explained that, within the framework of 'environmental design', a teacher can elicit motor responses by designing the environment to 'bring out' the skill. It seems that this approach to teaching and learning sits most comfortably with a cognitive approach to learning whereby children learn through problem solving and skill application. Wherever a teacher feels that he or she wishes to place the learning emphasis, there is an accompanying choice of teaching style.

Teaching styles in physical education

Muska Mosston (1966) first introduced the term '*spectrum of teaching styles*' to describe a range of choices facing the teacher in relation to teacher behaviour. The term 'teaching style' does not refer to individual idiosyncrasies or measures of efficiency in teaching, but behaviour governed by a pattern of decisions made in relation to the learner, the task and the environment (Gallahue, 1996, p. 235).

Mosston's original spectrum of teaching styles has undergone a number of revisions (see Mosston and Ashworth, 2002), most recently to include two 'clusters' of styles – the first centred on the *reproduction* of past knowledge, and the second aiming to *produce* new knowledge (for the learner). Physical education for primary aged children should lean towards the latter group of indirect styles of teaching, especially where learning intentions are not solely centred on physical skill acquisition. The so-called 'indirect styles' of teaching facilitate the discovery of existing concepts, as well as the development of alternatives and new concepts.

The link between indirect styles of teaching and child-centred strategies should be seen as a convergence of philosophies. Notions of 'learning to learn' and, in physical education, 'moving to learn', suggest that learning can take place through experimentation, problem solving and self-discovery. Furthermore, the process of learning to learn is seen as equally important as the acquisition of a specific skill and ultimately more transferable beyond the physical education and sports context. Despite the advantages of indirect teaching styles, some teachers appear reluctant or unable to use them productively. The dependence on direct styles (such as 'command') may prevail where the teacher is most concerned with maintaining discipline or where the predominant learning intention is to develop technique.

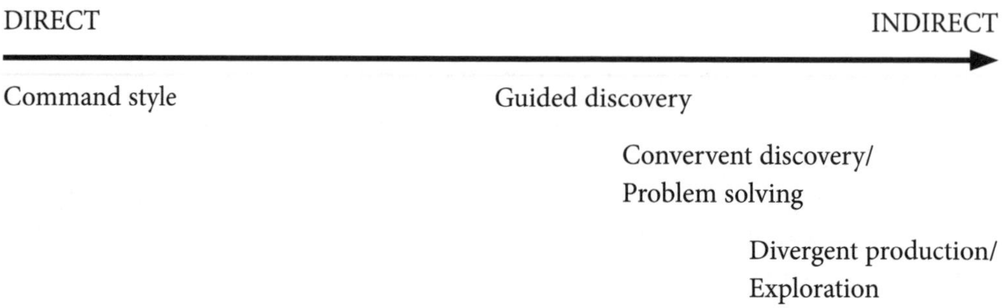

DIRECT   INDIRECT

⟶

Command style   Guided discovery

                                                             Convervent discovery/
                                                             Problem solving

                                                                                    Divergent production/
                                                                                    Exploration

Figure 5.4 A range of 'teaching styles'

Cooperative learning in physical education

Cooperative learning is used here as a generic term for various small group interactive instructional procedures and encompasses a variety of broadly constructivist approaches to teaching and learning. Within these approaches, children work together on tasks to help themselves and their peers learn. Advocates of cooperative learning techniques (see for example, Hohmann and Weikart, 1995) suggest that cooperative methods share the following five characteristics:

1 Children work together on common tasks or learning activities that are best developed through group work.
2 Children work together in small groups, most commonly containing two to five members.
3 Children use cooperative, pro-social behaviours to accomplish their common tasks.
4 Activities are structured so that pupils need each other to accomplish their common tasks or learning activities.
5 Pupils are individually accountable or responsible for their work or learning.

In the physical domain, movement skill learning generally occurs in a group setting requiring cooperative behaviours for successful participation (Gallahue, 1996). Cooperative learning simultaneously models interdependence and provides students with the experiences they need to understand the nature of cooperation (Johnson and Johnson, 1989). Research clearly indicates that cooperation, compared with competitive and individualistic efforts, typically results in (a) higher achievement and greater productivity, (b) more caring, supportive and committed relationships, (c) greater psychological health, social competence and self-esteem, (d) enhanced critical and creative thinking, and (e) positive attitudes towards subject and school.

Creating an environment for cooperative learning

The teacher needs to make a conscious, planned decision to include tasks that require children to share, discuss, argue, rationalize, find solutions and come to decisions together. Fisher (2000) recognizes, however, that young children will not cooperate simply because it is in the teacher's plans. Children will collaborate and communicate when they see the need to do so.

> To encourage cooperation between young children, teachers should plan activities and work areas that encourage spontaneous interactive learning opportunities and in which children see a purpose in talking together, working together and learning together. (Fisher, 2000, p. 103)

Cooperative learning requires effective communication (listening and speaking skills), mutual compromise, honesty and fair play and team work. Physical education has clear potential for the use of these approaches across all activity areas, especially where learning intentions include reference to social an affective learning.

Encouraging the learner to discover for him or herself

When considering options presented by Mosston's spectrum of teaching styles, primary physical educators are encouraged to seek methods through which children can learn to learn in addition to learning new skills. **Guided discovery** teaching centres on the use of questions intended to facilitate a small discovery by the learner. In the 'purest' form of the guided discovery teaching style, each question is designed to elicit a single, correct response by the learner, during which the teacher is able to provide feedback and praise in response to the learner's discovery. The role of the teacher (or LSA) is more obvious within this style than in other styles mentioned below. The teacher's role is specifically geared to facilitating, shaping and influencing movement outcomes and can result in children showing greater versatility, increased skilfulness and clarity of intent and outcome (Davies, 2003).

A variation on the guided discovery style is **convergent discovery**, where children are challenged to discover the solution to a movement task with the teacher simply providing feedback and clues without providing the solution. This style fosters a greater level of decision making amongst the learners, and a wider range of possible 'correct' responses. A final variation is the **divergent production** style, in which children are engaged in exploring a range of possible responses. The teacher presents movement challenges or questions that do not require one specific solution – any reasonable attempt at the task is seen by the teacher to be acceptable. This is sometimes called 'free exploration' (e.g. Davies, 2003) and allows children to move in any way they wish. This style focuses on the learning *process* itself and not on the *product* of learning.

Teaching strategies and interventions when using indirect teaching styles

The use of a combination of teaching styles may help to provide a focus for this intervention, in particular in planning when to observe actions and provide some specific instruction. Gallahue (1996, p. 241) provides what he calls a 'limitation model' (see Figure 5.5) in which teaching involves a combination of indirect and direct teaching styles progressing in order from (1) free exploration/divergent production, to (2) Guided discovery, to (3) problem solving, to (4) specific skill instruction.

In recognizing that all children learn differently it would be wrong for a teacher to use only one teaching style. Choice of style may depend on a range of factors related to the **learner** (stage of development, level of attainment, level of cognitive understanding, fitness level, affective characteristics, motivation), **environment** (facilities and equipment, time, safety considerations, numbers in group), **task** (difficulty, complexity, risk) and **teacher** (philosophy, personality, lesson objectives, ability to adapt, class control and confidence). Ultimately, the selection and use of teaching styles should be based on what we know about the learner's phase and stage of motor development and an ultimate aim of providing an appropriate next step in the learning process.

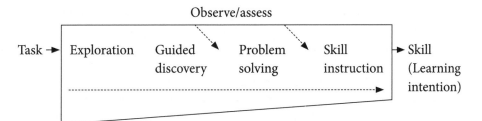

Figure 5.5 The 'limitation' model of teaching and learning (adapted from Gallahue, 1996)

Summary

The effective teaching of primary physical education relies on a range of teacher behaviours, styles and strategies, all of which can be deliberately planned to help bring about learning. Beginning teachers are encouraged to seek parallels with approaches in other subjects – after all, children do not suddenly learn in completely different ways as they leave the classroom and enter the hall. There are, however, a range of additional factors for the teacher to consider in physical education that relate to this shift in context, all of which must be thoughtfully reviewed in the planning stage. The 'physical education classroom' can become a vivid, colourful and multisensory learning environment within which all children can learn and where the educator can maximize space, time and the children's natural disposition for learning in the physical domain.

Key Questions

1 How do I go about planning for physical education?
2 Is teaching and learning in physical education different to teaching and learning in other subjects?
3 What are the key features of the planning, teaching and assesment cycle in primary physical education?
4 How can I make the best use of resources (including other adults) to support learning in primary physical education?
5 What choices do I have with regard to my own teaching styles and behaviours?

Learning tasks

1 Review school-based planning for primary physical education during a school placement. Reflect on the extent to which projected learning meets children's specific needs and consider ways in which changes can be made to both planning frameworks and subject delivery.
2 During school-based experience, seek out an opportunity to observe a small group of children during physical education. Consider the level of attainment they are demonstrating and begin to identify

priorities for their future learning. How do these observations and future planning ideas correspond to actual plans? What changes could be made for the subsequent lesson?

3 Identify one piece of ICT hardware or software that you would like to use in your physical education teaching. Identify how this resource will enable you to improve pupil achievement, motivate pupils to learn in physical education and/or support your class management.

4 Consider your own preferred teaching styles in physical education. To what extent are you encouraging pupils to solve problems and be 'self-directed' learners? What factors influence your choice of teaching style and how could your own teaching change to reflect pupil needs?

5 At a relevant stage of ITT, seek out an opportunity to plan collaboratively with an experienced colleague. Where possible, this should include both medium-term and short-term planning and the subsequent teaching of planned lessons. Reflect on the process throughout, recording what went well and what could be improved in the future.

Links to the Framework of Professional Standards for Teachers

The content and focus of this chapter have direct relevance to the following Qualified Teacher Status (QTS) standards (TDA, 2007) for those training to teach in primary schools: Q3, Q6, Q10, Q11, Q19, Q21, Q28.

Useful websites

www.afpe.org.uk

The Association for Physical Education (afPE). Contains general information about membership and links to specific services, such as relevant health and safety guidance and links to professional development opportunities.

http://www.qca.org.uk/downloads/4031_afl_principles.pdf

Qualifications and Curriculum Authority. Contains a wealth of information regarding planning, teaching and assessing. This specific link outlines principles of assessment for learning.

http://www.ofsted.gov.uk/publications/annualreport0405/4.1.10.htm1

Office for Standards in Education. Contains links to all subject reports. This link is to the 2004/5 report for primary physical education.

www.nc.uk.net/http://www.teachernet.gov.uk/teachinginengland/detail.cfm?id=498

Current National Curriculum guidance. Advice about use of adults other than teachers.

www.dfes.gov.uk/ictinschools

DfES guidelines and up-to-date source of information regarding the use of ICT to support learning, teaching and management.

http://www.ncaction.org.uk/subjects/pe/ict-sft.htm

National Curriculum in Action

http://www.afpe.org.uk/public/downloads/baalpe_ptr_poster.doc

Health and safety poster useful for displaying in school for pupil and teacher reference.

References and further reading

Auxter,D., Pyfer, J. and Huettig, C. (2001) *Principles and Methods of Adapted Physical Education and Recreation*. Boston: McGraw-Hill.

BAALPE (2004) *Safe Practice in Physical Education and School Sport* (6th edn). Leeds: Coachwise.

Bailey, R. (2001) *Teaching Physical Education: A Handbook for Primary and Secondary School Teachers*. London: Kogan Page.

Bailey, R. and MacFayden, T. (eds) (2000) *Teaching Physical Education 5–11*. London: Continuum.

Casbon, C. (1999) 'National Curriculum Review: Key points in the review of the order', *British Journal of Physical Education*, **30**(1), 6–7.

Costa, A. L. (1991) 'The Search for Intelligent Life', in A. L. Costa (ed.) *Developing Minds: A Resource Book for Teaching Thinking*, Volume 1 (Revised edn). Alexandria, USA: Association for Supervision and Curriculum Development.

Davies, M. (2003) *Movement and Dance in Early Childhood* (2nd edn). London: Paul Chapman Publishing.

Dewey, J. (1933) *How we Think: A Restatement of the Relation of Reflective Thinking to the Educative Process*. Boston, MA: Heath.

DfEE (1988) *Education Reform Act*. London: HMSO.

DfEE/QCA (1999) *The National Curriculum for England and Wales*. London: QCA.

DfES (2003a) *Every Child Matters*. London: HMSO.

DfES (2003b) *Excellence and Enjoyment: A strategy for primary schools*. London: DfES.

DfES (2003c) CD 'Success for All: An Inclusive Approach to PE and School Sport' (available from Publication Centre, email: dfes@prolog.uk.com).

DfES (2004) *Children Act*. London: HMSO.

DfES/DCMS (2003) *Learning Through PE and Sport – A Guide to the Physical Education, School Sport and Club Links Strategy*. Annesley: DfES Publications.

DfES/QCA (2005) *Do You Have High Quality Physical Education and School Sport in Your School?* Annesley: QCA.

Fisher, J. (2000) *Starting from the Child, Teaching and Learning from 3 to 8* (2nd edn). Buckingham: Open University Press, p. 103.

Gallahue, D. L. (1996) *Developmental Physical Education for Today's Children*. Duboque, IW: Brown & Benchmark, p. 235.

Gallahue, D. L and Donnelly, F. C. (2003) *Developmental Physical Education for all Children* (4th edn). Champaign, IL: Human Kinetics.

Graham, G. (2001) *Teaching Children Physical Education*. Champaign: Human Kinetics.

Graham, G., A. Holt-Hale, S. and Parker, M. (2004) *Children Moving: A Reflective Approach to Teaching Physical Education* (6th edn). Boston, MA: McGraw Hill.

Hohmann, M. and Weikart, D. P. (1995) *Educating Young Children, a Curriculum Guide from High/Scope Educational Research Foundation*. Michigan: High/Scope Press.

Hopper, B., Grey, J. and Maude, T. (2000) *Teaching Physical Education in the Primary School*. London: Routledge Falmer.

Johnson, D. W. and Johnson, R. T. (1989) *Cooperation and Competition: Theory and Research*, Edina, MN: Interaction Book Co.

McCall, R. M. and Craft, D. H. (2000) *Moving With a Purpose*. Champaign, IL: Human Kinetics.

Mosston, M. (1966) *Teaching Physical Education*. Columbus, OH: Charles E. Merrill.

Mosston, M. and Ashworth, S. (2002) *Teaching Physical Education* (5th edn). San Fransisco, CA: Benjamin Cummings.

Ofsted (2004) *Annual Report of Her Majesty's Chief Inspector of Schools, 2005/5: Primary Physical Education*. London: HMSO, available at: http://live.ofsted.gov.uk/publications/annualreport0405/4.1.10.html. [accessed 1 June 2006].

Penney, D. (1999) 'Physical Education: In Changing Times is it Time for a change?', *British Journal of Physical Education*, **30**(4), 4–6.

Penny, S., Ford, R., Price, L. and Young, S. (2002) *Teaching Arts in Primary Schools*. Exeter: Learning Matters.

Pollard, A. (2005) *Reflective Teaching: Evidence-informed Professional Practice* (2nd edn). London: Continuum, p. 210.

QCA (1999) *The Review of the National Curriculum in England: The Secretary of State's proposals*. London, QCA.

QCA (2005) *Physical Education: 2004/5 Annual Report on Curriculum and Assessment*. London: QCA.

Rink, J. (2006) *Teaching Physical Education for Learning*. Boston, MA: McGraw-Hill.

Severs, J., Whitlam, P. and Woodhouse, J. (2003) *Safety and Risk in Primary School Physical Education*. London: Routledge.

Siedentop, D. and Tannehill, D. (2000) *Developing Teaching Skills in Physical Education* (4th edn). Mountain View, CA: Mayfield Publishing.

Stephenson, A. (2003) 'Physical Risk-taking: Dangerous or Endangered?' *Early Years*, **23**(1), 36–43.

Training and Development Agency for Schools (TDA) (2007) *Draft Revised Professional Standards for Teachers in England*. London: TDA. Available from http://www.tda.gov.uk/upload/resources/pdf/d/draft_revised_standards_framework_jan_2007.pdf [accessed 5 March 2007].

TTA (1999) *Using ICT to Meet Teaching Objectives in Physical Education*. London: TTA, p. 3.

Young, M. F. D. (1998) *The Curriculum of the Future: From the 'New Sociology of Education' to a Critical Theory of Learning*. London: Falmer Press.

Teaching Activity Areas

Variety's the very spice of life that gives it all its flavour.

William Cowper

Introduction

The focus of this chapter is on the activity contexts detailed within the prevailing NCPE documentation. The curriculum advocates a breadth of study across six activity areas, namely games, gymnastics, dance, athletics, outdoor and adventurous activities, and swimming and water safety. Each of these activities provides a unique set of challenges and considerations for the primary practitioner. To maximize the potential that each activity area holds for children to learn to move and move to learn, the primary physical educator will need activity-specific subject knowledge, an understanding of how teaching and learning can be managed within each context, and an appreciation of the educational value of each activity.

It is possible that future national curriculum in physical education will not include specific activity areas and that a broader skill theme approach will be advocated. In many ways, we would support this notion and encourage teachers to be innovative and flexible in their approaches to teaching and learning. In order to personalize learning and provide individually relevant experiences, it may indeed be necessary to view activity areas in the broadest possible sense; perhaps skateboarding (entailing a plethora of stability skill themes) can be addressed within gymnastic activities, or roller hockey played in games activities? This said, a broader aim of physical education should also be to introduce children to the full range of activities available for engagement throughout life – we would do a disservice to all if this neglected those activities that are relevant to society's sporting and cultural histories and traditions.

This chapter addresses key issues facing the teacher within each activity area, suggests approaches to teaching and learning that reflect the uniqueness of each activity, and provides sample activities to support the primary practitioner. This chapter will definitely not, however, provide schemes of work for teachers to follow off the shelf; this would cut against the grain of developmental physical education, and we hope that all primary physical educators will be committed to planning to meet the needs of their pupils, not those in mind when a hypothetical plan was written.

Key points

- A focus for learning within the six activity areas of the NCPE is a vehicle to ensure breadth and balance of children's experiences and should not be construed as a 'sports-down' approach to teaching and learning.
- Teaching and learning in each activity area of the NCPE brings a unique set of challenges to the teacher and unique learning experiences for the children.
- Lesson content within each activity area should build from a 'skill theme approach' and seek to apply skills and movement concepts in a range of different activities.
- The teacher should consider and utilize movement vocabulary relevant to each activity area, seek transference of skills and concepts, and use this vocabulary to inform feedback and feed-forward.

Teaching dance activities

A rationale for the teaching of dance in primary school settings might include a reference to the rich cultural traditions the activity area has in society, or even a global dimension that can witness different dance forms across cultures. It might also include the importance of building on children's apparent readiness to physically respond naturally to sound, rhythms, beats and music. There may also be reference to the transferability of skill learning that complements and benefits from movement concepts accrued in gymnastic activities in the school setting. However, the benefits to children from experiencing a variety of dance activity in their formative years cannot be underestimated if we accept the following premises:

- Dance activity presents its own set of unique physical challenges, is demanding of stamina, strength and suppleness, poses athletic and agility tasks within its content, and requires an understanding of how the body operates in response to a range of different stimuli.
- Dance activity is a creative art form which encourages children to bring to their learning their own ideas, imaginations and interpretations.
- Dance activity promotes both expressive and communicative physical movement response, and allows for children to express their own moods and feelings through display of outward movement.
- Dance is artistic in its product and we should aim therefore for variety and contrasts within all taught sessions.
- Dance is a friendly and fun activity which promotes sociability, is cooperative by nature, and builds on individual work that can be shared with partners and groups, and in a variety of different roles within the context under focus.
- Dancing is essentially a fun thing to do which contributes to the enjoyment to be derived from engagement with a wealth of possible activities on offer.
- Within a lifelong physical education model, dance activities can claim to be relevant to all age groups and something that can stay relevant throughout the life cycle.

Dance is a unique part of the primary curriculum, blending as it does learning from across the spectrum, with obvious links to music and physical education generally, but also drawing from, and contributing to, a full range of experiences throughout the primary age range. The NCPE emphasizes the importance of introducing simple movement actions to young children through the concepts of dance. These are:

- travelling, jumping (and landing), twisting, turning, gesture and stillness;
- the use of movements to show moods, emotions and feelings;
- a range of responses to simple rhythms and contrasting stimuli.

When planning activities for children, teachers need to consider basic movement concepts such as strong and light movement, high and low action, fast and slow speeds, and following different pathways and directions in their movement patterns. Basic knowledge and understanding of how to move, extending children's personal movement vocabulary, and participation with others alongside the teacher are all important aspects of learning in this area of activity.

Cross-curricular links are a good starting point for dance activities and give an identity to the activity area unique amongst others. For example, dance can draw from English Language input, drawing on poetry, simple rhymes, stories and drama elements. The use of percussion, voice and sounds, as well as a variety of music can be a useful starting point to invoke a movement response. Similarly, topics of interest such as 'Minibeasts', 'Seasons', 'Festivals', 'Transport', and 'Ourselves', for example, can be used to provide a starting point for children's work. All of these immediately give dance a link to learning in other subject areas like science, mathematics, history, religious education and geography.

As in other areas of physical education, the process of learning through dance activity involves children in planning, performing and evaluating. With experience and practice, children's ability to plan their movement responses to a range of stimuli improves, and they become not just more capable themselves but also begin to appreciate the performances of others. A growth in personal competence (and self-confidence) can enhance appreciation of what others are doing in dance and lead to exciting opportunities for evaluating and improving work.

Dance vocabulary and themes

The key themes for dance development revolve around a focus on *what* the body is doing, *where* the body is performing, *how* well it is doing this, and with *whom* the actions and movements are performed. In essence, dance provides children with a unique learning opportunity to communicate through body language, focusing on action, space, dynamics and relationships. This is achieved by providing learning opportunities which focus on the following aspects.

What the body is doing – Actions such as jumping, twisting, turning, travelling, rolling, stretching, curling, gesturing; what individual body parts are doing independent of each other but also in unison with one another – hands, feet, hips, elbows, head, knees, etc.; the symmetry or asymmetry of body action; what the top part of the body is doing as opposed to the bottom part, for example gesture using the top part, travel and support actions for the bottom part.

Where the body is performing (i.e. space) – At different levels (high, medium, low, deep, shallow); in different directions (forwards, backwards, sideways, diagonally, up, down); in movement action size (big and using lots of space, little using smaller more defined space); in extension or contraction with action performed near to the body or stretching away from the body; in body shape (a 'pin piercing shape', making a shape to enclose the body like a ball, a 'screw twisting' shape, etc.); in patterns or pathways such as circles, lines, curves, figures of eight, in a spiral, a zig-zag, etc.; in personal space of one's own or in the general space shared with others.

How the body is performing (quality of performance) – Weight, as in strong, powerful, vigorous, forceful, gentle, light, delicate, airy; time, which can be sudden, quick, fast, hasty, slow, unhurried, leisurely, gradual; space usage that can be straight, direct, linear, wavy; flow which can be careful, controlled, exact, precise, easy, fluent.

With whom action is performed (relationships) – partners, trios or groups involving mirroring, complementing, matching, leading and following, meeting and parting; with scope for circling and surrounding.

Children can learn to increase their own repertoire of skills in all four of the above noted areas but it is significant to note that dance is more than just a combination of skilful actions that are joined together in response to a particular stimuli, rhythm or beat. The dance-making process involves children in drawing from their own personal movement vocabulary in order to be able to respond in their own particular way or in response to particular step patterns suggested as part of the taught experience. They acquire such skills as a result of building their personal movement vocabulary from an exposure to such basic content as found in Table 6.1. Children will be able to move from very independent and personal initial responses, where the skills and timing elements are unique to them, but with a growing awareness of space and pattern as they work alongside others. This progression will begin to facilitate shared learning and contribute to a building up of skills and a widening movement repertoire as children are exposed to the variety of dance movement opportunities that come their way through the primary years.

Table 6.1 Basic movement vocabulary for primary dance activities

Physical Skills	What, Where, How, When				Social	
	Body	Space	Weight	Time	People	Stimuli
START	WHOLE PARTS	PERSONAL	Strong	Slow	Self	MUSIC
STOP	Hands	Near	Firm	Sustained	Others	Classical
TRAVEL	Feet	Far	Hard	Slower	Teacher	Popular
Walk	Knees	Above	Gentle	Decelerate	Partner	National
Jog	Elbows	Below	Light	Quick	Trio	Traditional
Run	Shoulders	In front	Soft	Quicker	Small group	Folk
Trot	Hips	Behind	Powerful	Fast	Large group	SOUNDS
Skip	Head	At sides	Tense	Sudden	Copy	Percussion
Slip	Arms	GENERAL	Relaxed	Accelerate	Contrast	Vocal
Slide	Leading	Forwards		A long time	Lead	Electronic
Gallop	Following	Backwards		A short time	Follow	WORDS
March	SURFACES	Sideways			Towards	Literature
JUMP and	Front	Up			Away	Poetry
LAND	Back sides	Down			Around	Prose
1 – 1 hop	Right	LEVELS			Pass	PICTURES
1 – other 1	Left	High			At same time	SCULPTURE
2 – 1	Top	Medium			After other	COSTUME
1 – 2	Bottom	Low			After one	Mask
2 – 1	Palms	PATHWAYS			another	PROPS
GESTURE	Soles	Straight				
Bend	Heels	Curved				
Stretch	Toes	Zigzag				
Twist		Angular				
BALANCE		Direct				
TURN		Flexible				
Open						
Close						

With an open-ended approach that facilitates all children accessing this part of the curriculum, drawing from their own skills base and movement knowledge, there is ample room for success for all children working at their own level. Once the base is established and can be successfully drawn from, then alternative teaching approaches can be adopted to promote an increasing range of step patterns, or particular movements which will bring greater control, flow and quality to overall performance. The important premise to work towards is that here is a part of the physical education curriculum where inclusion of all can be facilitated within a flexible approach that each individual child can access from what they already know and can do. The key is to build on this and extend the possibilities through experimentation and exploration of ideas and different starting points, whether they are story, drama, words and phrases, or percussion or music.

Learning episode 6.1: Starting points for dance activities

A Year 5 class teacher has recently attended a borough-wide INSET about engaging boys in reading. The facilitator suggested that some boys would respond better to stories with particular themes, such as historic battles, mythical Gods or Roman gladiators.

The class teacher returns to school and sees an improvement in attention during literacy when stories with such themes are used. Whilst supervising a lunchtime break she sees some of her pupils re-enacting scenes from the morning's story which was centred on the adventures of Perseus. The teacher sees that the children are engaged by the story and so plans the following week's dance lesson to draw on the characters within the story. The character of Medusa, in particular, provides rich stimuli for body actions and the class is able to interpret a visual stimulus by moving in monstrous, scary and slithery ways. To further strengthen the link between physical education and literacy, the teacher also adjusts the timetable so that the dance activities lesson follows the classroom-based literacy lesson.

Assessing pupils' performance in dance activities

When assessing children's performance in dance, teachers are looking for progress having been made in an individual child's ability to perform an increasing range of movement actions and skills. They will be looking for evidence which suggests that children have developed a range of movement skills which allow them to travel in different ways and on different body parts, are able to jump and land in a number of ways and that they are becoming increasingly controlled in their movement generally. They will be assessing how children move their whole bodies, the various isolated parts of it, and how they can show it working in unison. Evidence about how children are becoming increasingly adept at using limited and greater amounts of space, how they share that with others and how they can follow different pathways as they travel is further testimony to becoming a skilled performer in this area.

Similarly, a developing 'dance awareness' is evidenced in children's ability to respond to different rhythms and beats; how they can repeat sequences of movement consistently; and their growing awareness of the beginning, middle and end of particular movement routines. The ability to share ideas with others (with partners and in groups) and to begin to appreciate others' efforts in response to provided stimuli gives an indication of growing knowledge and understanding beyond just the physical demands of the activity. Overall, a teacher looking for signs that children have moved their learning forward in this area will be able to draw on a host of indicators in ascertaining progress and responsiveness to developing kinaesthetic awareness.

Teaching games activities

In some schools, games activities (often presented as traditional 'sports') dominate the physical education curriculum and our work in schools regularly unearths plans that refer to 'football' or 'netball' rather than a more explicit use of the terminology of the NCPE. Games activities should certainly form part of the 'core' physical education experience across both Key Stages in the primary school, but in no greater measure than dance or gymnastic activities. Teachers should not resort to games teaching simply because this is their own area of strength and experience. Whilst some children will have the necessary skills and conceptual understanding to compete in recognizable versions of team sports before others, others will find cooperative games and developmentally appropriate variations more appealing. Games activities should not therefore simply entail football or netball training for the benefit of the footballers and netballers; carefully differentiated activities, using a variety of equipment and teaching strategies are required to ensure relevance to all children within curriculum physical education. Without this, '15-a-side bench ball' or '15-a-side rounders' becomes the norm, arguably with little learning taking place.

Games activities introduce children to the range of skills and conceptual ideas needed for future participation in a wealth of adult and community sports settings. Indeed, such skills are often seen by children as a currency for socialization – not least in the playground where informal, child-led games require a base of skills for participation and acceptance (some research has shown how increased games skills can lead to less incidents of bullying at break time). There is clear potential within games activities for learning about rules, respecting and cooperating with others and accepting winning and losing with equal grace. The contribution that games activities can therefore make to child development across physical, social, affective and cognitive domains is therefore apparent, yet practitioners must fully embrace this potential by giving careful consideration to how games activities are framed in the teaching and learning context.

Games activities provide children with opportunities to develop and apply skill themes in cooperative and increasingly competitive contexts. Travelling with and without objects in space, sending them to others, receiving them back again and thinking how to first cooperate with and then 'outwit' others are the key themes that run throughout all types of games. Quality physical education seeks the progressive development of these skills to show increasing accuracy, variety and versatility of actions in increasingly competitive contexts.

The question therefore is not one of competition *or* cooperation, but one of *when* to introduce appropriate competition to the teaching and learning context. Because not all children will be ready to perform skills under the increased pressure that competition brings, it is important for the teacher to consider *how* and at *what time* competition is introduced. Pressure is applied in games activities through defending, restricting space and reducing opportunities to score (e.g. by reducing numbers of goals or making goals smaller). Under the increased pressure that competition brings, the time to process information and decide how to act in response to external stimuli (position of the ball and opponents, judging of space and time and so on) is reduced, which makes the demands of the task greater.

For children whose skills are not yet 'mature' in pattern (see Chapter 4), this can lead to deterioration of performance or, in the worst case, an avoidance reaction where the child says 'I can't do that'. In such circumstances, the more able begin to dominate activities and the less able become inconspicuous. The challenge for the teacher is to ensure that the more able are provided with opportunities to shine whilst taking their learning forward, and for the less able to grow in confidence and ability. Getting the pace of progression towards

Table 6.2 A selection of games activity skills and strategic concepts

Locomotion	Manipulation	Stability	Strategic concepts
Running – different speeds and directions Side slip Jumping	Throwing Kicking Ball rolling Sliding (e.g. a bean bag) Static ball strike Catch Trap Stop Dribble with hands Dribble with feet Dribble with stick Volley Strike moving ball	Ready position Stopping and turning Landing Cross laterality Twist and turn Dodge	Placing of object away from opponent(s) Shot variation (speed, distance, height) Keeping possession Creating an extra person (overlap, attacker in space, etc.) Drawing defenders to particular areas – create space elsewhere React and anticipate opponents movements (field placing, etc) Marking (1 on 1, zone) Apply pressure to opponent(s) by reducing space and time

competition right for every child can be extremely motivating and empowering for pupils; getting this wrong could lead to children being 'turned off' from games forever.

When planning and teaching within games activities, teachers must ensure that they have considered all safety factors that relate to the space used, the people taking part and equipment used. In games activities, this will specifically relate to:

- clear, clean and appropriate playing surfaces (especially those that are multi-purpose);
- correct storage and safe fixing of equipment (e.g. securing of goalposts);
- correct attire for children to allow free movement;
- clear expectations stressed at the outset of each lesson (e.g. class rules);
- clear instructions and use of resources to scaffold learning where appropriate.

Classification of games activities

In the NCPE, games activities are described within three broad categories:

- net games
- striking and fielding games
- invasion games.

An additional category – 'target games' – is sometimes used where the focus is on accuracy, control and aiming. Although the NCPE does not specifically refer to such games, these can be viewed as early progressions for many striking and fielding and net games where an element of control over an implement or object is required before pace and power can be developed. This said, some skills (such as the overarm throw) may be best developed to a mature pattern by neglecting accuracy in the first instance. Asking a child to throw *as far as she/he can* may be the required suggestion to encourage the child to step into the throw and fully extend the arm in preparation for release. Where accuracy is the only concern, a stilted, 'dart-throwing' arm action is the most appropriate response. The choice of activity and the specific interaction provided by the teacher is therefore of critical importance and should be firmly linked to the desired learning intention.

The broad classification of games activities should not be seen as mutually exclusive, as many skills are transferable across the categories and some games can be played as 'hybrids' of two or more. The descriptions provided below will help the beginning teacher to understand what the distinctive elements of each type of game are and how they will look when approached within primary physical education.

1. Net games (sometimes called net-wall games)
Adult versions of net games include tennis, badminton, volleyball, squash and table tennis. The net (and wall in squash) is therefore a barrier, over (or against) which participants send an object (usually a ball). Participation in these games requires an ability to control an object with the designated implement (racket or with body parts as in volleyball), and

the games generally take place on 'courts'. The implement is to be kept within the dimensions of the court (therefore being 'out' or 'in') and points are awarded for doing this to the detriment of one's opponent(s).

At first, children will need to gain individual control over the implements and objects using specific skills (striking, volleying, smashing, serving, etc.) to accurately judge the pace and weight of the shot within the designated boundary. Before this can be achieved, a degree of familiarity with the implement (such as a racket) needs to be gained. The racket should be viewed as an extension of the arm, so initial hand–eye coordination is at first required. When a racket or bat is introduced for the first time, the length and weight of the racket should be minimal, therefore minimizing difference between a throw and catch to palm and a hit and catch from bat. Variety of task is possible through using a range of types of bat and ball, forms of boundary (e.g. chalk line, rope along ground, bench, and cane between skittles) and numbers of children engaged in the activity.

2. Striking/fielding games

Adult versions of striking/fielding games include cricket, rounders, softball and baseball. They are characterized by sending an object away from oneself (by striking, throwing or kicking) and then attempting to score 'runs' by travelling towards or between designated bases or zones. Whilst the striker attempts to score, the defending team attempts to limit the runs by returning the object back to another designated space or person. In addition to limiting the number of runs scored, the defenders (or 'fielders') also attempt to limit the strikers' attempts in a number of different ways. Generally, the fielders catch, stump or bowl the strikers 'out' so that the two teams swap roles. Striking and fielding games are sometimes referred to as 'lions den' games ... the batters or strikers enter the lions den to try and outwit the full defending team – often as an individual or in a pair.

3. Invasion games

Adult versions of invasion games include hockey, netball, football, rugby, basketball and lacrosse. They are characterized by trying to get an object (such as a ball) into a goal or zone that is defended by somebody else or another team. Such games are normally played on a pitch that gives a clear indication of direction of play and therefore which territories (such as goals, end-lines, halves of pitch) are to be attacked or defended. Keeping possession of the ball is a priority in these games in order to create scoring opportunities. By moving the ball between team-mates, attacking teams will try to move defenders and create 'holes' in the defence through which to score. Games activities in each category encourage an emphasis on specific skills, ostensibly combinations of locomotor and manipulative skills, but also those that require balanced posture. In addition, games encourage problem solving and strategic awareness by team members who need to think through specific tactics and techniques to successfully achieve learning outcomes (such as score a goal). The teaching of games activities should ensure that children are afforded ample opportunities to plan and discuss a range of tactics and strategies within games that they themselves have created.

Teaching gymnastic activities

Gymnastic activities in the primary curriculum provide children with the unique opportunity to become increasingly controlled and skilful in their physical movements. In this area of learning children can experience a range and variety of movement tasks and activity that takes them upside down, where their feet are sometimes higher than their heads, and where they can work on a range of different surfaces at various levels away from the ground, and at heights that bring excitement and challenge to their repertoire of movement action. They can learn to move at different speeds and begin to combine increasingly complex series of movement and actions at various levels following a mixture of different pathways. In doing so, children's abilities to jump (and land), to perform different rolling actions, to balance on a variety of body parts, and to transfer body weight are nurtured and developed, which in turn promotes both movement competence and at the same time personal confidence.

It can be argued that the basic skill competencies that all children need to master in order to lead a future healthy and active lifestyle can be encapsulated within a well designed, continuous, progressive gymnastics curriculum. The control, coordination and discipline learnt from gymnastic activity provides the basis from which all areas of movement draw, including the very important elements to daily life such as locomotion, general stability and manipulative skills. The contribution this activity area makes to learning in other physical education activity areas is an added consideration to be borne in mind when justifying the importance of gymnastic activities. It is therefore alarming to note the reduction in curricular gymnastic activities in some primary schools where a 'fear factor' regarding safety, class discipline and teacher subject knowledge prevails. Beginning teachers are encouraged to prepare their own justifications for delivering high quality gymnastic experiences and to be aware that in some schools gymnastic activities will not be an existing curriculum priority.

The development of a movement vocabulary that promotes, for example, a variety of responses to ways of travelling, using space, making different body shapes, balancing on different parts, jumping and landing skills and working at different speeds, is very clearly required in the performance aspects of other 'core' physical education activities. Teachers' awareness of the potential for transferability of skill learning will enhance the overall knowledge, skills and understanding referenced as part of NCPE requirements. It could also be added here that as children do acquire greater control, accuracy and versatility in their motor competence, so gymnastics can also bring a discipline to their general movement performance.

A rationale for why we should provide a gymnastic experience for children throughout the primary years then may therefore look like this:

Why? – To support the need the need for children to become increasingly controlled in their general physical movement and motor competences. Gymnastic activities are primarily concerned with gross and fine motor development and contribute markedly to gradual and progressive improvement in coordination, balance, flexibility, strength and stamina.

What? – To broaden children's abilities in jumping and landing skills, rolling actions, and taking weight on different body parts, and to promote a range of different travelling actions.

Where? – The ability to display the broadening range of skills on the floor, initially on low level apparatus surfaces and increasingly on the varied surfaces offered by a full provision of gymnastic apparatus, including that which provides the potential for work at increased heights and levels (and on different types of surfaces).

How? – Through a full range of teaching strategies and an approach that promotes children succeeding at their own level – utilizing teaching methods that focus on promoting the individual child's learning and success in physical activity.

When? – Consistently through well thought through planned units of work over concentrated periods of time, consolidating what has gone before and extending children's repertoire of skilful body actions.

By posing the question 'what would be the result of children not experiencing learning in this particular area?' we gain further insight into its importance. If this were the case then a vital and integral cog in children's all round development would be missing, and there would inevitably be a shortfall in their physical performance capabilities. Furthermore, the wider brief of physical education should not be understated. The subject generally, and gymnastic activity specifically, makes a major contribution to speaking and listening skills, children's aesthetic and artistic development and their ability to develop problem-solving skills, as well as nurturing interpersonal and observational skills. These are all invaluable life skills and part and parcel of the wider curriculum.

What we want children to learn through their gymnastic activities are the skills that combine to make them more skilful, not just for their own physical education but also for their everyday needs. The identification of action words to movement application is key to learning in this area, with the emphasis on using a vocabulary that children understand and can interpret. Table 6.3 illustrates how particular movement themes (some of which are identified within National Curriculum frameworks) are linked to the various components of learning in and through gymnastic activity.

Table 6.3 Movement vocabulary for primary gymnastics

Gymnastic activity themes	Skills	Body	Spatial	Dynamics	Apparatus	Relationships	Movement skill vocabulary
Space	*Stability*	*Whole body*	*Personal*	*Speed*	*Portable*	*Individual*	On to
Use of apparatus	Balance	Large parts	Near	Go and stop	Mini apparatus		Off
Movement tasks	Stillness	Small parts	Next to	Fast	Hoops	*Partner*	Across
Supporting body weight	Dynamic	Fixed	Far away	Slow	Cones		Between
Transference of weight	Inverted	Free	In front	Quicker	Skipping ropes	*Groups*	Up
Lifting parts high	On different body parts	Near	Behind	Accelerate	Beanbags		Down
Travelling		Far	At the side	Decelerate	Skittles	*Class*	Over Under
Feet together and apart	*Locomotion*	Leading	Following	Slower	Canes	Work alone	Around
Curling and stretching	Walking	Following	Leading	Short time	Discs	Work with others	Next to
Use of space	Jogging	Isolated		Long time	Mats	Copy	Far away from
Transferring weight	Skipping		*General*	Sudden	Benches	Mirror/match	Through
Joining movements	Galloping	*Surface*	Directions	Stillness	Linking planks	Contrast	Underneath
Directions	Running	Front	Forwards		Nesting tables	Support actions	Into
Parts together and apart	Jumping	Back	Backwards	*Weight*	'A' frame	Talk and discuss movement	Out of
Lifting and lowering	Rolling	Side	Sideways	Strong	Ladders		Near to
Shape	On different parts	Top	Diagonal	Powerful	Movement tables		Towards
Speed	Continuous	Bottom	Up/down	Firm	Boxes		Away from
Twisting and turning	Paused	On different parts		Light	Stools		Height
Sequences			*Levels*	Soft	Foam equipment		Length
Levels	*Manipulative*	*Shape*	High	Tension			Width
Partner work	Grasp	Arrow	Low		*Fixed*		Obstacle
Flight	Grip	Ball	Medium	*Time*	Frames		
Pathways	Hook	Wall	Near floor/surface	At same time	Ropes		
Symmetry and asymmetry	Hang	Twist	Away from the floor/surface	Within a set time	Beams		
Balance and continuity	Spring	Gesture		After another	Bars		
Flow	Push	*Size*		Before another	Poles		
Strength and lightness	Pull	Big		Use same space			
	Slide	Small					
		Medium					

By breaking down the detail of provision for primary age groups we can track the progression of skill learning that should ensue from the Foundation Stage through to the point where children move to secondary education. Teachers will appreciate the need to identify the progression expected across the primary age range, seeing both where the children they are faced with teaching gymnastic content to have come from, and where they need to go to in their learning. General pointers characterizing what we might expect, and therefore need to plan for, are described in relation to each primary Key Stage below.

The Foundation Stage and Key Stage 1

It is important that teachers develop a background knowledge of children's play and movement experience. Some children will have attended playgroup settings, or nursery classes which may well have provided a variety of physical experiences, but others may not have benefited from such opportunities and may exhibit a marked lack of physical confidence. The basic work must therefore allow these young children to explore the simple actions of jumping, rolling, balancing and climbing as well as finding out which parts of the body are needed to support itself when it is still, or which can assist it to move, for example hands and feet, shoulders, seat, etc. During this exploration the children should be made aware of where the body and its parts are moving, whether it is moving on the spot, in the larger area of the hall or on or around apparatus. As the child becomes more skilful he or she should be encouraged to join together actions to form a simple movement phrase or pattern. Initially the children should be restricted to linking two actions which lead smoothly from the first to the second, for example a jump to land under control, then roll of a kind that the child can do.

The teacher's choice of words, which promote movement responses from the children and need to be understood by them, is of great importance at this stage. The personal vocabularies of children can be increased by their greater appreciation and understanding of the meaning of words which have been used to stimulate, extend and enhance body actions, for example moving along, through, up, down, stepping, sliding, etc. Other words may be used which increase children's awareness of space and help them to grasp concepts, for example backwards, sideways, behind, forwards, in front of, left, right, etc.

By the end of the infant period most children are adventurous and able to move confidently, freely and safely on the floor and on a variety (albeit still relatively low) of apparatus. This is not to say that they will not seek further tests of their abilities, so part of the teaching strategy must be to provide extended opportunities to increase their repertoire of skilful actions, through demonstration, further practice and application in other areas of the curriculum.

Key Stage 2 – Years 3 and 4

Much of the material for 'lower juniors' should reinforce and extend the basic work of the infants. In setting tasks, teachers should always refer to specific action words and body parts to achieve a clear response from the children. Greater control and appreciation of body form and outline should be expected, together with an increased awareness of the movement of other children in close proximity, especially when working on apparatus. This displays increased spatial awareness not just of the space the individual uses to perform their actions and movements, but also of others using similar (and therefore restricted) space of their own as all work and share the activity area.

It will be necessary to continue to encourage children to link movements together in simple, yet developing sequences. A combination of more than three or four actions is likely to be within the capabilities of most children of this age, although there will be marked differences in terms of the continuity achieved, the skill levels attained, the range of actions performed and the overall quality of the work produced.

When setting tasks on the floor or on the apparatus, the teacher's choice of language continues to be very important. A great deal of the work continues to be exploratory, and quick responses to tasks set for lower juniors are emphasized and encouraged, since too detailed analysis or description of actions can lead to a lack of spontaneity and (potentially) lower quality work being produced. The keynotes in this age group are clearly action, participation and involvement.

Early work with a partner should be carefully considered. Many children do not find it easy to match the movement of others, or to adapt their own ideas to working with someone else. However, working at simple tasks with a partner can be both challenging and enjoyable, and may help some children to clarify their movements and ideas. Shared, verbal reflections on each other's performances are a vital part of the learning at this stage, bringing with it a growing appreciation of movement for its own sake.

This is a period therefore when children should be encouraged to observe the movement of others. By careful and informed observation they can learn a great deal which will help to improve or add variety to their own work. The ability to observe and extract from what they have seen, what is significant in the movements and actions observed, should be developed by asking children to look for particular features of the work. For example, what parts of the body are being used to support the weight? At what speed is the body moving? Does the body movement change direction during the sequence?

Demonstrations by the teacher or children should be short and used sparingly. The point of any demonstration should be clearly established and positive teaching points made as a result. One further point here – ensure that any demonstrations are within the attainment of the children being taught. Nothing detracts more from potential performance than to see action demonstrated beyond the scope of the majority of children. Look to spread the opportunities to display their work, and use half class watching half class, or groups showing a range of movement response, rather than isolating individuals to show what they can do – remember, this an area that is immediately visible to others and though some revel, others can be reluctant and shy to publicly display their efforts.

Key Stage 2 – Years 5 and 6

At this stage children will achieve a higher level of skilful response to tasks set by the teacher, provided that the earlier work to develop strength, suppleness and an appreciation of quality of movement has been successfully carried out. The children by this stage should be able to respond to the demands of thoughtful, sustained and concentrated work. Their own choice of actions can be refined to produce movement sequences appropriate to the problems and tasks set by the teacher. Their awareness of body movement should equip them to select actions which flow naturally from one action to another. An example would be the choice of an appropriate movement to follow an inverted position using the momentum created by overbalancing and controlling and adapting it to produce the next phase of the sequence, for example handstand into controlled forward roll, or a shoulder stand into a log roll.

The ability to observe the work of others should be further developed so that constructive, positive criticism is expected and encouraged in the pursuit of quality work being produced. The exploration of tasks with a partner or in small groups is an important aspect of the work at this stage and may lead to a greater variety of response and a greater appreciation of the needs, strengths and limitations of others. It may also help the less skilful child to work with those who are more confident.

Ultimately at this stage of development there should be an expectation that the complexity, individuality and creativity of movement will be qualitatively driven. Children should be expected to work hard on improving their sequences of movement, becoming increasingly adept at moving from floor to apparatus and vice versa, and to sustain their performance levels to improve the flow and continuity of the actions that make up the overall performance. The teacher's ability to monitor such developments, and to consistently encourage children to move their learning forward, is a hallmark of effective teaching in this period in readiness for the demands that a more formal approach to teaching gymnastics might take in Key Stage 3.

As with all aspects of physical education, an integral assessment tool to be employed by teachers is their ability to observe, analyse and evaluate what they see children doing in their lessons. In essence this can be summarized under four key headings:

1 Is the class working safely? With care, under control, in response to the particular tasks set.
2 Is the class answering the task? Listening, understanding, appropriateness of response, challenge.
3 How well is the task being answered? Appropriateness of the idea(s), quality of the performance produced.
4 How can the teacher help? Feedback, and further guidance, clarification, teaching points, demonstration, discussion, suggestion, praise, encouragement, criticism, reflection on the effort.

A specific approach to take when monitoring children's progress in gymnastic activities is to utilize the plan, perform and evaluate process model as shown in the accompanying templates for Key Stages 1 and 2. The reference to associated health, safety and Personal,

Social, Health Education (PSHE) elements gives a perspective on broader educational components. By coding progress as suggested and allowing for further commentary such record sheets can be utilized both formatively and summatively.

Key Stage 1 Gymnastics

Assessment and recording pupil progress

By the end of the key stage pupils should be able to:

Pupil's name:	
Plan • Joining together linked movements and actions, e.g. jumps, rolls and balances	**Comments**
Perform • Skills – performing basic gymnastic actions with increasing control and precision, showing a change of direction, shape or speed • Skills – performing chosen specific skills from the basic actions of jumping, rolling, balancing, travelling on hands and feet and in climbing, hanging and swinging	
Evaluate • Recognizing own and others individual actions and skills and within joined movement sequences	
Health • Recognize the importance of warming up before exercise and warming-down as a conclusion to activity • Recognize that exercise causes the heart to beat faster, that there is a knock-on effect to body temperature, that breathing can get faster, and that the body can get tired	
Safety • Lift, carry, site, assemble and dismantle apparatus with teacher supervision • Safely share the workspace provided including when working on apparatus	
PSHE • Collaborate and cooperate with others in gymnastics work • Comment constructively on own and other's work	

Key: 1 = Working towards 2 = Achieved 3 = Achievement 'plus'

Key Stage 2 Gymnastics

Assessment and recording pupil progress

By the end of the key stage pupils should be able to:

Pupil's name:	
Plan • Extended sequences of at least 5 or 6 movements joined together and including changes of speed, shape and direction and performance at different levels on floor and apparatus	**Comments**
Perform • Skills – performing selected gymnastic skills which increasingly show clear body shape, extension, accuracy and control • Skills – sequencing selected actions which are linked together with increasing control, flow and continuity • Skills – extended, repeatable and more complex sequences which have defined start and finish positions • Skills – performing gymnastic actions that match the context, e.g. floor to apparatus, individual, pairs or group work	
Evaluate • Using given criteria – to provide accurate and insightful feedback to self and others • Identify accurately the component parts and features of a sequence • Comment on the quality of actions in relation to speed, direction, and body shape achieved	
Health • Display increasing knowledge of which particular activities are suitable for gymnastics warming up • Understanding of the need to combine pulse-raising activity and stretching exercises for warm up and warm down parts of each lesson	
Safety • Safely apply lifting, carrying, siting, assembly and dismantling of apparatus skills • Safely sharing the workspace and the apparatus with due concern for own and others' safety	
PSHE • Work collaboratively and cooperatively with others • Display understanding and sensitivity for others' abilities	

Key: 1 = Working towards   2 = Achieved   3 = Achievement 'plus'

Teaching swimming activities and water safety

Of all the physical education activity areas, swimming activities and water safety has a unique right to claim 'life skill' relevance; being able to swim can certainly save lives in emergency situations, and swimming is also a recreational activity that can be continued throughout adulthood. The non-weight bearing nature of swimming, together with the excellent benefits for cardiovascular development suggest that swimming is a suitable health based activity that should be accessible by all. Whether future Olympic competitors, recreational swimmers or individuals benefiting from the therapeutic nature of water-based activity, swimming activities have a direct relevance to all children.

The teaching of swimming activities and water safety is a compulsory component of the NCPE. Coverage of the swimming programme of study must take place within the primary age phases, although schools have a choice as to whether this is done in Key Stage 1 or 2, or indeed both. The teaching of swimming in schools is, however, somewhat problematic and many teachers have concerns regarding:

- their own subject knowledge;
- health and safety issues;
- travel time to nearest pools;
- changing the children and implications for child protection;
- incurred costs.

The teaching of swimming activities in the primary school is often achieved best when a trained swimming 'instructor' works alongside a class teacher in a local authority swimming pool. This has the benefit of pool-side lifeguards too, although it carries a cost and transport implication. Time spent travelling to the pool also erodes learning time within the activity itself and schools must weigh up the pros and cons of different approaches. There is certainly a major issue with regards charging parents for National Curriculum teaching and learning, and school managers must make every effort to ensure that every child has true access to learning in this activity area.

Where schools have their own 'learner' pools on site, clear health and safety guidelines should be issued which all staff should understand and follow. These should comply with both local authority and nationally recognized best practice guidelines (see BAALPE, 2004). Trainee teachers are urged (as in all activity areas) to check such guidelines fully and to be aware of their own legal position with regards status as a trainee. As a starting point for the swimming context, we would urge all trainee teachers to:

- seek out additional opportunities to develop subject knowledge in swimming (such as through teacher courses run by the Amateur Swimming Association and the Swimming Teachers' Association);

Table 6.4 Key swimming themes and vocabulary

Water confidence and familiarization	Floating and propulsion	Water safety
Hygiene, changing and drying	Resting in the water	Water dangers in the environment

Entry and exit
  Side/steps
  Jump in
  Shallow entry dive
	Floating in the water
	
	Propulsion
	  Push/glide
	  Front/back
	  Stretched position
		Closed and open water
		  environments
		
		Survival skills
		
		Surface dive

Walking and locomotion practices
  Individual
  In pairs
	Turning and tumbling
	
	Collecting objects
		Sculling
		
		Treading water

Playing with a ball	Stroke techniques Front crawl	Knowledge of how to be rescued
Playing with a hoop	Backstroke Breast-stroke	Knowledge of how to rescue others
Nursery rhymes and action songs	Butterfly	
Standing to horizontal and back to feet, using float or side of pool	Arm action Leg action Body position	
Different body positions and shapes	Breathing	
Breathing practices		
Blowing bubbles on and under water surface		
Blowing ping-pong ball		
Washing face		
Open eyes under water		
Crouch down under water		
Travelling under and through		

- be fully aware of risk assessment and emergency procedures as relevant to the swimming context;
- seek opportunities to become trained in pool-relevant first aid and life-saving (e.g. through courses run by the Royal Life Saving Society);
- seek support and guidance from more experienced colleagues.

Where swimming activities are taught by a visiting or pool-based instructor, we strongly urge the class teacher to remain with the class and to be a key part of the lesson. The class teacher is the person with the best knowledge of children's broader learning and can share delivery with the instructor to ensure that the children not only receive skill-specific instruction and feedback, but that wider learning opportunities are maximized and developed. The class teacher will have a greater knowledge of the aims and purpose of the curriculum too and will be best placed to draw out learning within social, cognitive and affective domains. The teacher can also use classroom-based learning to prepare and review children's swimming learning. Swimming-specific health and safety 'rules' are best addressed before arriving at the pool, for example alongside the development of children's awareness of their own bodies in the water.

The pool context is not ideal for detailed explanation of conceptual knowledge and understanding, so the classroom (utilizing links to other curriculum areas) can be effectively used in addition to pool-based learning. Classroom-based preparation for a swimming unit of work could include:

- children creating a health and safety poster to display on pool side (laminated);
- children considering their own preparation – bringing the correct kit, suitable food to eat before and after, hygiene, changing and drying;
- reviewing prior learning and considering different techniques for moving in the water;
- designing water-based games that they can play with others;
- creating visual resources to support their own and others' work in swimming and water safety.

The teacher should also consider methods that will be used to scaffold learning in the water. The potential for extensive use of voice is limited, so a clear start and stop signal using body language (or whistle in case of emergencies) is advised. All children must understand what they have to do when they hear the signal to stop (e.g. stand up with feet on the bottom and look to teacher, or swim to the side, hold on to rail and look to teacher). The teacher's place during the lesson is on the pool side, and consideration should be given to where children are positioned to see and hear instructions, feedback and guidance. The use of simple 'cues' (introduced in the classroom, reinforced in the changing room and utilized on pool side) is an effective way of imparting feedback through few but meaningful words, body actions and pictures. The use of gestures to reinforce positive behaviour is also encouraged – a timely 'thumbs up' to reward good effort and listening for example, can be very beneficial.

The need for mixed ability teaching is very evident in the swimming context. Some children will be true beginners (learning to swim for the first time in school), whereas other classmates will have been 'swimming' from infancy. By the end of Key Stage 2 some children will already be competitive swimmers in club and representative squad structures and have progressed much further than the existing NCPE aim of swimming at least 25 metres unaided. Creating distinct

---

Learning episode 6.2: Preparation for a swimming unit

Malcolm is a Year 3 class teacher, and although he is not a confident swimmer himself, is looking forward to working with the children in his class in the forthcoming five-week unit of work at the local pool. During the first week of term, Malcolm has used time in the classroom to prepare children for their swimming and water safety work. The children have created a poster to display in the classroom and on pool side that reminds them of the main ways in which they can propel themselves in the water. They have also created their own swimming diaries that will provide a written record of their learning (and will be completed during the bus journey back to school). Finally, Malcolm has liaised with parents to ascertain the level of prior learning in swimming and has met with the swimming instructor to discuss individual learning needs.

learning zones (by using lane ropes or markers on the side of the pool) is one way of ensuring that sufficient space (and appropriate depth of water) is available for children at different ability levels. It is crucial that the teacher checks children's understanding of the task before saying 'off you go' and that keen observation during the task provides indication of children's progress.

The focus for learning in swimming should be through the 'four aspects' of physical education described in Chapter 5. In swimming, three main areas for specific focus are:

- developing confidence in the water;
- developing a range of techniques through which children can propel themselves in the water;
- developing an awareness of safety considerations and 'dangers', together with a range of skills that can be used to keep self and others safe.

The focus should not therefore be solely on developing 'strokes', although children's ability to swim on front, back and side and to use different body parts in different ways will be developed from exploratory beginnings to more recognizable and applicable 'strokes' of front crawl, breast-stroke, backstroke and butterfly. The early stages of swimming experiences should focus on ways of entering and exiting the pool, regaining the standing position and gaining confidence whilst getting the face wet and being fully submerged.

See key swimming themes and vocabulary in Table 6.4.

Athletic activities

Here is the area of the physical education curriculum where children can learn to run faster or for longer, jump further or higher, or to throw a range of projectiles (balls, plastic and foam javelins, discus and shot) in different ways over greater distances. In addition to where similar activity occurs elsewhere (in games, dance or gymnastic activities, for example), this is an area that can engage children's natural propensity for vigorous and enthusiastic participation in events that require them to utilize measuring tapes and stopwatches that accurately record achievement. The running, jumping, throwing, hurdling and relay activities children will encounter within this activity area are all enjoyable and central to our natural ability to move, indeed crucial in different ways to all sporting activities, based as they are on the natural physical movements we all make in everyday life. Furthermore, such activities are key contributors to normal growth and development and as such should be recognized as vital to children's all round physical education.

In athletic activities children can experience a varied and challenging series of events and practices designed purposely to improve, develop and refine the technical and skilled performances of running, jumping and throwing. They experience basic and simple tests with measurements of 'How fast?', 'How far?' and 'How high?' which allow children to measure, compare and improve their own performances, and be aware of their progress from lesson to lesson and over time. Additionally, children can experience competition in athletic activities which includes competing against previous personal bests, against each other, and in groups against other teams. This can include involvement in competitions that they and others have combined to plan, create, experience, reflect on and develop, and might also include participation in a major event like a school sports day, inter-school competition or 'mini youth games'.

The motivational aspects of athletic participation, inspired by the excitement and pleasure of actively monitoring progress and seeing improvement, make this an area that builds naturally on such a big part of what makes up so many major team games. The practice to improve the skills of running, jumping and throwing has an appeal to children, particularly when they can see and witness its potential across a range of learning domains – this might be the place where children finally understand what a metre is, and how 3.28 is a different measure (for the long jump) than running a distance in 3.28 minutes.

Beyond the reasons already stated, it is clear that athletic activity in the primary PE curriculum plays a significant and important part in the development of skills and through the development of fitness, both being elements that are essential to successful physical activity. Success in athletic activities can undoubtedly support and foster success in other areas of the PE curriculum.

In the early years and throughout Key Stage 1, teaching should be concentrated on helping children to perform and extend their abilities in the basics of running, jumping and throwing. This will contribute to the improvement of coordination skills as well as to good posture and overall body control. It is crucial, therefore, that children during this period have opportunities to access the resources conducive to supporting this learning, are able to explore and experiment with space and equipment which meet such objectives, and are supported and guided to improve their abilities through structured and semi-structured activity sessions (the more regular the better).

At Key Stage 2 the skills are developed and refined, taking account of the stage of general physical development children will have reached by this stage. Particular techniques can now be taught, for example how to maintain a straight running pathway or 'run a bend' on an oval track, or how to maximize force and power when executing an overarm throw, or take off on a preferred foot when jumping for distance or height. Although such skills will be advanced in other areas, like gymnastics, dance and games, it is only in athletics that these skills are used to their maximum in response to the challenge to go faster, higher and further. As Couling and Dickinson (1993, p. 2) suggest:

> It is therefore essential that a continued emphasis should be placed on athletics activities within the PE programme, for therein lies the key to physical and personal development over the whole range of the subject.

The particular movement vocabulary for teaching and learning in primary school athletics is as follows:

Key Stage 1 – An emphasis on increasing accuracy, speed, height, length and distance of general movement performance. (It should be noted that current NCPE guidance does not specifically include athletic activities in Key Stage 1, although the content described here can be achieved within games, gymnastic and dance activities and an overarching 'skill theme' approach.)

Key Stage 2 – Building on and applying the above to the basic actions of running, jumping and throwing; to incorporate measuring, comparing and improving performance, and to experience competition of various kinds.

Running – General running activities involving a change of pace and direction in team and individual activities; a particular focus on keeping the head still and effective use of the arms and legs.

Jumping – A range of jumping activities emphasizing run up, take off, flight and landing; position of the head and the effective use of arms and legs.

Throwing – A variety of throwing activities requiring different techniques (one handed, two handed, underarm, overarm), using a variety of projectiles for accuracy and distance, e.g. balls of various sizes, quoits, shuttlecocks, beanbags as well as 'junior' athletics equipment like foam javelins, shots and discus.

The following teaching pointers provide progressive learning experiences for children participating in athletic activities, with specific technical aspects that apply once the very basic movement competence is in place. Within this are the specifics of what to look for when monitoring children's progress as they experience the range of activities a balanced athletics programme should offer. The need to ensure access for all to such activity is well catered for in athletics because of the specific nature of the events covered. Care needs to be taken with regard to ensuring equal opportunity with an emphasis on monitoring personal performance against previous attainment.

Running activities
- Arm action: for running fast; for running distances.
- Leg action: speed of stride; length of stride.
- Acceleration: coordination of arms and legs; body position (particularly the head – 'keep it still and looking forward!').

For 'sprinting'
- Running on the balls of the feet.
- Appropriate arm action for acceleration – 'fast arms make the legs go faster'.
- 'Fast' legs – leg speed governs how fast you can go!

- Appropriate leaning body position for acceleration.
- Working on keeping the head looking forward.

For 'starts'

- Use a start signal, e.g. 'Get-set, go', developing to 'To your marks, set, go'.
- Practise using the safety area and jogging back initially over short distances.
- Practise standing starts; develop to partner helping to place feet to help grip, ensuring a 'push away' with stronger foot from behind, up to, but not on start line.
- Increase sprint distance to 30 metres for Year 5 and 35 metres for Year 6 (and more for competent performers).

For 'hurdling'

- Establish preferred take-off foot (likely to be take-off foot for long and high jump activities and linked to foot preference in kicking – take-off foot is often the opposite foot to preferred kicking foot).
- Encourage work on straight leading leg to clear the middle of the hurdle and maintain speed.

For relays

- If the leader puts back the right hand, the follower taps the left hand and passes on the right. This teaches the correct relay passing technique. Vice versa for left hand.
- A and B must change on the correct side. The receiver must not look back for the quoit/beanbag/baton because this slows the change-over.
- Introduce a third person.

Jumping activities

- Preparation for jumping: a standing jump (no run up) with the swinging of arms coordinated with the bending and springing from knees and ankles which begins the action.
- Take off: coordination of arm and leg action to propel the body into the air, forwards or upwards.
- Flight phase: keeping head and arms up as long as possible.
- Landing: safe, active, springy landing with rebound, especially on hard surfaces.
- Coordination: in take off and between phases, as in a combination jump (e.g. three steps).

Two feet to two feet jumping (standing start):

- Preparation.
- Coordination: the timing of arm and leg actions and the height of the jump are instrumental in improving length ('Stay in the air as long as possible').

(Safety: encourage active landings which do not skid onto the seat, and which might jar the base of the spine.)

One foot to two feet jumping (standing start initially):

- One foot to two feet using a three-/five-stride approach (a short approach is recommended to concentrate the effort on the jump).
- Measure the jump from the take off to landing point.
- Encourage safe landings.
- Children can set out individual challenges using ropes and beanbags.

Combination jumping (standing start):

- The landing phase of one jump merges with the preparation for the next jump. It is therefore important to keep the body upright on each landing to avoid a shorter jump on the next phase, and to keep the jumps of equal length.
- Set out ropes so that children can practise this coordination progressively.
- Ask children to find out how far they can jump using two or three steps; two or three hops; two or three two-footed jumps.
- Ask them to combine these techniques to find their best distance.

Throwing activities

- Body position/stance: a sideways stance is usual in all throwing, slinging, pushing actions.
- Transference of weight: from the rear foot to the front foot during the throwing action.
- Arm action: for overarm throwing, slinging, one-handed and two-handed pushing, the object being thrown is moving before it is released. The heavier the object, the more important it is to begin its movement in order to throw it a long way.
- Twisting the trunk in slinging and pushing aids the process of moving the object the furthest distance before it is released.
- Grip: for throwing, slinging and pushing – increasingly a finger grip rather than a palm.
- Force: the faster an action is performed, the longer the potential throw.
- Trajectory: the optimum release point to propel the object the furthest distance is at approximately 45 degrees to the ground.

For slinging:

- Straight-arm action, one-handed.
- Encourage turning/twisting the trunk to impart extra force to the quoit/discus.
- Follow through with rear foot and arm in direction of throw.
- Children often bowl the quoit instead of slinging with a straight arm.
- Emphasize low start, high finish position (approximately 45 degree trajectory).

For pushing:

- Which position, sitting or standing, gives the longest throw? Why? (In a standing throw, use the trunk to give added leverage.)
- Sitting: concentrate on correct grip and pushing action. The elbow should be fixed and high, the object resting on the fingertips and fingers. The forearm moves. The palm faces the front all the time (a common fault is for the elbow to drop, resulting in throwing rather than pushing).
- Standing: concentrate on turning the trunk to start the object moving before release.

(Safety note: throw light equipment; throw into a free space; train your class routines and systems for throwing, i.e. adequate spacing arrangements, working with partners taking turns to throw and collect when all throws have taken place. Group throwing activities require teacher supervision.)

Teaching outdoor and adventurous activities

Outdoor and adventurous activities (OAA) are perhaps the most misunderstood area of the NCPE. In a similar way to adults' perceptions of games as being football, hockey, netball and cricket, many teachers equate OAA with rock climbing, abseiling, canoeing and potholing – 'specialist' activities that are clearly beyond the scope of most class teachers! Whilst such activities can be introduced to primary aged children during residential experiences and by appropriately trained, qualified and experienced staff, curricular OAA can provide meaningful opportunities for children to experience very distinct learning tasks.

Current requirements of the NCPE suggest that Key Stage 2 pupils should be taught to:

- Take part in outdoor activity challenges, including following trails, in familiar, unfamiliar and changing environments.
- Use a range of orienteering and problem-solving skills.
- Work with others to meet the challenges. (DfEE/QCA, 1999, p. 19).

School-based OAA can help children to develop self-awareness and self-confidence, problem-solving skills, group cohesion, trust and communication. Although not a statutory requirement until Key Stage 2, young children can also benefit from exploring their school environments through orientation-type exercises – both indoors and out. Treasure hunts, dinosaur expeditions or 'photo trails', for example, also hold exciting potential for cross-curricular development, particularly from work in literacy, geography and science. Many schools and early years settings have embraced the learning potential of the 'outdoor classroom' and this area of physical education can fully utilize this approach. 'Constructivist' approaches to teaching and learning can also be fully utilized as children work together to solve problems, identify solutions and create new understandings.

OAA perhaps holds most potential for learning in affective, social and cognitive domains. When OAA is taught well, children can learn so much about themselves and each other; links to PSHE are also meaningful and relevant within many tasks. Because OAA is not a statutory requirement in Key Stage 1, many schools leave the teaching of OAA until late Key Stage 2 – often taught as a self-contained unit within a Year 5 or 6 residential experience. This could be seen as a missed opportunity to develop physical learning tasks, orientation, problem solving, cross-curricular and communication skills throughout the primary years. Where OAA is a central feature of learning across both primary Key Stages, teachers often report improved behaviour, class cohesion, pupil confidence and problem-solving abilities.

Orientation and orienteering

The range of possible activities in school-based OAA should not be restricted to orienteering, although this particular focus does provide an opportunity for children to develop understanding and specific skills. Map work, the eventual use of a compass to aid route planning and application of these skills to work in unfamiliar territory (for example, in a local park) are central themes of the OAA curriculum that can have very simple beginnings. The activities listed below show how orientation-type activities can be developed progressively over time in both familiar and unfamiliar environments.

Examples of 'orientation' activities

- Guided tours
- Following written or spoken directions
- Photo trails
- Treasure hunts
- Travelling to and from school safely and around the local vicinity (include road safety)
- Creating and using a map of the classroom or hall
- Creating and using a map of the playground, school fields and grounds
- Identifying and travelling around distances, scale, spaces and landmarks from a simple map
- Using Ordnance Survey maps
- Using web-accessed maps, plans and aerial photography
- Using compass directions
- Setting a compass to a map
- Use of control markers and cards
- Orienteering in school grounds and cross country (local park)

The health and safety considerations for this kind of OAA activity should follow recognized good practice for all physical education. A risk assessment should be completed for any activity that involves new environments and teachers must pay particular attention to the fact that children will be operating across a much larger area than in other physical education lessons. Sites should be chosen without hazards such as open water, steep banks or close proximity to roads and railways. Where such features exist, an adult can be positioned to ensure that children are kept away from them. In most cases, children should work together with others in pairs and small groups and should be encouraged to come up with solutions together.

Problem solving, cooperation, trust and challenge

Residential OAA centres place a high priority on trust-building exercises in the outdoor and adventurous context; not only do these help children develop a sense of team work and cooperation but also serve as excellent ice-breakers for more challenging work to come. In the residential experiences that many schools choose to use for OAA delivery, it is fascinating to see how different characters and personalities grow and develop across the course. A teacher can often learn more about a child within such activities than any other – particularly when asking a child to overcome personal fear. This also serves to foster a better inter-pupil understanding of strengths and weaknesses and reinforces the importance of encouragement and peer support.

There is every reason to incorporate this kind of activity in school-based physical education and not to save this for 'one-off' trips. The same themes can be explored in the school grounds, making OAA not only physically challenging, but relevant from a 'life skills' perspective. Interestingly, a recent academic review regarding educational benefits of physical education and sport (Bailey *et al.*, in press), describes affective gains seen within OAA activities, particularly when aimed at specific groups of children and young people.

There is a wide range of activities that can be used to foster cooperation and trust and the recommended reading at the end of this chapter will provide richer descriptions of specific games and tasks that can be used during lessons. Many of the possibilities listed below as examples will already be familiar to class teachers and can be easily incorporated into curriculum lessons. The possibilities are almost limitless and we encourage teachers to explore new ideas, especially those which engage the children themselves in the creation of challenges and tasks.

Parachute games Parachute games typically involve a group of children who are positioned to hold the outside of a large piece of cloth or 'parachute' and asked to cooperate with each other to achieve a variety of goals, such as manoeuvring balls, ropes and beanbags, travelling underneath the parachute or moving the parachute to create different shapes. The key to all such games is cooperation.

Leading and guiding In these activities, some pupils are given responsibility of leading others (via verbal commands, arm signals and so on) through, around and across a space. The use of blindfolds adds a greater level of challenge, although their use should be introduced with care – the removal of visual perception can be a frightening experience for some children.

Trails and courses A trail can be created in a variety of ways – using specific materials such as string, paper, crumbs or flour to 'show the way' and for children to follow. The trail can also incorporate a series of obstacles across, under or through which the children have to manoeuvre. Obstacle courses can be created using gymnastic and simple games apparatus, or other resources such as tyres, milk crates, barrels, existing play equipment, and the like. The obstacles can be seen as stepping stones or safe zones in quicksand for example, challenging the teams of pupils to cross without touching the ground. In such activities, the use of carefully considered, unhurried actions should be stressed.

Searches and rescues In these activities, children are challenged to find specific materials or items located in a designated area. Variations along a theme can include egg hunts, letter hunts, finding pieces of a shipwrecked boat, 'buried' treasure and so on. The search can also lead to a 'rescue' situation where the team is challenged to retrieve an item from within a designated area using specified equipment (such as ropes, poles, etc.). Such rescues can also be used as separate activities.

Communication games These games challenge children to work together to solve a physical problem. For example, ask six children to line up along a bench and then to reorganize themselves in a specified order (e.g. date of birth, alphabetical, height and so on) without stepping off the bench. The task can be repeated without verbal communication. Other problem-solving activities where communication and elements of leadership are essential include 'river crossing' type games, made more challenging by the requirement to carry a piece of equipment or containers of water!

The above ideas are adapted from PEAUK, BAALPE, NDTA 1995, pp. 31–44.

Residential experiences

We have little doubt that a well planned and effectively led residential experience can contribute to the physical education curriculum in a major way. Effective use of specialist staff should provide the 'icing on the cake' for primary aged children, particularly when they come away with new skills, improved self-confidence and personal growth. During such trips, it is essential that the primary class teacher and other accompanying adults are engaged fully in the educative process and do not simply hand the children over to the specialists with a sense of abdicated responsibility. School staff should:

- Liaise in detail with the centre staff to ensure that the programme is geared to specific needs of the class.
- Visit the centre in advance to meet staff and carry out a risk assessment (with the specific needs of the class in mind).
- Ensure that time is spent at school in preparing children for upcoming challenges. Some of the activities described above will introduce key themes for further development, whilst other specific skills can be introduced in other activity areas (e.g. climbing can be practised on wall bars before application to a climbing wall at the centre).

- Communicate fully with parents and carers and ensure that a full account of the children's learning is produced on return to school (using for example a diary approach or even video footage).
- Use time away from school to work pastorally with children and to work towards broader learning objectives.

The choice of residential centre should be made very carefully. In our experience, some of the best providers do not market themselves and are run by not-for-profit organizations. A high quality of staff is of paramount importance – not just as experts in climbing and canoeing, but best when this specialist knowledge is combined with an understanding of the broader goals and objectives of the primary school curriculum.

Summary

The current framework for teaching primary physical education in England (the National Curriculum) provides scope for a rich breadth of experience that is difficult to match within other curriculum areas. Through a carefully planned and well-taught physical education curriculum children can learn, in and through specific actions, skills and concepts that are not replicable in other classroom-based subjects. The task of delivering such a rich and varied curriculum is, however, a challenging one, and teachers must carefully focus planning efforts to maximize the opportunities that curriculum physical education lessons provide. Each activity area has its own distinct elements that cannot be ignored and children's entitlement to a broad curriculum content should be nurtured and protected by all those seeking to develop primary physical education.

Key Questions

- Why does current curriculum documentation suggest a breadth and balance of activity areas?
- What are the unique learning benefits for each of the six NCPE activity areas?
- Do schools currently maximize learning across all six areas of the NCPE?
- What are your own professional development needs in each of the the six activity areas and how can you identify opportunities to meet these needs?

Learning tasks

- Identify a stimulus for dance activities and use this starting point to suggest what, how, where and with whom a series of dance lessons will progress.
- Design a non-traditional game for primary aged children that will foster the development of specific, named skills as well as tactical awareness.
- Observe a gymnastic activities lesson and identify the key learning that is taking place. Suggest ways in which learning could be taken forward in the subsequent lesson.
- Consider the current requirements of the NCPE at Key Stages 1 and 2 with regard to OAA, swimming and athletics. Could each of these activity areas be introduced effectively in Key Stage 1 and what areas of skill transference to and from other activity areas can be identified?

- What will the future primary physical education curriculum look like? Will it be focused on six distinct activity areas?

Links to the Framework of Professional Standards for Teachers

The content and focus of this chapter have direct relevance to the following Qualified Teacher Status (QTS) standards (TDA, 2007) for those training to teach in primary schools: Q7, Q8, Q11, Q12, Q13, Q19, QQ25.

Useful websites

http://www.britishorienteering.org.uk/asp/makepage.asp?PID=SCHOOLS

The national governing body for orienteering and information relevant to school-based OAA.

http://www.standards.dfes.gov.uk

Links to schemes of work within each activity area.

http://www.britishswimming.org/

National Governing body for swimming.

http://www.sta.co.uk/

Swimming teachers association.

http://www.ndta.org.uk/

The National Dance Teachers Association (NDTA) is a membership organization led by a team of teachers and dance education professionals.

http://www.eoe-network.org/

The European Institute of Outdoor Adventure Education and Experiential Learning (EOE) develops theoretical foundations for the field of outdoor activities.

http://www.outdoor-learning.org/

The Institute for Outdoor Learning encourages outdoor learning by developing quality, safety and opportunity to experience outdoor activity provision and by supporting and enhancing the good practice of those who work in the outdoors.

http://www.sportengland.org/index/get_resources/resource_ul.htm

Sport England site with links to all relevant national governing bodies.

A small selection of NGB sites:

http://www.british-gymnastics.org/
http://www.england-netball.co.uk/game/events.cfm
http://www.thefa.com/GrassrootsNew/School/
http://www.ecb.co.uk/kids/
http://www.ukathletics.net

References and further reading

BAALPE (2004) *Safe Practice in Physical Education and School Sport* (6th edn). Leeds: Coachwise.

Bailey, R., Armour, K., Kirk, D., Jess, M., Pickup, I. and Sandford, R. (in press) The Educational Benefits Claimed for Physical Education and School Sport: An Academic Review. *Research Papers in Education*.

Balazik, D. (1995) *Outdoor and Adventurous Activities for Juniors*. London: A&C Black.

Benn, T. and Benn, B. (1992) *Primary Gymnastics – A Multi Activities Approach*. Cambridge: University Press.

Butler, P. (2000) *Becoming an ASA Assistant Teacher*. London: A&C Black.

Cooper, A. (1993) *The Development of Games and Athletic Skills*. Hemel Hempstead: Simon & Schuster.

Cooper, A. (1995) *Starting Games Skills*. Cheltenham: Stanley Thornes Ltd.

Couling D. and Dickinson, D. (1993) *Athletics in the National Curriculum – Key Stage 1 and Key Stage 2*. London: AAA.

Cregan A. and Noble J. (1999) *Swimming Games and Activities* (2nd edn). London: A&C Black.

Davies, A. and Sabin, V. (1995) *Body Work: Primary Children, Dance and Gymnastics*. Cheltenham: Stanley Thornes Ltd.

DfEE/QCA (1999) *The National Curriculum for England and Wales*. London: QCA.

Lowden, M. (1989) *Dancing to Learn*. Basingstoke: Falmer Press.

Elkington, H. (1997) *Swimming: A Handbook for the Teaching of Swimming*. Cambridge: Cambridge University Press.

Hall, J. (2002) *Dance for Infants* (2nd edn). London: A&C Black.

Hopkins, D. and Putnam, R. (1993) *Personal Growth Through Adventure*. London: David Fulton Publisher.

Martin, B. (1995) *Hunting the Griz*. Nottingham: Davies Sports.

Martin, B. (1997) *Finding the Griz*. Nottingham: Davies Sports.

Maude, P. (1997) *Gymnastics*. London: Hodder & Stoughton.

McFee, G. (1994) *The Concept of Dance Education*. London: Routledge.

McNeil, C., Martland, J. and Palmer, P. (1992) *Orienteering in the National Curriculum*. Doune, Perthshire: Harveys.

Noble, J. and Cregeen, A. (1999) *Swimming Games and Activities* (2nd edn). London: A&C Black.

O'Neill, J. (1996) *Athletic Activities for Juniors*. London: A&C Black.

PEAUK, BAALPE, NDTA (1995) *Teaching Physical Education, Key Stages 1 & 2*. Reading: PEAUK.

Price, L. (2003) *Primary School Gymnastics*. London: David Fulton Publisher.

QCA. (2000) *Schemes of Work for Physical Education*. London: QCA.

Read, B. (1995) *Teaching Children to Play Games – a Resource Pack for Primary Teachers*. Leeds: Coachwise.

Shreeves, R. (1985) *Children Dancing*. London: Ward Lock Educational.

Smith, B. and Kibble, S. (1993) *A Devon Approach to Physical Education: Outdoor and Adventurous Activities at Key Stages 1, 2 and 3*. Torquay: Devon Learning Resources.

Smith-Autard, J. M. (1994) *The Art of Dance Education*. London: A&C Black.

Smith-Autard, J. M. (1996) *Dance Composition*. London: A&C Black.

Training and Development Agency for Schools (TDA) (2007) *Draft Revised Professional Standards for Teachers in England*. London: TDA. Available from http://www.tda.gov.uk/upload/resources/pdf/d/draft_revised_standards_framework_jan_2007.pdf [accessed 5 March 2007].

YMCA (1999) *Teaching Swimming Fundamentals*. London: Human Kinetics.

Current Issues in Primary Physical Education

Chapter outline

Education, education, education . . .

Tony Blair

Introduction

This book is being written during a period of unprecedented central government investment in physical education and school sport in the UK. The Physical Education, School Sport and Club Links (PESSCL) strategy (DfES/DCMS, 2003), with its focus on quality and quantity of physical education and sport in schools, also sits alongside wider initiatives such as Every Child Matters (DfES, 2003a), Excellence and Enjoyment (DfES, 2003b) and the national agreement for raising standards and tackling workload (ATL *et al.*, 2003). Whilst teachers may feel that they have been victims of 'initiative overload' in recent years, it is clear that children, in part, lie at the heart of policy innovation. This represents an exciting opportunity for those who wish to develop the quality of primary education in general and physical education in particular.

The status of physical education within the UK political landscape has been strengthened by the formation of one professional association for the subject, the Association for Physical Education (AfPE). The 2006 inaugural conference of this Association included what could be seen as a 'call to arms' for primary physical education. Concerns have been raised by a succession of researchers and professional bodies over a sustained period of time. Most recently, the state and status of primary physical education has been identified as an area needing urgent attention by:

- A declaration issued at the Second World Summit on physical education, held in Magglingen, Switzerland, 2005;
- The UK physical education profession mission statement issued January 2005;
- The Independent Sports Review, published in 2005.

This chapter presents a range of themes that can be construed as 'current issues' in primary physical education. Each issue is set against the prevailing education policy driven backcloth, and concerns are raised that we hope will contribute to the emerging debate within the profession.

Key points

- Primary physical education has been seen as a problem by researchers and professional bodies for many years.
- Primary physical education cannot be separated from the social and political milieu in which it is sited.
- Primary physical education can capitalize on prevailing policy and all teachers can play a role in revitalizing and maintaining the subject's contribution in school.
- Whatever the political climate of the day, it is the individual teacher's personal conviction to the subject, demonstrable through a commitment and passion for physical education, that will influence the subject's potential to contribute widely.

Research in primary physical education

Primary physical education is generally an under-researched area both in the UK and worldwide. Much research within primary physical education has focused on the ITT process and comparatively little has been investigated within school-based pedagogy and practice. It is startling to note the lack of primary-focused papers delivered at major international and domestic research conferences, despite the repeated identification of primary physical education as a 'problem'.

The reasons for this are relatively straightforward, in that the vast majority of physical education 'specialists' in the UK are initially trained as secondary teachers. Structures of university programmes often result in primary physical education ITT being delivered in isolation from secondary departments, frequently by a 'one person band' without significant support from a team of colleagues. In such circumstances, research may not be a priority and the lone voice is faced with internal battles to stem reduction in teaching time and a low status for the subject. In such circumstances, the development of a body of researchers in the field is difficult.

Whilst many of the issues raised in recent primary Ofsted reports are similar to those for secondary subject delivery, there is a case for arguing that primary physical education *is different* to secondary physical education and should therefore be treated as a special case within initiatives, policies and strategies. Table 7.1 highlights some of the perceived differences between secondary and primary physical education. A fundamental question to ask in this regard is whether primary physical education exists solely to prepare children for secondary physical education, or whether primary physical education makes a different contribution to wider education objectives, thus helping to prepare children for life.

A further point for debate is whether secondary school physical education can learn from approaches in the primary school. In this regard, issues of 'specialism' in primary physical education could be viewed as something of a 'red-herring'. Through ITT and professional development, primary teachers clearly become highly skilled in their work with young children. Secondary teachers (particularly those who have undergone intensive ITT within one year and school-based routes) may indeed be specialists in one or more activity areas of the physical education curriculum, but may not have specialist knowledge of young children and how they learn. This is a somewhat simplistic view (and possibly even a stereotypical view) of teachers in the different age phases. Any notion of primary physical education specialism must, however, consider how such different areas of strength can be more closely aligned.

It is important for primary physical educators to consider the implications of these differences for their own practice, particularly at a time when national strategies have attempted to release secondary specialist physical education teachers to work in primary schools (see the PESSCL strategy section later in this chapter).

Table 7.1 Perceived differences between primary and secondary school physical education

Primary physical education	Secondary physical education
Generally taught in schools by class teachers (although there has been recent shift in this as a consequence of PESSCL and remodelling workforce agenda)	Taught in schools by trained specialists
Managed in schools by subject leaders who may not have any experience, further training or support	Managed in schools by physical education specialists
Taught in multi-purpose facilities	Taught in specialist, purpose-built facilities
Small budget allocations	Significant budget allocations
Whole child philosophy of education, with 'play' construed as an important component of learning	Perceived performance/sport led philosophy
Constructivist teaching and learning	Greater focus on skills-based teaching/coaching
National Curriculum as a broad and balanced curriculum	National curriculum progressively leads to specialism in activities
Non-examined	Opportunities for accreditation and examination

Issues for exploration

In 2002, the Physical Education Association of the United Kingdom (PEAUK) highlighted five key research areas to 'encourage research that will address current political and professional priorities, and build upon existing studies' (Harris and Penney, 2002). The five areas were:

- Assessment in physical education
- Physical education, PSHE and citizenship
- Inclusive physical education
- Continuity and progression in physical education
- Effective partnership between physical education and sport.

This list was originally compiled as a consequence of an interrogation of subject inspection reports. It was clearly focused on investigating issues that impact on pedagogical quality. The topics we have chosen to highlight below are not dissimilar and our list is by no means exhaustive. We believe the topics addressed represent concerns that are impacting on the quality of primary physical education in today's schools and that they have been brought into sharp focus by prevailing policy. Although the examples given are pertinent to the English perspective, similar issues exist within European and international contexts.

The issues we present as relevant to primary physical education are:

- the nature and impact of government policy on primary physical education;
- the state and status of primary physical education;
- definitions of 'quality' in primary physical education;

- the relationship between physical education and sport;
- ITT and continuing professional development for primary teachers;
- curriculum innovation and alternative visions for primary physical education;
- the health agenda;
- including all learners in primary physical education.

These issues are not presented below in any particular order; they are intertwined and any attempt to separate them for the benefit of this chapter would be impossible. Instead, we introduce each issue against the backcloth of initiative and policy and discuss the themes as 'matters arising'.

We encourage trainee and practising teachers to engage in their own 'action research' to help raise the quality of learning experience for all children. This model of research is thought to develop reflective practice, promote collaboration amongst colleagues and link research and practice through the investigation of real-life contexts (Cohen, Mannion and Morrison, 2000, p.79). The action research process is often represented as a spiral or cyclical process (Kemmis and Wilkinson, 1998), as shown in Figure 7.1 below.

Through action research, it is possible for pre-service and practising teachers to significantly add to the body of evidence within primary physical education and for findings to be useful where it matters most, that is in schools. Where this is linked to school development plans, the impact of action research can be very powerful.

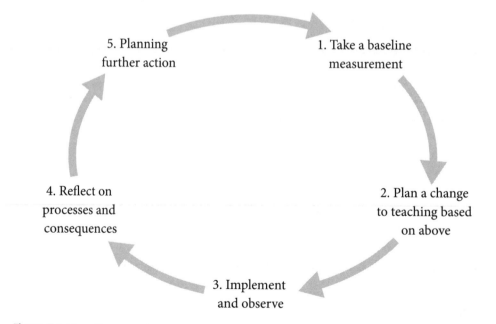

Figure 7.1 The action research process

Overarching government initiatives

On election to power in 1997, Tony Blair famously stated that education would be a priority for his new government. Since then, a plethora of initiatives has impacted on the working practices of all teachers in England, bringing some criticism of 'initiative overload'. In line with all other government departments, Public Service Agreement (PSA) targets have been established for education. In relation to physical education, two targets are of significant interest:

> Enhance the take-up of sporting opportunities by 5 to 16 year olds so that the percentage of school children in England who spend a minimum of two hours each week on high quality PE and school sport within and beyond the curriculum increases from 25% in 2002 to 75% by 2006 and to 85% by 2008.
>
> Halt the year-on-year rise in obesity among children under 11 by 2010 in the context of a broader strategy to tackle obesity in the population as a whole.
>
> (HM Treasury, 2004).

The setting of numeric targets is problematic in education where outcomes of schooling are as much to do with individual feelings, moods, behaviours and engagement as they are with quantities and definitions. Despite the best efforts of the government (DfES/QCA, 2005) and others (see, for example, Kirk, 2004) to define outcomes of quality physical education, many practitioners are still unclear as to what this actually looks like in relation to the NCPE (Ofsted, 2005).

Within primary schools, timetable and facility constraints, together with a perceived low level of subject knowledge amongst many teachers, has meant that pupils in Key Stage 1 are less likely to receive two hours of weekly provision than those in Key Stage 2 (ibid.). In addition, the physical education curriculum in primary schools has a tendency to be disrupted by preparation for national tests and local events (ibid.), seemingly exasperated by the hall being sidelined in the build-up to the Christmas play.

Evidence gathered within school audits by our own student teachers suggests that the status of physical education in primary schools is variable. This appears to be dependent on the enthusiasm and commitment shown by individual members of staff and school leadership teams.

Indicators of subject status in primary schools include:

- amount of curriculum time devoted to physical education;
- wider contribution to whole school improvement by physical education as evidenced in action plans;
- coverage of full breadth of National Curriculum content;
- experience and qualifications of subject leader;
- allocation of time and money to physical education in-service training and continuing professional development;

- budget allocations;
- facility usage and priority for non-physical education activities;
- celebration of pupil achievements in physical education within newsletters, on notice boards and in assemblies;
- learning support assistants involvement in physical education lessons;
- assessment, recording and reporting of pupil progress in the subject;
- use of out of school hours learning time for physical activity, sport and dance.

Whilst many schools have approached curriculum mapping with greater degrees of flexibility since the publication of *Excellence and Enjoyment* (DfES, 2003b), the negative impact of the National Literacy and Numeracy Strategies lingers. The Speednet (2000) survey claimed that half a million teaching hours was lost in primary physical education owing to the dominance of English and mathematics resulting from these strategies. It appears that in many schools and ITT curricula, the 'core' subjects still hold the balance of power in relation to time and status. As long as physical education is not inspected by Ofsted as a 'front line' subject in primary schools (or within ITT establishments) expectations about the quality and quantity of teaching and learning will be difficult to enforce.

The 'obesity' PSA target represents an intent by government to impact on what appears to be an alarming rise in proportions of children and young people who are categorized as 'overweight' and 'obese'. There is a seemingly endless stream of reports that draw attention to the 'problem' of children's escalating body weight and perceived links to health. Whether or not this area of concern lies within the scope and influence of physical education is open to debate and some urge the profession to 'rid itself of the reductive tendencies of the obesity discourse and rediscover there is more to life and education than making children thin' (Evans *et al.*, 2005).

Our own research (Pickup and Price, 2006) has highlighted trainee teachers' awareness of children's health issues and a manifestation of this within personal philosophies for teaching primary physical education. It is clear that some entrants to the primary profession believe that they have a role to play in fostering healthy and active lifestyles amongst children. It is important that all teachers are assisted in developing an appropriate, reflective, sensitive and compassionate approach to this issue.

In both examples of PSAs given above, the government has declared a clear message of intent around which measures of accountability have been built (Linn, 2003). What this means in terms of policy, practical implementation and pedagogy is less clear, although attempts have been made to give schools more explicit guidance. Turning rhetoric into action and progress is the challenge that faces those charged with delivering high quality physical education.

We now scrutinize in more detail three examples of specific government intervention and consider implications of each for to the delivery of primary physical education.

The Physical Education, School Sport and Club Links Strategy

Over £1 billion has been invested in English physical education through the PESSCL strategy between 2003 and 2006, a very serious commitment by government to the subject area. The strategy is designed to help meet the two hours per week PSA centred on 'high quality physical education and school sport' for children and young people aged 5–16. The long-term aim, by 2010, is to offer all children at least four hours of sport every week made up of:

- two hours of high quality PE and sport – delivered within curriculum time;
- an additional two to three hours of high quality sport experienced beyond the school day, delivered by a range of school, community and club providers.

Reflecting on the broad aims of this strategy, it is difficult to be critical of an initiative that has visions of improvement and high quality for all at its core. However, in an effort to ensure that primary physical educators are empowered to capitalize on the opportunities this brings, two ensuing concerns are highlighted below:

Table 7.2 Component parts of the PESSCL strategy (adapted from information contained on http://www.teachernet.gov.uk/teachingandlearning/subjects/pe/nationalstrategy/)

PESSCL strand	Overview
Sports colleges	Specialist status can be applied for by any maintained secondary school in England. The specialist colleges are a regional focal point for promoting excellence in physical education and sport.
School Sport Partnerships	Families of schools, usually clustered around a specialist sports college are intended to strengthen links, extend opportunity and raise quality. New positions have been created within this infrastructure to manage the partnership and to fulfil particular roles, such as School Sports Coordinators and Primary Link Teachers. In addition, competition managers have recently been added to this framework.
Teacher professional development	A comprehensive range of new, locally delivered 'modules' for primary and secondary teachers centred on high quality physical education.
Step Into Sport	A leadership and volunteering programme in sport for young people aged 14–19.
Club Links	Strengthening the links between schools and local clubs to increase active membership of children and young people. This strand also includes the setting up of multi-skills clubs for primary aged children, with a focus on fundamental movement skills.
Gifted and talented	Aiming to improve identification of and provision for gifted and talented children and young people in physical education.
Swimming	The only activity area to be named specifically within a dedicated strand, reflecting the true 'life skills' nature of swimming and water safety. Extra resources to support delivery of swimming have been created for teachers.
QCA physical education and sport investigation	An ongoing study which is collating evidence from schools around the country regarding the role of high quality physical education and school sport in raising whole school attainment.
Sporting Playgrounds	The latest addition to the national strategy following successful piloting. This strand aims to raise levels of physical activity, leadership and citizenship skills by revitalizing primary school playgrounds.

1. Definitions of high quality

Definitions of 'high quality' have been provided by DfES and QCA in an attempt to support teachers' work in this area. This guidance is presented as 'pupil outcomes', in other words the actions, words and behaviours that pupils will demonstrate as a consequence of high quality physical education and school sport. These outcomes are laudable, yet no differentiation is offered in relation to age, stage of development or experience of pupils. Does high quality primary physical education look the same as high quality secondary physical education? Is high quality physical education the same for all children, or do the learning needs of some children necessitate a different view of high quality?

To implement high quality physical education, primary teachers must begin to consider what it looks like within their own context, with the specific needs of their children borne in mind. This has a clear resonance with the principles of developmental physical education listed in Chapter 1 and advocated throughout this book. Furthermore, a teacher's view on what high quality physical education looks like in their lessons should surely include a reference to the *amount of learning* taking place.

2. Sport down or child up?

The physical education versus sport debate has been evident amongst professional groups for some time. For example, Kay (2003, 2005) suggested that 'physical education may, in the very near future, cease to exist' and that the 'very nature of sport is to exclude and eliminate the many until the elite are found'. Others, however, see the attempt to separate out the two activities as futile and that both activities should be embraced as educationally worthwhile. It would be nonsense to suggest that well structured sporting activities with high quality teaching and learning at their core are not of educational value. Whilst the activities of teaching and coaching can be theoretically separated, the distinction is less clear in practice. We would argue that the best physical educators are high quality teachers, coaches, mentors, leaders, observers and facilitators all rolled up into one.

Thinking about the distinction between physical education and sport is an important reflective activity. If sport in the primary school equates to 'games' and adult versions of these, then this would seem to be a narrow interpretation of the aims, goals and purpose of physical education. If, on the other hand, participation in adapted versions of sport to meet identified learning needs takes place within a broad, movement-based curriculum, then this would seem appropriate and worthwhile.

Sport Education (see for example, Siedentop, 1994; Penney *et al.*, 2002; Siedentop, Hastie and van der Mars, 2004) has gained popularity as a framework for curriculum planning and intervention and offers a view of physical education that can aid innovation. In addition, the principles of Sport Education have been applied to dance, health and outdoor education activities and the definition of sport in this sense is broad.

It is clear that 'sport' holds great appeal to government and policy makers. This is surely to be expected, as sport permeates society and, as some would argue, is a 'vote catcher'. Our focus in schools must surely shift away from debating the name we attach to what we do, to doing what we do more efficiently. Part of this process must be to articulate clearly the aims of primary physical education. This articulation will help children, their parents, community sports clubs, school management teams and wider government agencies to be more aware of the purpose of high quality physical education and the lifelong impact it can have. This is particularly pertinent in light of the aims of *Every Child Matters*, outlined later in this section.

There are several components of the PESSCL strategy that suggest the approach advocated is a 'top-down' model. These include:

- provision is for children and young people aged 5–16 (i.e. there is no early years or pre-school/ Foundation Stage strand);
- a proliferation of the term 'sport' in terminology (such as specialist sport colleges, school sport coordinators and so on);
- the assumption that a secondary trained physical education teacher can positively impact on primary practice;
- the appointment of competition managers to develop an infrastructure for locally arranged school matches and tournaments.

At the same time, a curriculum review being led by QCA is beginning within Key Stage 3. From a developmental physical education perspective it is disappointing that developments and change are not being led from the bottom up, in other words from the very youngest children within full-time care and education settings.

The Primary National Strategy

Excellence and Enjoyment – A Strategy for Primary Schools was launched by the DfES in 2003 and set out the vision for the future of primary education, to 'focus on raising standards while not being afraid to combine that with making learning fun' (DfES, 2003b, p. 3) The strategy aims to empower primary schools to take control of their curriculum, and to be more innovative. The document also encourages schools to network together and learn from others in sharing and developing good practice. Partnership with parents and making wider links in communities are also encouraged. This strategy has clear potential for teachers seeking to raise the profile and status of primary physical education. The principles of 'learning to move' and 'moving to learn' bring wide scope for cross-curricular linkage and effective primary physical educators will be able to draw on these curriculum links.

A 'topic-based approach' whereby key concepts are revisited through several subjects has reappeared in many primary schools. Teachers, too, appear to have embraced having greater control over their own teaching. For us, the dominance of 'literacy and numeracy hours' within morning timetables (whilst school halls, fields and playgrounds lay dormant) was a notion that sidelined already low status subjects to the fringes of the curriculum. It is now encouraging to see many teachers developing core subject knowledge through foundation subjects and even sometimes physical education taking a prominent and early place in daily timetables. The implications of this have brought wider benefits:

- morning physical education activity can help energize and motivate children to learn throughout the remainder of the school day;
- children can be allowed to wear physical education kit to school on the days where physical education takes place, thus reducing changing time and the infringement on learning time;
- timetabling of physical education has become more flexible – not everyone wants to use the facilities at the same time;
- children are allowed to explore conceptual links across subjects and their general ability to 'think and learn' is strengthened through the use of the body as a tool for this;
- the transition from Foundation Stage to Key Stage 1 can become smoother as the six areas of learning (in the Foundation Stage) can be carried forward into subjects within cross-curricular approaches.

Every Child Matters

Every Child Matters is arguably the most significant piece of present day government intervention in education and children's services in England. The original 'Green Paper' was issued by the DfES in 2003, largely in direct response to the horrific circumstances surrounding the death of Victoria Climbie. Victoria Climbie was tortured and killed by her great aunt and her aunt's partner in North London, 2000. The inquiry into her death highlighted a range of endemic issues within health, child protection and social care and led to a wholesale and holistic review of children's services.

The Green Paper raised enormous levels of debate amongst professionals working with children and young people and led to the publication of a Children's Act (DfES, 2004) which provided legislative leverage for developing more effective and accessible children's services. The cross-departmental document entitled *Every Child Matters: Change for Children* as published in November 2004 and mapped out five broad aims for the development of all children and young people, regardless of background, from birth to 19 years. The five aims are for all children to:

- be healthy
- stay safe
- enjoy and achieve
- make a positive contribution
- achieve economic well-being.

These aims encourage all those working with children to liaise closely together and to share information, ideas and resources to help children achieve. Local Children's Trusts will help this process and also consult with children and young people. This approach is, we would argue, developmental in nature and fits within the ecological approaches to human development outlined in Chapter 2. In relation to primary physical education, it is pertinent to consider the role that the subject can play in meeting such holistic goals. Whilst there is an obvious connection to 'being healthy' within a subject that includes physical activity and developing knowledge of fitness, further connections can be made where learning intentions are concerned with affective, social and cognitive development. In a subject where ample opportunities exist to develop leadership, communication and goal-setting amongst children, the role of physical education within the context of *Every Child Matters* seems critical. It is also important to note that Ofsted inspection frameworks will begin to reflect the five outcomes and view the role of the school within the wider community context. In schools where physical education has low status, a subject leader may wish to use the framework to demonstrate the subject's potential contribution and apply some pressure to management and colleagues to reconsider the role of physical education in school.

Workforce reform

The day-to-day working practices of teachers in England have changed as a consequence of a national agreement signed between teaching unions and government in January 2003. This agreement led to alterations in teachers' conditions of service as well as implications for school management within the *Every Child Matters* agenda. A fundamental change in the practice of the class teacher is that 10 per cent of timetabled teaching time is now allocated for planning, preparation and assessment activities (known as PPA time). This release from the classroom to engage with critical tasks to support teaching and learning has been widely welcomed and has gone some way to address concerns over work-life balance. However, the management of this time (in particular how and by whom the teaching is 'covered') appears to have ramifications for physical education.

It is clear that some headteachers have approached this issue with a view to releasing staff from teaching subjects where they lack confidence, subject knowledge and experience. In some cases, the 'cover' is provided by colleagues within the school, although an increasingly common practice is the use of external 'specialists' or commercial providers. There is significant professional concern regarding the deployment of adults other than teachers during curriculum physical education. Guidance issued by the Association for Physical Education (see web links at the end of this chapter) encourages schools to ensure that the employment of a coach satisfies three main criteria:

1 They only assist or support the work of qualified teachers.
2 They are directed and supervised by a qualified teacher.
3 They have satisfied the headteacher that they have the appropriate skills, knowledge, experience and expertise to carry out the required work.

In addition, we would encourage subject leaders and headteachers to consider the personal rationale or philosophy for primary physical education that the external 'specialist' may bring. This is likely to underpin their practice and an exposure to the principles of child-centred education may not have been experienced by sports professionals who do not have Qualified Teacher Status. Interview questions for appointment to these roles can explore these issues and, together with an exposure to continuing professional development opportunities, can ensure appropriateness of curriculum activity.

We would not immediately dismiss the notion of physical education being delivered by non-qualified teachers as, in certain situations, this may genuinely raise the quality of experience for children. However, this ought to be viewed as a short-term approach during a period of time when ITT and CPD for primary teachers is being reviewed and developed. The PPA issue has implications for the trainee primary teacher during school-based experiences and we encourage providers of primary ITT and student teachers themselves to ensure that:

- the delivery of physical education by external coaches does not reduce the trainee's time to observe, reflect and teach within the subject area;
- subject-specific mentoring in primary physical education must be carried out by an appropriately qualified teacher;
- the trainee is not the person who provides PPA cover and his/her teaching practice in physical education should be supervised by a qualified and experienced teacher at all times.

The long-term impact of workforce remodelling on primary physical education is unknown. It is an area that requires immediate research focus and consideration by practitioners, policy makers, advisers and headteachers alike.

Initial Teacher Training

The delivery of National Curriculum primary PE in England has long been seen as a problem. Whilst some concerns relate to an apparently low status of the subject in schools compared to the focus given to other subjects (Warburton, 2001), others relate to the 'preparedness' of teachers to deliver and raise issues regarding the perceived quality and quantity of ITT in this subject.

Over the past three decades, professional bodies have (so far unsuccessfully) sought to establish a minimum allocation of time within undergraduate and postgraduate training routes to teaching (PEA, 1987; CCPR/NAHT, 1992; CCPR, 2005). Research has consistently highlighted perceived weaknesses of ITT in relation to primary trainees' needs in physical education and our own work has started to conceptualize these needs more fully (Pickup, 2005). We suggest that there are three broad categories of trainee primary teacher in relation to physical education. There are those we would describe as 'avoiders', who have a negative perception of the subject on entering ITT; 'enthusiasts' occupy the opposite end of a continuum and arrive with a commitment to the subject largely born out of positive personal experiences; the others occupy a 'middle ground' and, through a combination of personal reflection, awareness of children's learning needs and commitment to the whole child can become enthusiasts. All trainees are influenced by a range of factors before, during and after the ITT experience but can be positively swayed. This process involves providing opportunities for reflective practice, positive, often perception-altering experiences during taught sessions and, critically, a positive experience of teaching physical education during school-based experiences. The sooner this happens after taught courses, the better.

Whilst it may not ever be possible to secure more time for all trainee teachers to study the subject in depth, we suggest that it is imperative that specific content and approaches towards the subject within primary ITT need to be considered fully by all pre- and in-service teachers and those charged with their professional development. On becoming a newly qualified teacher it is then crucial that a positive socialization into the profession is continued and supported. Local authority induction programmes, opportunities for attending CPD as part of the PESSCL strategy and opportunities to engage in professional debate with colleagues are an important part of this process.

The health of the nation

The UK PE profession's 2005 position statement (BAALPE *et al.*, 2005, page 8) claimed that the subject 'can make a significant contribution to the health and well-being of the nation's children and young people, helping to prevent overweight and obesity and to improve the quality of life'. Despite these claims, the health of children continues to be a concern and a plethora of statistics suggests a rapid rise in the numbers of children and adults who are overweight or obese and leading sedentary lifestyles. An estimated two million children under the age of five are thought to be overweight worldwide, with Western European countries rapidly catching up with the United States in this regard. In the UK it is thought that inactivity costs the National Health Service £8.2 billion per annum (DoH, 2004) and that we currently have the first generation of children whose life expectancy is shorter than their parents (CCPR, 2005).

Children appear to have a natural exuberance for movement and seemingly boundless energy. Despite this, it appears that some young children are experiencing uncharacteristically inactive lifestyles. Causes of this are numerous and include:

- parental concerns regarding safety in the local community;
- limited availability of spaces in built-up areas for activity;

- increased traffic on local roads;
- less children walking or cycling to school;
- an increasingly technological society resulting in greater choice in leisure time;
- perceived barriers to active participation.

Guidance has shifted somewhat as a better understanding of appropriate levels of activity for a child has emerged. Evidence suggests that regular moderate physical activity is beneficial to health and that children should be given opportunities to engage in a variety of activities (at different intensities and for varying durations) on a daily basis. Corbin, Pangrazi and Welk's (1994) 'Lifetime Physical Activity Model' is an example of this advice. In the UK, current guidance issued by the Chief Medical Officer suggests that children and young people should achieve a total of at least 60 minutes of at least moderate intensity physical activity each day. This should include, at least twice per week, activities to promote bone health, muscle strength and flexibility.

It is widely accepted that body weight cannot be separated from wider issues of health and society. It is a complex sociological, physiological and psychological issue and one that cannot be tackled by achieving greater levels of physical activity alone. In an attempt to tackle the problem of rising incidences of obesity amongst children in England, the government has recently announced a programme of weighing all 4 and 11 year olds in primary schools in 2006. These measurements will be used to calculate a Body Mass Index (BMI) for children, an index used widely for such purposes, despite some concerns over its suitability for application to childhood populations.

Physical educators in the primary school should be a little concerned with this programme and the implications the results may have for practice. *If* controlling children's weight falls within the scope, possibilities and philosophy of primary physical education (and some see this as a big if), then a physical *activity* model as opposed to a physical *education* model may be encouraged by policy makers in the near future. Lining children up in the playground at the start of every day for compulsory aerobics and physical jerks may hold some appeal for those wishing to burn off children's calories, but is a concept that would set physical education back almost a hundred years. The developmental physical educator will be concerned with a wider aim of motivating children to take part in physical activity throughout life as a consequence of the quality of learning experienced in physical education lessons. This will see lessons that include all pupils (those who are overweight, underweight, those who are dyspraxic or have a specific special educational need, for example) within learning intentions and which serve to promote the development of self-esteem and confidence as part of the educative process.

Including all learners

The issues of 'inclusion' and 'inclusive education' in schools has become increasingly relevant in the UK where there appears to have been a year on year rise in the number of children with identified special educational needs (SENs) being taught in mainstream schools (DfES, 2001, cited in Vickerman, 2003). There appears to be widespread regional variation in these figures however, suggesting that particular Local Authorities (LAs) are doing more than others to be 'inclusive' (CSIE, 2005).

The NCPE makes a strong case for inclusion, alongside the expectation that teachers will provide each child with opportunities to experience success and achieve their individual potential (DfEE/QCA, 1999, p. 28). The inclusion of pupils within mainstream education is defensible educationally, morally and ethically, although the ability of all teachers to be able to include the full spectrum of children's learning needs within their teaching is less certain. To aid the teacher, a range of practical materials has become freely available, including CD-ROMS, teaching packs, adapted equipment and lesson plans. In addition, the PESSCL CPD strategy for all teachers includes a module that relates to this exact issue. Such resources generally equip teachers with a range of strategies and sample activities to help engage all learners across an ability spectrum. Activities can be planned that are:

- *open activities* where all children participate in the same activity and differentiation is 'by outcome';
- *modified activities* that have specific, adapted features that have been changed to cater for individual needs;
- *parallel activities* that are similar to the main task but significantly different and may need to take place on an adjoining area or pitch;
- *separate activities* where children with a particular need take part in alternative provision;
- *disability sport activities* that are formally recognized versions of sports with specific rules.

This range of strategies for inclusion will go some way to help the teacher meet individual learning needs. The above choices represent different degrees of differentiation required and will help provide a solution to the teacher's problem of how to include all pupils. This does, however, also demonstrate a deeper issue with regard disability and physical education – the viewing of pupils as a 'problem' to which there needs to be a 'solution'. The issue is more broadly linked to views of ability and pupil achievement in physical education, largely based on physical performance rather than cognitive, social or affective goals. For some, a radical rethink of physical education is required if we are to really include all pupils in physical education (see for example, Fitzgerald, 2005). The principles of developmental physical education with a central concern for teachers to 'start from the child' would seem appropriate, whether pupils are those with SEN, are identified as gifted and talented, or are those who are meeting expectations of NCPE.

Gifted and talented pupils

In a recent publication issued by the National Academy for Gifted and Talented Youth (NAGTY), Deborah Eyre, Director of NAGTY, highlighted key features of provision for gifted and talented children in primary education:

- primary schools have recognized the needs of the majority of their most able pupils, but that they are catered for by provision of additional activities and events rather than in everyday classroom practice;
- children not only need to develop skills, knowledge and understanding, but also the ability to think, learn and solve problems;
- all children, regardless of ability, can benefit from classroom approaches such as the use of probing questions and exploration of connections between topics;
- whilst achievement is an outcome we would like for children, we should also be aiming for well-rounded, thoughtful learners, ready and confident to take on new challenges and new opportunities.

Adapted from NAGTY/DfES (2006)

The definition of what is meant by 'gifted and talented' has attracted some attention from theorists and practitioners in recent years. The government say that 'gifted' refers to the top 5 per cent of the school population in 'academic' subjects and 'talented' to the top 5 per cent in other subjects. This perhaps suggests that some notions of being highly able are more important than others, and that there is a difference in how this ability should be perceived. This is problematic in physical education where learning takes place across all developmental domains. Should we say that our most able choreographers in dance activities or strategists in games activities are 'gifted' whilst those children who are the most physically able are 'talented'?

Bailey and Morley (2006) have suggested that we should look at notions of gifted and talented children within five ability sets. These are cognitive, creative, social, personal and physical abilities. This would seem to tie closely with the four aspects of NCPE and provide all children with an opportunity to develop knowledge, skills and understanding in some or all of the abilities. Alternative visions of talent development seem to match more closely with developing sporting ability and performance. The model provided by Istvan Bayli (2002) outlines a Long Term Athlete Development (LTAD) approach, which outlines a staged approach to elite performance. Whilst this framework fits neatly with the importance of fundamental skill development as outlined earlier, Bailey and Morley's work is more relevant to the broader educational objectives of primary school physical education.

At a practical level, teachers have two main considerations. Firstly, how to identify talented pupils in physical education, and secondly, how to support their learning. At a simplistic level, a talented pupil will exceed expectations in the NCPE in one or more of the four aspects in one or more of the activity areas. In the primary age phases, the demonstrable ability, however, may be as much to do with having greater opportunities to practice or greater encouragement from parents, than simply being genuinely more able than others. The difficulty in predicting talent is evident in the primary school years and the practitioner should be wary of attaching labels to children too early. The answer of course lies in the quality of experience for all children and the developmental approach of creating optimum conditions within the environment, the task and the individual. From our experience in schools, teachers' perceptions of talent in primary physical education tend to be linked with pupils' extracurricular activities and selection for town or district squads rather than a genuine assessment against specific criteria.

Gender and primary physical education

There are two broad questions to be considered with regard to gender in primary physical education:

1 Is primary physical education equitable for boys and girls (i.e. do all children have the same opportunities and breadth of experiences)?
2 Should the primary physical education curriculum be the same for both boys and girls?

Gender issues in physical education have been studied widely. Girls are thought to be more sensitive to the holistic goals of physical education and less competitive than boys. Some studies suggest that girls also have a lower perception of their ability than boys. (See for example, Birtwhistle and Brodie, 1991; Tannehill et al., 1994). Shropshire, Carroll and Yim (1997) suggested that primary aged boys are more willing to participate in physical education than girls, and that boys are less negatively affected by environmental conditions such as cold weather. Girls, they argued, are also more positive in respect to views of the teachers, whereas boys feel more strongly about inequality in feedback and teacher interaction.

It is agreed that socialization into gender-stereotyped behaviours starts during early childhood (Pomerleau et al., 1990) and so we suggest that all teachers reflect on their own views of 'inclusion and diversity' in this regard. It is clear that in the physical education context the choices that the teacher makes in planning, giving feedback and interacting with pupils are aspects of teaching and learning that can reinforce gender construction. Physical activity per se plays an important role in gender construction, exemplified in 'traditional', single-sex secondary school physical education lessons where boys and girls take part in separate activities, often taught by same-sex members of staff (Wright, 1996). Physical activity in the playground during break times can also demonstrate gendered notions of appropriate activities.

There is debate amongst the wider profession, however, regarding the merits of both single-sex and mixed-sex groupings, and on both sides of the argument positive and negative consequences have been suggested (see Table 7.3).

Table 7.3 Perceived positive and negative impact of gender groupings in physical education (collated and adapted from a review of literature by Lines and Stidder, 2003)

	Perceived benefits	**Perceived weaknesses**
Single-sex PE	At Key Stage 3, can have a positive effect on pupil achievement	Reinforces stereotypical views of 'male and female' activities
	Easier to manage the class	Restricted opportunities for both boys and girls
	Contact sports can be played	Develops 'subcultures' amongst staff and a boys' and girls' department
	Higher pupil perception	Non-stereotypical activities remain marginalized
Mixed-sex PE	Breaks down gender barriers and overcomes stereotypes	Doesn't address cultural differences
	Pupils benefit from staff expertise regardless of gender	Reduces girls' participation, achievement and self-esteem
	A natural transition from Key Stage 2 to Key Stage 3	Concerns over physical contact
	Supports inclusive principles of National Curriculum	Underachievement by boys in games
	Opposes practices that promote aggression and bullying	Boys misbehave in order to 'impress'
	Emphasis on social and affective learning	Boys receive more reprimands than girls
	Enables modifications of traditional games to include non-contact rules	Majority of teacher intervention with boys (to overcome above)
		Girls less committed than boys in this context

The majority of primary physical education is taught in mixed groups, so a move to single-sex groupings on transition to Key Stage 3 can itself be a 'culture shock'. This may be particularly true for boys rather than girls owing to the presence of few males in primary education. The impact of teacher gender on strategy and style of teaching has recently been studied and findings suggest that pupils, contrary to popular belief, do not think that men teach any differently than women. Little has been done to investigate the impact of teacher gender within primary physical education, however; this would be an interesting focus for future research projects, particularly at a time when so few men are employed as primary class teachers across the UK.

A major consideration is the teacher's own interests and strengths, and the extent to which lesson planning and delivery are dictated by these. If activity content is largely governed by the teacher's personal confidence, then pupils' voices in the planning process will remain unheard (Williams and Bedward, 2001). This serves only to reinforce existing gendered constructions; female primary teachers are more likely to have experience and knowledge of netball than they are of football and rugby; the few male primary teachers are more likely to have experience of football than they are of dance and gymnastic activities. When this cycle remains unbroken, the teachers themselves, through teaching areas in which they have experience and confidence, will serve only to reinforce these stereotypes.

In essence, it is thought that the structure provided by the NCPE is based on a male notion of what constitutes 'success'. As a result, girls are judged on the same basis as boys, regardless of their cultural, social or physiological and anatomical needs. This is clearly juxtaposed against principles of developmental physical education where, in essence, every child is viewed as an individual learner with specific needs. It is also clear that it is not just girls who can be marginalized within a 'macho' approach to physical education and games. In considering the balance of the primary physical education curriculum, it is therefore important that we have a broad understanding of children's development and a return to these underpinning tenets for practice will assist the practitioner to remain focused on the needs of the child.

Summary

Whether or not primary teachers value the subject and perceive it to be an important aspect of the curriculum, it is clear that children themselves consistently rate physical education as one of the most enjoyable subjects in school. The development of a personal rationale, or philosophy, for the role of physical education in the primary curriculum is a key requirement for teachers and a concept we return to in Chapter 8. If new entrants to the profession are to be 'agents of change' and impact on the work of colleagues in this subject, then they must also be informed advocates and be prepared to argue the case for quality physical education provision. Current initiatives centred on education broadly and physical education specifically, provide a wealth of opportunities for the subject to be developed. For some, the creation of new infrastructures has been the priority, whilst for others, the raising of quality has been the most pertinent issue. It is clear, however, that at a time of unprecedented government investment in the subject and with 'London 2012' on the horizon, the health, fitness and the physical education of all children and young people will remain on the political agenda for some years to come.

Key Questions

1 What specific government policies have impacted on the quality of primary physical education?

2 How can physical education contribute to the desired outcomes of *Every Child Matters*?

3 Has the quality of physical education been enhanced through changes to working practices for primary teachers in today's schools?

4 What has been your own experience of primary physical education ITT and how has this been influenced by the issues explored in this chapter?

5 Can primary physical education make an impact on the perceived health problems afflicting the world's populations?

6 To what extent are all learners included in primary physical education?

Learning tasks

1 Talk with the subject leader for physical education in school. Consider the extent to which they are aware of the PESSCL strategy and how it has specifically helped to raise standards.

2 Identify a sample of children to talk to in school. Talk to them about issues of inclusion and ask them the extent to which they all feel 'included'. Consider the extent to which the curriculum is truly inclusive.

3 Write a paragraph to explain your own personal philosophy for primary physical education; consider within this your own views on sport and physical activity and the emphasis placed on these in curriculum time.

4 Consider the curriculum of the future. How would it look different to what we have today? Are any specific groups of children catered for differently than they are today?

5 Reflect on the extent to which your own physical education teaching is inclusive. Are any pupils in your class catered for to a lesser degree? Are all pupils, regardless of ability, provided with the opportunity to fulfil their potential?

Links to the Framework of Professional Standards for Teachers

The content and focus of this chapter have direct relevance to the following Qualified Teacher Status (QTS) standards (TDA, 2007) for those training to teach in primary schools: Q7, Q8, Q13, Q16, Q18, Q24.

Useful websites

A selection of sites with information about the PESSCL strategy:

http://www.culture.gov.uk/NR/rdonlyres/278A9606-081B-4BDC-A3E5-3048D10E253E/0/learningthru.pdf

http://www.teachernet.gov.uk/teachingandlearning/subjects/pe/nationalstrategy/

www.qca/pess

http://www.youthsporttrust.org/page/pesscl/index.html

http://www.sportengland.org/index/get_resources/school_sport/pesscl.htm

http://www.teachernet.gov.uk/_doc/8704/2005 Ofsted%20PESSCL%20Report.doc

Ofsted report on PESSCL

http://www.standards.dfes.gov.uk/primary/?version=2

Details of the current Primary National Strategy

Resources and research relating to provision for gifted and talented pupils:

www.talentladder.org

www.talentmatters.org

A variety if sites with information on *ECM*:

http://www.opsi.gov.uk/acts/acts2004/20040031.htm

http://www.everychildmatters.gov.uk/_files/F9E3F941DC8D4580539EE4C743E9371D.p

http://www.everychildmatters.gov.uk/aims/

Information regarding *Remodelling the Workforce*

http://www.afpe.org.uk/public/downloads/ppa_briefing_note.pdf
http://www.remodelling.org/remodelling/nationalagreement.aspx

UK National Summit Declaration 2005:

http://www.afpe.org.uk/public/downloads/national_summit.pdf

Magglingen International Summit:

http://www.who.int/moveforhealth/publications/PAH_2nd_world_summit_2005_en.pdf

References and further reading

ATL, DfES, GMB, NAHT, NASUWT, NEOST, PAT, SHA, TGWU, UNISON, WAG (2003) *Raising Standards and Tackling Workload: A National Agreement*. (Accesed via www.remodelling.org, 23 June 2006.)

BAALPE, CCPR, PEAUK and PE ITT Network (2005) Declaration from the National Summit on Physical Education, London, 24 January 2005. 4. Available from: http://www.afpe.org.uk/public/downloads/national_summit.pdf [accessed 12th June 2005].

Bailey, R. and Morley, D. (2006) 'Towards a Model of Talent Development in Physical Education', *Sport, Education and Society*, **11**(3), 211–30.

Bayli, I. (2002) 'Long Term Athlete Development: the systems and solutions', *Faster Higher Stronger*, 6–9.

Bennett, A. (2000) 'The National Action Plan for Women's and Girls' Sport and Physical Activity', *British Journal of Teaching Physical Education*, **31**(3), 6–8.

Birtwhistle, G. and Brodie, D. (1991) 'Children's Attitudes Towards Activity and Perceptions of Physical Education', *Health Education Research*, **6**, 465–78.

Campbell, K. (1999) *Women-friendly Sports Facilities, Factfile*. London: Sport England.

Capel, S. and Piotrowski, S. (eds) (2000) *Issues in Physical Education*. London: Routledge Falmer.

CCPR (2005) CCPR hosts Physical Education Summit (Press Release, 25 January 2005). Available from: http://www.ccpr.org.uk/anitem.cfm?AnnID=212 [accessed on 18 February 2005].

CCPR/NAHT (1992) *National Survey of Physical Education in Primary Schools – A Sporting Chance?* CCPR/NAHT: London.

Centre for Studies in Inclusive Education (CSIE) (2005) Segregation Trends – LEAs in England 2002–2004. Placement of pupils with statements in special schools and other segregated settings. Bristol: CSIE.

Cohen, L., Manion, L. and Morrison, K. (2000) *Research Methods in Education* (5th edn). London: Routledge Falmer.

Corbin, C., Pangrazi, R. and Welk, G. (1994) 'Toward an Understanding of Appropriate Physical Activity Levels for Youth', *Physical activity and fitness research digest*, **1**(8).

DfEE/QCA (1999) *Physical Education. The National Curriculum for England Key Stages 1–4*. London: QCA.

DfES (2003a) *Every Child Matters*. London: DfES.

DfES (2003b) *Excellence and Enjoyment: A Strategy for Primary Schools*. London: DfES.

DfES (2004) *Children's Act*. London: DfES.

DfES/DCMS (2003) *Learning Through PE and Sport: A Guide to the PE, School Sport and Club Links Strategy*. London: DfES.

DfES/QCA (2005) *Do You Have High Quality PE and Sport in Your School?* Annesley, DfES Publications.

Department of Health (2004) At Least Five a Week. Evidence of impact of Physical Activity and its relationship to health. A report from the Chief Medical Officer. London: DoH.

Evans, J., Rich, E., Allwood, R. and Davies, B. (2005) 'Fat Fabrications', *British Journal of Teaching Physical Education*, **36**(4), 18–20.

Fitzgerald, H. (2005) 'Still Feeling like a Spare Piece of Luggage? Embodied Experiences of (Dis)ability in Physical Education and School Sport', *Physical Education and Sport Pedagogy*, **10**(1), 41–59.

Harris, J. and Penney, D. (2002) 'Research in Physical Education: Priority Areas for Investigation', *British Journal of Teaching Physical Education*, **33**(2), 6–10.

Hayes, S. and Stidder, G. (eds) (2003) *Equity and Inclusion in Physical Education and Sport.* London: Routledge.

HM Treasury (2004) 2004 Spending review PSAs. London: HM Treasury. Available from: http://www.hm-treasury.gov.uk/spending_review/spend_sr04/psa/spend_sr04_psaindex.cfm [accessed 12 August 2006].

Kay, W. (2003) 'Physical Education, R.I.P.?', *British Journal of Teaching Physical Education*, **34**(4), 6–10.

Kay, W. (2005) ' "A rose is a rose by any other name", but physical education and sport are not the same', *The Bulletin of Physical Education*, **41**(1), 15–22.

Kemmis, S. and Wilkinson, M. (1998) 'Participatory Action Research and the Study of Practice', in B. Atweh, S. Kemmis and P. Weeks (eds) *Action Research in Practice: Partnerships for Social Justice in Education.* London and New York: Routledge.

Kirk, D. (2004) 'Framing Quality Physical Education: The Elite Sport Model or Sport Education?,' *Physical Education and Sport Pedagogy*, **9**(2), 185–95.

Kirk, D. and Tinning R. (eds) (1990) *Physical Education, Curriculum and Culture: Critical Issues in Contemporary Crisis.* London: Falmer Press.

Laker, A. (2000) *Beyond the Boundaries of Physical Education.* London: RoutledgeFalmer.

Lines, G. and Stidder, G. (2003) 'Reflections on the Mixed and Single Sex Debate', in S. Hayes and G. Stidder (eds) (2003) *Equity and Inclusion in Physical Education and Sport.* London: Routledge. 65–87.

Linn, R. L. (2003) 'Accountability: Responsibility and Reasonable Expectations', *Educational Researcher*, **32**(7), 3–13.

McNamee, M. J. and Parry, S. J. (1998) *Ethics and Sport.* London: Routledge.

NAGTY/DfES (2006) *Effective Provision for Gifted and Talented Children in Primary Education.* Warwick: NAGTY.

Ofsted (2005) *Every Child Matters: Framework for the Inspection of Schools.* London: HMI.

Penney, D. and Evans, J. (1999) *Politics, Policy and Practice in Physical Education.* London: E & FN Spon.

Penney, D., Kinchin, G., Quill, M. and Clarke, G. (2002) 'A New Way Forward', *Physical Education and Sport Today*, **9**, 20–3.

Physical Education Association (PEA) (1987) *Report of a Commission of Enquiry, Physical Education in Schools.* London): PEA.

Pickup, I. (2005) 'Physical self-perceptions of trainee primary teachers: working out and working in the physical domain'. Paper presented at the British Educational Research Association Annual Conference, University of Glamorgan, 14–17 September 2005.

Pickup, I. and Price, L. (2006) 'The Primary Physical Educator: Reflections on Becoming a Physical Education Specialist', *Physical Education Matters*, **1**(2), 41–7.

Pomerleau, A., Bolduc, D., Malcuit, G.and Cossette, L. (1990) 'Pink or Blue: Environmental Gender Stereotypes in the First Two Years of Life', *Sex Roles*, **22**(5–6), 359–67.

Renold, E. (2000) ' "Coming out": Gender, (Hetero)sexuality and the Primary School', *Gender and Education*, **12**(3) 309–26.

Shropshire, J., Carroll, B. and Yim, S. (1997). 'Primary School Children's Attitudes to Physical Education: Gender Differences', *European Journal of Physical Education*, **2**, 23–38.

Siedentop, D. (ed.) (1994) *Sport Education: Quality Physical Education Through Positive Sport Experiences*. Leeds: Human Kinetics.

Siedentop, D., Hastie, P. A. and van der Mars, H. (2004) *Complete Guide to Sport Education*. Champaign, IL: Human Kinetics.

Skelton, C. (1996) 'Learning to be "Tough": The Fostering of Maleness in One Primary School', *Gender and Education*, **8**(2) 185–98.

Speednet (2000) 'Primary School Physical Education – Speednet Survey Makes Depressing Reading', *British Journal of Physical Education*, **30**(30), 19–20.

Tannehill, D., Romar, J., O'Suillivan, M., England, K. and Rosenberg, D. (1994) 'Attitudes Towards Physical Education: Their Impact on How Physical Education Teachers Make Sense of Their Work', *Journal of Teaching in Physical Education*, **13**, 406–20.

Thorne, B. (1993) *Gender Play: Girls and boys in school*. Buckingham: Open University Press.

Training and Development Agency for Schools (TDA) (2007) *Draft Revised Professional Standards for Teachers in England*. London: TDA. Available from http://www.tda.gov.uk/upload/resources/pdf/d/draft_revised_standards_framework_jan_2007.pdf [accessed 5 March 2007].

Vickerman, P. (2003) 'Success for All: Developing an Inclusive Approach to Physical Education and School Sport for Children with Special Educational Needs', *The Bulletin of Physical Education*, **39**(3), 154–61.

Warburton, P. (2001) 'Initial Teacher Training: The Preparation of Primary School Teachers in Physical Education', *British Journal of Teaching Physical Education*, **4**, 6–8.

Williams, A. (1989) *Issues in PE for the Primary Years*. Basingstoke: Falmer Press.

Williams, A. (1993) 'Who Cares about the Girls? Equality, Physical Education and the Primary School Child', in J. Evans (ed.) *Equality, Education and physical education*. London: Falmer Press, pp. 125–38.

Williams, A. (ed.) (2000) *Primary School Physical Education: Research into Practice*. London: Routledge.

Williams, A. and Beward, J. (2001) 'Gender, Culture and the Generation Gap: Student and Teacher Perceptions of Aspects of National Curriculum Physical Education', *Sport, Education and Society*, **6**(1), 53–66.

Wright, J. (1996) 'The Construction of Complementarity in Physical Education', *Gender and Education*, **8**(1), 61–79.

Subject Leadership in Primary Physical Education

Leadership is the art of getting someone else to do something you want done because he wants to do it.

Dwight D. Eisenhower

Introduction

This chapter examines the role and function of the primary physical education subject leader. Effective leadership undoubtedly plays an important part in ensuring the quality of primary physical education; the very best subject leaders are also champions for the subject and are able to motivate others to teach high quality physical education. Carrying out the role is demanding and should not be underestimated or taken lightly. Being a physical education subject leader cannot be done without a degree of personal investment of time, effort and vigour, but will undoubtedly reap dividends with regard to job satisfaction, professional aspirations and pupil achievement. The personal attributes, knowledge, skills and understanding required to become an effective subject leader are discussed in this chapter, alongside examples of specific tasks that can be incorporated into day-to-day work in this role. At a time of increased focus on the subject and its role in the wider child-centred focus of government policy, the need for well informed and dynamic primary physical education leaders is clear.

Key points

- Effective subject leaders will act as champions for physical education in the primary school and need to be prepared to articulate its importance.
- Subject leaders may be appointed at relatively early stages of their teaching careers and the development of interpersonal skills is an important aspect of achieving success.
- Leadership can take many forms and the style and strategies used for leadership depend on expected functions of the role and the specific school environment.
- Subject leaders should engage in professional dialogue with a wider community of practice through local collaboration and by maximizing opportunities for continuing professional development.

The importance of leadership

It is widely accepted that professional, high quality leadership is a prerequisite for school effectiveness (MacGilchrist, Myers and Reed, 2004). There is no reason to believe it is any different for *subject* effectiveness and the role of the primary physical education subject leader is crucial in ensuring that every child receives high quality physical education. The context created in England by *Every Child Matters* and the PESSCL strategy has brought physical education to the fore, and subject leaders will need to engage in professional dialogue and debate that will influence policy and practice.

It is possible that any primary teacher may be asked to fulfil the role of physical education subject leader at some stage of their careers. It is an unfortunate fact of life that in some schools the physical education leadership role is allocated to the newest or youngest member of staff, or the teacher who once confessed to having played netball at school! This may sound a comical situation for teachers to find themselves in, yet it appears to be worryingly common. There are very few genuine primary physical education specialists entering the profession (as evidenced by the low number of ITT courses available with a significant allocation of time in this regard), something that has been partly addressed through the professional development of teachers within the PESSCL strategy. It is clear, however, that the role is not always warmly embraced, is often misunderstood and is sometimes undervalued – all indicators of a low status for physical education in school.

It is our hope that all subject leaders will tackle the demanding role with a relish that will help raise standards and status for physical education in their school. Where this is not the case, we must find alternative ways for teachers to benefit from strong leadership through working in partnership with others, as part of a wider school sports partnership network, through liaison with local providers of ITT and an engagement with professional subject associations such as the Association for Physical Education (afPE).

What is leadership?

Leadership can mean different things to different people and a variety of organizations have tried to define and nurture this concept in a multitude of settings. Most notably, the world of business has a plethora of gurus willing to write and talk on this topic, often drawing on the worlds of professional sport, politics and armed conflict for inspiration! The value of such analogies for primary school subject leaders is open to question, although the need to be strategic, political and doggedly persistent will have some day-to-day relevance for the role.

Choosing a leadership style

Flamholtz and Randle (2000, page 259) discuss the 'Leadership Effectiveness Framework' which views leadership as a 'process whereby an individual influences the behavior of people in a way that increases the probability that they will achieve organizational goals'. The achievement of teaching and learning goals can be aligned to what Flamholtz called 'operational leadership', a process of influencing members of an organization (in this case a primary school teaching and support staff) to achieve goals (such as the outcomes of high quality physical education defined by DfES/QCA) on a regular basis. In this framework, the leader selects a style that best suits the demands of the task in hand *and* the people in the team. The six possible styles are categorized in Table 8.1, based on the degree of freedom that the leader intends to give to others in the decision-making process.

The categorization shown in Table 8.1 is a continuum, and we will all be able to think of leaders who we know from within each category. It is highly unlikely however, that a primary physical education subject leader will be completely autocratic, or at least it is improbable that such an approach would be continued for long. At the same time, a 'laissez-fair' approach is unlikely to help in the achievement of common goals and so the adoption of a leadership style that values and utilizes the opinions of others would seem most relevant.

Table 8.1 Leadership styles

Leadership style	Definition	Physical education leadership example
Autocratic	Declares what is to be done without explanation	Imposition of a new curriculum map and associated lesson plans
Benevolent Autocratic	Declares what is to be done with an explanation	Implementation of a new scheme of work, introduced at a whole staff meeting
Consultative	Gets opinions before deciding on the plan presented	Review of staff professional development needs through a questionnaire and subsequent organization of courses
Participative	Formulates alternatives with group, then decides	Canvasses opinion regarding curriculum change and then decides on the best course of action
Consensus	All in group have equal voice in making decisions	Staff meeting facilitated by subject leader, but outcomes generated by teachers are carried forward into new physical education policy
Laissez-faire	Leaves it up to group to decide what to do	Physical education teaching and learning left to the individual teachers without intervention from subject leader

The second classification of leadership styles that we have space to consider here as relevant to primary schools is that suggested by Goleman, Boyatzis and McKee (2002), known as 'emotional leadership'. This concept views leadership based on the desired emotional impact incurred on those being led. The six styles listed below are not mutually exclusive, and leaders can adopt one or more styles to tackle particular circumstances.

The visionary leader – This style aims to move people towards a shared vision, telling them where to go but not how to get there – perhaps most closely aligned to the autocratic leader. Information is, however, shared openly to give knowledge and power to others. We would expect this style to have most impact in primary physical education where an experienced and well respected leader is working with more inexperienced colleagues. This may not be the most effective approach for a newly appointed subject leader to take.

The coaching leader – This approach requires the leader to nurture colleagues though one-to-one conversations, offering advice and helping teachers to identify strengths and weaknesses. This is a highly reflective process and is not a short-term approach to leadership. However, individuals can be positively motivated in this way and real changes to practice can result. The coaching leader in primary physical education needs to be highly confident in her/his own subject knowledge and have keenly developed interpersonal skills.

The affiliative leader – This approach tends to value emotional needs of colleagues more highly than professional or strategic needs. It is unlikely to lead to confrontation and if significant change to curriculum delivery is required, is unlikely to produce the desired results. However, when done well, affiliative leadership can result in a very cohesive teaching team.

The democratic leader – This approach values input and participation of others in a decision-making process. This approach would engage all teachers in decision making and facilitate discussion regarding the issues within primary physical education. This approach can be used effectively to gain support, particularly when colleagues are initially sceptical of proposed changes.

The pace-setting leader – This approach seeks to challenge colleagues, to set goals and to raise expectations. Such a leader must lead by example and will challenge poor performers in an attempt to demand improvements. In such circumstances, the subject leader may see him/herself as the 'star attraction', which may not be the best approach unless the 'team' is competent and highly motivated.

The commanding leader – The commanding leader is thought of as an authority figure and generally maintains a distance from the workforce. He or she generally expects full compliance and takes a powerful stance, but can seem cold and distant. The approach may well suit a headteacher at a time of crisis but does not appear to hold much sway for the physical education subject leader who will often need to persuade colleagues to reflect on their practice.

As with the Flamholtz continuum of leadership styles, the types of leadership centred on valuing and cooperating with others and working together to achieve common goals hold most appeal in respect of primary physical education. Fletcher and Bell (1999) found that subject leaders were reluctant to be autocratic, particularly reticent of any perceived need to instruct, direct or criticize colleagues, creating a potential dichotomy between role expectations (as dictated by senior management or even central government through Ofsted, the DfES or the TDA).

A collaborative approach to subject leadership would also appear most appropriate because:

- where colleagues are valued and involved, a shared sense of purpose can be fostered;
- relatively inexperienced subject leaders can recruit support from the wider school team;
- any low self-perception of subject leader's own 'expert' knowledge can be overcome through shared dialogue;
- limited time afforded to carry out the role can be maximized by shared working;
- subject leadership should enable others to achieve, but an autocratic approach could lead to disaffection amongst colleagues.

The approach to leadership in primary physical education will undoubtedly be shaped by a range of personal and contextual factors. A 'developmental' view of leadership would conclude that style and strategy of leadership will be unique to the individual. The personal attributes of the leader (including their own stage of professional development), the nuances of the school context, and expected outcomes of the role, will all interact to create particular requirements for leadership. Whatever these may be, there are several core tasks for the subject leader to which we now turn our attention. The first task to be faced by the newly appointed subject leader is to gain a full understanding of role expectations.

Appointment to the role

Regardless of the contextual background of an appointment to a leadership role, the effective primary physical education subject leader *must* possess five personal and professional assets to successfully carry out the role:

1 Enthusiasm and strength of conviction regarding the value of physical education.
2 Good subject knowledge together with sound teaching and learning experience.
3 An ability to reflect on and through his/her own practice and the 'bigger picture'.
4 A clearly articulated and appropriate personal rationale for the subject.
5 Strong interpersonal and professional skills to encourage others to embrace the subject. This will require both empathy and strength of character.

In the most favourable circumstances, a knowledgeable and enthusiastic subject leader can play a crucial role in the wider life of the school and help bring physical education to the fore. In this situation, the subject leader will usually be supported by both senior management and colleagues and will have access to meaningful professional development opportunities. He or she will also be afforded opportunities to work with colleagues to improve practice throughout the school as part of a whole school approach to professional development and physical education will be included in school improvement plans.

The subject leader may at times need to stake a claim for increased curriculum time, request improvements to equipment and resources, seek an increase to the budget, and so on. This should be done from an informed position and will be most effective when the case is founded on a strong personal rationale. In addition to having some subject-specific knowledge, a wider understanding of leadership is required, as highlighted by the TTA (1998, cited in BAALPE, 2003, p. 6):

> Subject leaders must have knowledge and understanding which is in part subject specific and in part generic to the leadership role. The knowledge and understanding required will change over time, and it is important that the subject leaders recognize their responsibility to remain up to date with developments in their subject area, and in other aspects of education relating to their role.

It is crucial for any subject leader to know what is expected of them. A careful review of a job description will give clues to the requirements of the post and different schools will have different desired outcomes.

The ten dimensions of subject leadership

In 1998, the TTA published 'standards for subject leaders' which were mapped around 'Ten Dimensions of Subject Leadership'. Whilst these standards have not yet been updated (and it is likely that they will, particularly to bring them in line with new TDA QTS standards, 2007), they still provide a further frame of reference within which physical education subject leaders can work. The list will be particularly useful for tracking subject leaders' own professional development and in planning to undertake a new leadership role.

1 Knowledge and Understanding
2 Planning and Setting Expectations
3 Teaching and Managing Pupil learning
4 Assessment and Evaluation
5 Pupil Achievement
6 Relationship with Parents and the Wider Community
7 Managing own Performance and Development
8 Managing and Developing Staff and Other Adults
9 Managing Resources

These principles are a combination of personal attributes and tasks that are required as part of fulfilling the role. Some of the principles suggest that the subject leader will be heavily engaged in tasks across the whole school, centrally planning lessons and units of work, assessing pupil progress and managing resources. Where subject leaders are seen as *the* expert in physical education it is perhaps difficult to avoid such tasks – although this would seem to fly in the face of developmental physical education which would argue that children's specific learning needs should be planned for in detail by the class teacher. The adoption of pre-written schemes of work is generally not encouraged and this stance may be one of the first challenges for the subject leader to face.

Communication

It is crucial that newly appointed post holders have clear lines of communication to all staff within the school. Because of the scope of the work involved, effective and regular communication must be possible with the headteacher and senior managers, teaching colleagues, learning support assistants, adults other than teachers (for example, sports coaches), local school sport partnership managers and link teachers, parents, the school site manager, domestic staff (such as lunchtime supervisors) and community sports clubs and groups.

Whilst a personal network of contacts will grow over time through attendance at festivals, meetings and through day-to-day work, the proactive subject leader can also make a habit of making regular contacts with key personnel. Practically, the school site manager is a key player in helping to ensure facilities and spaces are adequately prepared for physical education and should be nurtured in this role. Members of staff who facilitate school lunches are extremely important and play a very big role in helping to ensure the hall is free and ready for indoor physical education in the afternoon. The subject leader should not underestimate the importance of establishing a positive relationship with these colleagues; a well timed 'thank you' card or Christmas gift can work wonders!

Communication with teaching colleagues and senior staff should be seen as a necessary functional requirement of the role, but also a political step to help raise profile and achieve 'buy-in'. Regular communication at staff meetings and through notices in the staff room are invaluable in helping to build a physical education profile and presence. Similarly, communication with parents should not only happen once a year in preparation for a sports day or residential trip; the use of newsletters or school website to share regular pupil achievements and celebrate the quality of physical education in the school is encouraged.

Specific activities for the subject leader

Whilst the specific duties of each subject leader will vary from school to school and person to person, it is likely that immediate tasks to be conducted will include the following eight key activities. These are suggested here as starting points for the newly appointed subject leader and will help to identify baseline information relating to the quality of physical education provision in the school.

Auditing provision and action planning

When starting a new subject leadership role, a 'subjective feel' for the quality of provision can be gained through interaction with colleagues, talking to pupils and by observing practice. A qualitative judgement regarding the state and status of the subject can be made from such observations, but may not be particularly useful for planning to bring about change. The following methods could be used to provide baseline data (which in some cases can be quantified) from which an action plan can be written:

- lesson observations of colleagues;
- team-teaching with colleagues;
- interviews with a variety of children;
- talking with parents;

- reviewing assessment records;
- looking at colleagues' physical education planning;
- talking with colleagues;
- reviewing Ofsted inspection evidence;
- quantifying time spent within each activity area;
- reviewing practice against current health and safety guidance.

Some observations and documentary evidence (such as the existing school physical education policy) will provide 'leads' for the subject leader to follow. Where this is the case, a specific focus on aspects of physical education such as quality of assessment, feedback, teacher subject knowledge, health and safety and so on, will prove fruitful. Subject leaders are advised not to spend too long looking at the broader picture – specific, measurable and realistic targets should be established as soon as possible. However, a broad and accurate view of the state and status of physical education in school will enable the new subject leader to articulate the need for change and to begin the planning process.

Such a review of whole school practice will also allow the subject leader to consider the quality of current provision against the school's objectives and the vision he or she may have for physical education. National Curriculum objectives, principles of developmental physical education, high quality outcomes of physical education or the five outcomes of 'Every Child Matters' could provide points of reference for such activities. A suggested list of criteria for auditing is given below and has been adapted from the principles of high quality physical education (DfES, 2003) discussed in Chapter 1. Figure 8.1 also provides specific questions for auditing purposes against each criteria.

Analysing strengths and weaknesses

Whatever framework is being used as a template for auditing the physical education curriculum, a subject leader should aim to engage a wide range of colleagues, pupils, parents and support staff in the review process. A tried and tested formula for such an exercise is SWOT analysis, made popular at the Stanford Research Institute in the 1960s and widely used in business settings. An example of a simple SWOT analysis for primary physical education is provided below:

Strengths	Excellent facilities (two indoor halls plus playground and fields) and links with local community sports clubs
Weaknesses	Low staff confidence and expertise – particularly in gymnastic activities
Opportunities	National Physical Education CPD programme accessible via local authority and HEI provider
Threats	Other subjects competing for the same INSET time.

Figure 8.1 A possible framework for physical education auditing: staffing and resources

Feature of high quality physical education and focus for audit	Indicator	Specific questions	Possible audit method
Staff CPD	Frequency, quality and content of physical education specific CPD	1 What CPD has been delivered and by whom in last 12 months? 2 How has information been shared and applied? 3 What further needs have been identified and how many future opportunities for physical education INSET can be planned?	• Staff questionnaires • Informal meetings and discussions • Feedback sheets • Review of quality of teaching and learning
Facilities	Availability of school facilities, regular maintenance and safe use throughout the day and week	1 What facilities do we have available for physical education? 2 What other uses are we competing with for the space? 3 How can we best plan the use of these spaces? 4 Who is responsible for maintenance and upkeep? 5 Are any additional facilities (e.g. in local community or at a secondary school) available for use?	• Physical inspection of resources • Photographic evidence • Liaison with local authority/advisory teacher regarding health and safety concerns • Discussion with local secondary school or Partnership Development Manager • Discussion with colleagues, including maintenance staff/site manager
Quality learning resources	Suitability of equipment and learning resources for all children in school	1 Is there a range of equipment (sizes, weights, colours, etc.)? 2 Is the equipment stored appropriately? 3 Is the equipment used? 4 What resources to support pupils' learning are available (e.g. task cards, posters, videos etc.)?	• Discussion with colleagues • Inspection of cupboards • Inventory of all resources • Lesson observations • Review of recent budget spends • Identification of spending needs
AOTTs: recruitment and training	Appropriate use of support staff in curriculum physical education and out of school hours learning	1 Are learning support staff used effectively to support learning in physical education? 2 Are AOTTs used to lead curriculum activities 3 If so, what recruitment and training strategies are in place? 4 Do AOTTs help to provide links to local sports clubs?	• Lesson observations • Discussions with learning support staff • Review of selection criteria for AOTTs • Review of supporting documentation for AOTTs • Check provision with nationally issued good practice guidelines (e.g. via afPE) • Questionnaire for AOTTS and LSAs re training needs

Combining the pinciples of SWOT analysis with reference points for high quality physical education would be an effective starting point for auditing provision against specific criteria – teaching and learning, physical resources, structures and pupil outcomes. For the developmental physical educator, a specific focus on teaching and learning will be a good start for this process. The principles listed in Chapter 1 provide a further list of criteria for review. Interestingly, current Ofsted inspection criteria for quality of teaching and learning include the following descriptive characteristics for inspection grades (adapted from Ofsted, 2005a).

Ofsted inspection grade	Extracts from Ofsted description
Outstanding	• Exceptional enjoyment and progress of the learners
Good	• Teaching is well informed, confident, engaging and precise
	• The work is well matched to the full range of learners' needs, so that most are suitably challenged
	• Teaching assistants and resources are well deployed
	• Assessment of learners' work is regular and consistent and makes a good contribution to their progress
Satisfactory	• The lesson is inadequate in no major respect, and may be good in some respects, as shown by the satisfactory enjoyment and progress of the learners
Inadequate	• Unsatisfactory progress, whether this is due to unsatisfactory teaching or the impact of bad behaviour
	• Learners' overall behaviour or attitudes are unsatisfactory, and the tone of the lesson is inimical to the development of learners' personal qualities
	The teaching is unsatisfactory because:
	• work is badly matched to the pupils' starting points
	• ineffective classroom management of behaviour
	• methods which are poorly geared to the learning objectives or which fail to gain the interest and commitment of the learners
	• inadequate use of resources, including assistants and the time available
	• poor assessment

The implications of the above criteria for the developmental physical educator are clear: only through well planned, meaningful, appropriate, relevant and enjoyable physical education within which tasks match the specific learning needs of the pupils, can we deliver the highest possible quality of physical education. This may provide an excellent 'lever' for discussions with colleagues and senior managers for those subject leaders who are seeking to raise quality of provision and argue the case for a developmental approach.

Action planning

The review process described above should be carried out within a specific time frame, beyond which an action plan and monitoring strategy should be implemented. The action plan should normally identify specific, measurable and realistic aims and objectives to be achieved by a set time (and by whom) and ideally should be mapped into a whole school improvement plan. An action plan should focus on one identified weakness of existing provision and be linked to clear strategies for improvement and methods of monitoring. The action plan is best written in collaboration with colleagues and it is crucial that all colleagues feel part of this process; without the help of colleagues, it is unlikely that success will be achieved.

Example action plan (derived from above SWOT analysis)

Date of plan: **Date implementation starts:**

Aim: To raise staff confidence and subject knowledge in gymnastic activities and improve pupil achievement in this activity area.

Objectives:

Objective	By when?	By whom?	Monitoring strategy
1. Agree a rationale for the teaching of gymnastic activities throughout the school.	By October half term	Subject leader, in consultation with sample of staff.	Written documentation to be included in school improvement plan and reviewed by senior management.
2. Plan and facilitate two whole school INSET sessions with a focus on learning in and learning through gymnastic activities.	First session before December, with follow up before Easter	Subject leader, in consultation with headteacher. Using identified needs (through Swot) to plan specific content.	Quality of staff evaluations post-session and use of ideas in curriculum lessons.
3. Arrange one planning workshop to review and write medium-term plans for all classes.	Start of autumn term	Subject leader and volunteer colleagues from each Key Stage.	Clarity of learning intentions and specificity to individual learning needs.

---

4. Produce a new health and safety policy specifically written for gymnastic activities.	Start of autumn term	Subject leader and volunteer colleagues from each Key Stage. Seek support from local authority or HEI where possible.	Increased pupil time spent on large apparatus because teachers are more confident.
5. Develop assessment for learning in gymnastic activities.	Start of term/ongoing	All class teachers.	Pupil self-assessment and digital photographs used to celebrate and monitor achievement.
6. Improve teaching resources for gymnastic activities by purchasing relevant DVD-based resources and by creating a bank of teacher-produced materials.	December	Subject leader and all teachers.	Completion of home-made resource bank and use by colleagues in lessons; installation of the resource 'Observing Children Moving' (PEAUL Tacklesport, 2003) in each classroom and trial use by subject leader.

Monitoring colleagues' teaching and pupils' progress

Through the writing of an action plan, a subject leader will have started to consider how progress will be monitored. The monitoring is twofold and takes into account the role of those delivering physical education (i.e. teachers, specialists, AOTTs and LSAs) as well as the resulting quality of pupils' achievement. It is important that colleagues do not feel threatened by the monitoring strategy – particularly those for whom physical education is, for whatever reason, not a priority – and that the process is supportive and empowering rather than onerous. It may not, for example, be advisable to demand to see physical education lesson plans and assessment records if teachers have not previously completed paperwork for physical education with enthusiasm!

As when working with pupils, the subject leader should not be afraid to lavish praise on colleagues who are willing to improve their physical education and should seek out opportunities to share achievements and good practice. Newly created resources such as posters and task cards can be displayed in the staff room for example, or specific successful teaching and learning methods discussed at staff meetings. If monitoring strategies are used overtly to help raise standards and to celebrate pupil outcomes, colleagues are most likely to embrace them. If, on the other hand, monitoring is carried out without immediate feedback, at a distance, and without impact on quality of teaching and learning and without sensitivity, colleagues are more prone to become disenchanted with planned changes. Possible strategies for sensitive/non-threatening monitoring include:

- informal chats in the staff room;
- email contact via school intranet post-lesson;
- planned workshops or discussion groups to share ideas;
- short questionnaires for teachers and support staff;
- questionnaires for pupils;
- photographic evidence from lessons (taken by teacher, learning support assistant or pupils);
- talk with pupils;
- self-review checklists for teachers to complete post-lesson;
- checklists for TA or trainee teacher to complete during lesson;
- pupil diaries;
- team-teaching with colleagues;
- teaching another colleague's class;
- monitoring of pupil outcomes, e.g. take up of extracurricular activities.

The monitoring and assessment of *pupils'* progress and achievement is at the heart of developmental physical education, as discussed in Chapter 5. The subject leader must be prepared to articulate the necessity for assessment as an integral component of the school's physical education policy and provide colleagues with ideas for assessment strategies. Without ongoing, formative assessment, it is not possible to plan to accurately meet the needs of all children, and a focus on assessment in any primary school physical education is likely to have an impact on standards. The subject leader should look for opportunities to link physical education with wider school assessment policies and staff professional development. Where, for example, 'assessment for learning' is being encouraged, examples from the physical education context can be included in materials and resources for colleagues.

The ten principles of assessment for learning (Assessment Reform Group, 2002) have clear potential for application to physical education:

1 Assessment for learning should be part of effective planning of teaching and learning.
2 Assessment for learning should focus on *how* pupils learn.
3 Assessment for learning should be recognized as central to classroom practice.
4 Assessment for learning should be regarded as a key professional skill for teachers.
5 Assessment for learning should be sensitive and constructive because any assessment has an emotional impact.
6 Assessment for learning should take account of the importance of learner motivation.
7 Assessment for learning should promote commitment to learning goals and a shared understanding of the criteria by which pupils are assessed.
8 Learners should receive constructive guidance about how to improve.

9 Assessment for learning develops learners' capacity for self-assessment so that they can become reflective and self-managing.
10 Assessment for learning should recognize the full range of achievement of learners.

Because these principles are little more than good practice in teaching and learning and almost impossible to refute, colleagues are generally able to accept their relevance. In physical education, the provision of examples and strategies through which they can be embedded in physical education teaching and learning are most useful. Subject leaders should consider how each of these principles would look in physical education lessons and be able to share these examples with colleagues.

Despite the clear need for assessment to be an integral component of high quality primary physical education 'the quality of day-to-day assessment is weak. Although teachers know their pupils well, too many are reliant on memory alone when assessing progress and writing reports for parents' (Ofsted, 2005b). When taught well, physical education is fast-moving. A class of energetic and engaged movers is almost impossible to assess fully all of the time and it would be unwise for a teacher to attempt to do so. Videoing of lessons and spending time after the event is a strategy that can be employed, although it is unlikely that the enormous amount of time that this takes will see this becoming a regular feature of day-to-day practice. Pupils' achievement in physical education in the primary school is visible, physical and can be missed in the blink of an eye. It is therefore vital that the observation and assessment of pupils' work carried out by the class teacher, support staff and the pupils is focused, explicitly linked to planned learning intentions and relevant within the context of a whole school physical education assessment policy.

Assessment in physical education can take many forms and is not limited to the teacher observing and ticking a pre-prepared matrix of behaviours or skill outcomes. Alternative methods include talking and listening to pupils, observing children's actions and behaviours, looking at video or still images during or after the lesson, and analysing and reflecting on pupils' written commentaries. The precise methods of assessment used during any one lesson should be chosen at the planning stage and a clear trail between learning intentions and assessment criteria should be apparent within lesson plans. Through the application of these methods, a pupil 'portfolio' or mosaic of evidence can be built up over time which in turn can be used as a basis for recording and reporting pupil achievement. It is *not* the role of the subject leader to assess the progress and achievement of all pupils in the school, but it is his or her responsibility to provide guidance and support in this process.

In our experience, it is likely that Ofsted's current view of assessment in primary physical education is a consequence of two factors:

1 Many teachers lack confidence and subject knowledge in physical education and are 'unsure of *what* to look for.'
2 Some teachers are unaware of *how* to assess in the physical education context.

The subject leader is therefore encouraged to:

1 Support colleagues' assessment of and for learning through writing effective policy documents.
2 Provide reference points to learning intentions and level descriptors.
3 Provide examples of assessment methods that colleagues can adopt.
4 Coordinate and monitor records of assessment.
5 Advise colleagues with regards reporting to parents and pupils.
6 Use assessment records to inform action plans and further physical education curriculum developments.

The school physical education assessment policy should start from the premise that *high quality physical education cannot be delivered without assessing pupils' work.* Regular assessment in physical education should become part of everyday practice and the subject leader must encourage colleagues to adopt a range of assessment strategies. The assessment policy must also make clear what exactly is being assessed, provide examples of likely evidence, suggest ways in which assessment information is to be used, explain how physical education reporting is to be carried out and suggest other ways in which the information is used (such as at Key Stage transitions to inform detailed planning).

Mapping the curriculum

In Chapter 1 we posed a question that is very relevant to the subject leader who may be charged with mapping and redesigning the physical education curriculum:

> What do we want children to be able to do and know at the end of 500 hours of learning?

The answer to this question will help the formulation of a long-term plan for physical education in school. The term 'scheme of work' is often used to describe such long-term planning across a particular period of time such as a Key Stage (Raymond, 1998) and is the basis from which medium-term and individual lesson planning can be completed. Where possible, the curriculum map should also take into account pupils' learning in the Foundation Stage and provide reference points for future learning in Key Stage 3. Pupils' learning in primary physical education does not happen in a vacuum divorced from life outside the primary school and a simple acknowledgement of this will help colleagues see their work in physical education as part of the 'bigger picture'.

'Standard' formats for schemes of work are generally constructed around Year groupings, terms and half terms, specific activity areas and number of lessons per week, as shown by the headings in the example for Year 1 in Figure 8.2 (provided as an example rather than a curriculum map to copy). A key consideration for the subject leader is how this map of the curriculum is constructed and, crucially, the terminology used. Curriculum maps in primary physical education tend to be blocked into discrete six-week units, dedicated to specific activity areas as suggested by the NCPE. The benefit of this is that the proportion of time allocated to each of the six activity areas can be calculated and monitored (and an appropriate balance and breadth maintained) and an overview of facility and resource requirements can be generated. This activity-led view can be problematic however, where long-term plans are dominated by sports-based terminology. Whilst this may be legitimate in respect to National Curriculum requirements, the dual message it gives to colleagues is that the activities are the most important aspect of the curriculum and knowledge of aspects of these activities (such as rules and coaching terminology) are prerequisites for effective teaching and learning.

Figure 8.2 Example of curriculum map for Year 1

Year group (example)	Term	Lesson 1 (activity focus)	Lesson 2 (activity focus)
1	Autumn – first half	Games activities	Dance activities
	Autumn – second half	Gymnastic activities	Dance activities
	Spring – first half	Gymnastic activities	Games activities
	Spring – second half	Gymnastic activities	Dance activities
	Summer – first half	Games activities	Gymnastic activities
	Summer – second half	Dance activities	Games activities

In the Figure 8.2 example, the 12 medium-term units during Year 1 (each of half term duration) have been divided equally between the required statutory activities for Key Stage 1. This does not weight the curriculum in favour of any one activity, but does not take into account availability of facilities (will the school hall be available for physical education in the last two weeks of the autumn term?) and weather conditions.

Subject leaders should ensure that terminology used is relevant to the language used in the National Curriculum of the day, and is also in keeping with the underpinning rationale for physical education expressed in the school's policy documents. The words rugby, football, netball and hockey do not actually appear in the NCPE, so should not be written in long-term planning documents. The phrase 'activities' should always be used alongside games, gymnastics and dance, for example, to reiterate that we are not coaching, necessarily, adult versions of sports.

The subject leader should also consider the duration of units of work and the frequency of lessons within specific activity areas. Some schools have found that 'blocking' activities (where both lessons per week within a half term are dedicated to one activity area) is an effective way of raising pupil achievement. In such cases, a medium-term unit of work extends beyond six lessons to 12 or 14, providing sustained opportunities to refine and develop knowledge, skills and understanding. This should be an option for consideration by subject leaders who must also ensure that the long-term balance and breadth of activities is maintained within statutory requirements.

Those subject leaders who are fully committed to taking a developmental approach will also want to consider alternative visions for long-term planning and curriculum mapping. If we refer back to the aims and goals of developmental physical education originally suggested in Chapter 1 (and provided again below), we should consider how the teaching and learning time available can be best used to fulfil these objectives.

AIMS of Developmental Physical Education
Overarching intent
Learning to move / Moving to learn
Becoming 'physically literate'

GOALS of Developmental Physical Education
Long-term purposes
Movement skill acquisition
Fitness maintenance and enhancement
Cognitive learning
Affective growth
Social interaction

Adapted from Gallahue (1996)

The continual revisiting of physical, social, cognitive and affective leaning intentions is made possible through the 'four aspects of the NCPE' and these will be a central feature of all long-, medium- and short-term plans. Movement skill acquisition, with a specific focus on developing mature patterns within fundamental and increasingly specialized skill themes should be the unique focus of the curriculum map, as it is this which is thought to unlock the door to a lifetime of physical activity and full range of activities. It is possible, therefore to map a curriculum based round the development of skill themes and movement concepts and the gradual application of these into more recognizable versions of sports and physical activities.

Graham, Holt-Hale and Parker (2004) provided a taste of how this could look in the North American context by mapping the teaching and learning focus on specific movement concepts and skill themes (see Chapter 4 of this book) throughout primary year groups. An adaptation of this for UK primary schools has been provided in Figure 8.3. This curriculum map is presented here as an example of what is possible and we are not suggesting that it is a definitive guide to when specific skills and concepts should be introduced. Developmental physical educators will adapt this to meet the needs of their pupils and the school context. It should also be noted that the ticks below represent a *major focus* on a skill or concept during teaching and learning, and that these can be learned at other times, but perhaps not as *the* major focus.

Figure 8.3 Movement concept and skill theme map from Reception Year 1 to Year 6 (adapted from Graham, Holt-Hale and Parker, 2004)

	Reception/ Year 1	Year 2	Year 3	Year 4	Year 5	Year 6
Movement concept focus						
Space	✓	✓	✓			
Levels	✓	✓	✓			
Directions	✓	✓	✓			
Pathways	✓	✓	✓			
Time	✓	✓	✓	✓	✓	
Weight			✓	✓	✓	✓
Flow			✓	✓	✓	✓
Knowledge of body parts	✓	✓				
Body shapes	✓	✓	✓			
Relationships with objects	✓	✓	✓	✓		
Relationships with other people			✓	✓	✓	✓
Skill theme focus						
Walking	✓	✓				
Running	✓	✓				
Hopping	✓	✓	✓			
Skipping	✓	✓	✓			
Galloping	✓	✓	✓			
Leaping	✓	✓	✓	✓		
Sliding	✓	✓	✓	✓		
Chasing, dodging		✓	✓	✓	✓	✓
Jumping and landing	✓	✓	✓	✓	✓	✓
Balancing	✓	✓	✓	✓	✓	
Transferring weight			✓	✓	✓	✓
Rolling	✓	✓	✓	✓	✓	✓
Kicking			✓	✓	✓	✓
Punting					✓	✓
Throwing			✓	✓	✓	✓
Catching			✓	✓	✓	✓
Volleying				✓	✓	✓
Hand dribbling			✓	✓	✓	✓
Foot dribbling			✓	✓	✓	✓
Striking with rackets			✓	✓	✓	✓
Striking with longer implements				✓	✓	✓

Once this approach to mapping, with a skill theme approach – as opposed to activity focus – has been carried out (ideally in collaboration with colleagues as part of whole school professional development), it is then possible to divide teaching and learning time across major lesson foci. When this is done, we can see that two hours per week curriculum time is arguably not enough to devote significant time to skill development. This serves to underline the importance of protecting and extending curriculum time (and not allowing colleagues to cancel existing lessons) and of providing enrichment activities as part of an out of school hours learning programme.

The 'alternative' approach to curriculum mapping introduced here will, for some schools, be a major shift in approach. It represents what may be possible now and more possibly in the future if teachers are afforded greater opportunities to develop their own subject-knowledge and subject specific pedagogy during ITT and CPD. A skill theme approach to curriculum mapping may also be more viable if and when statutory orders and National Curriculum content change – all very possible within the current climate of educational development and initiative.

Whatever the approach to curriculum mapping taken by a subject leader, it is imperative that the scheme of work helps to maximize learning time, ensures balance and breadth of activity, promotes progression and continuity, and is clearly linked to the school physical education policy and stated aims. The long-term plans should also be cognizant of learning in other curricular areas and seek to draw out conceptual connections in pupils learning. For example, it would be a missed opportunity if an autumn topic on 'fireworks' did not include creative dance work in response to the range of stimuli that this provides.

Writing a physical education policy

School policies are generally linked to improvement planning and are required to reflect the overall philosophies and aims of the school. A school policy is a formal publication of how the school ethos affects each curriculum area (Easton, Golightly and Oyston, 1999), and a curriculum policy should act as a simple statement of purpose and provide a framework for action (Pollard, 2005). It is imperative, therefore, that the school physical education policy is not just the vision of the subject leader, but that it is truly a position statement that represents the views of all staff. It is likely then, that the subject leader will need to spend time reviewing the existing policy, talking with pupils and colleagues about areas for improvement and clarification to disseminate new content in a collaborative manner. A school physical education policy should always be seen as a working document that evolves over time in response to changing conditions, whole school foci and requirements.

A primary physical education policy can be structured using the following headings for guidance:

• General organization and management of the subject
• Policy statement

- – Physical education curriculum link to whole school ethos
- – Underpinning rationale
- – Teaching and learning styles, differentiation, progression and continuity
- – Pupils (dress, non-participation, valuables)
- – Assessment, recording and reporting procedures
- – OSHL, community links and external agency involvement, including policy for use of PPA time and the employment of adults other than teachers (AOTTs)
- – Cross-curricular dimensions
- – Inclusive practice and special educational needs
- – Use of ICT to support learning
- – Resources, equipment and facilities
- – Health and safety, risk assessment and accident procedures (including activity-specific content)
- – Policy on physical contact (e.g. support in gymnastic activities)
- – Weather conditions policy
- – Quality assurance procedure
- – Communication with parents
- Curriculum documentation
  - – Aims and objectives
  - – Overall syllabus, schemes and programmes of study
  - – Units of work
  - – Sample lesson plans
- OSHL provision
  - – Rationale, aims and objectives
  - – Club provision and timetable
  - – Details of teams, tournaments and festivals
  - – Details of whole school events
- Subject evaluation and development
  - – Monitoring procedures
  - – Annual report
  - – Staff continuing professional development
  - – Liaison with wider community of practice (subject advisers, HEI providers, national subject association).

(Adapted from Raymond, 1998)

Although this list may appear to be daunting in the first instance, it is likely that most of the required information is already to hand. Recent developments in the subject must be taken into account, however, and it is advisable for subject leaders to stay abreast of developments through communication with the local authority, HEI provider and subject association. In particular, the school health and safety policy for physical education carries with it the most important and potentially calamitous implications when not written or implemented with full awareness of current nationally recognized principles of good practice.

Severs, Whitlam and Woodhouse (2003) maintain that *good practice is safe practice* and, although teachers cannot be expected to be 'perfect', they must teach within frameworks that could be deemed as 'regular and approved practice'. Individual teachers have a *legal* duty of care for the health and safety of their pupils and, as qualified teachers, are expected to know how pupils act and react in curriculum activities. It is vital that the subject leader reiterates this to colleagues and support teachers and that school policy documents reflect best practice guidelines. In addition to a legal duty of care, all teachers have a *professional* duty of care as outlined within contractual agreements and a *moral* duty to ensure that pupils remain safe, unthreatened and engaged in enjoyable, purposeful and relevant activity. Teachers must ensure that they fully explain, reiterate and check pupils' expectations throughout lessons and should be encouraged to see this as an integral component of effective physical education teaching and learning.

The requirements for 'regular and approved practice' provided by Severs, Whitlam and Woodhouse (2003, p. 5) match up well to principles of developmental physical education outlined throughout this text. In particular, it should come as no surprise to those committed to taking a developmental approach to physical education, that:

> Lesson content should be geared to the range of ability and experience levels of the pupils in the class and reflect the requirements laid down in the school's physical education policy document and schemes of work devised for each year.

It is imperative that the subject leader fully understands the scope of his or her responsibility with regards to risk assessment and maintenance of equipment, facilities and resources and that this is agreed (in writing) with the headteacher. In the face of the increasingly litigious nature of the world and a society apparently gripped by a risk anxiety (Scott, Jackson and Backett-Milburn, 2001) it would be unwise to adopt a 'laissez-faire' approach to leadership in this regard; the subject leader must ensure that clear, concise and easily digested information is presented to colleagues and that this supports high quality teaching and learning in the subject.

A school physical education health and safety policy, contained within an overarching physical education policy document, should provide clear guidance for all teachers, trainees and others working in the school and should include:

- A statement stressing the importance of health and safety and stressing the legal duty of care.
- An informed statement that explains the educational value of challenge and the need to 'manage' risk.
- Specific activity guidelines which include procedures and routines for specific pieces of equipment or certain environments.
- Guidelines that outline procedures for care and maintenance of facilities and equipment, to include all spaces used for physical education. It is advisable to remind all colleagues of their own duty to report damaged or faulty equipment as part of normal operating procedures.

- An explanation of the school policy regarding the use of voluntary or employed helpers who are not qualified teachers.
- Guidance regarding planning formats and the use of assessment to determine pupils' learning needs in particular activities.
- The school's commitment to ongoing staff development.
- Details of the school insurance policy.

The management of risk is best done by considering the relationship between the people involved in the activity, the context within which the activity takes place and the organizational factors of the activity itself. There is a fine line between removing all risk to create a very safe but sterile and uninspiring environment and retaining some features of *acceptable risk* to allow children to learn through challenge. Many writers on this subject concur that risk taking is a necessary experience for children to become problem solvers and effective thinkers (see for example, Costa, 1991; Tishman, Jay and Perkins, 1993).

In addition to reviewing policies and procedures, it is likely that the subject leader will be responsible for carrying out (or arranging for external contractors to carry out) regular equipment and facility checks, completion of risk assessments and arranging staff development. It is vital that the subject leader keeps documented evidence of all procedures implemented and carried out – something that could also be termed 'negligence avoidance'. Formats for physical education risk assessment are available within the recommended reading at the end of this chapter, together with further signposts to information on this theme. Figure 8.4 below is a template that could be followed and adjusted to suit individual school requirements.

Subject leaders should be familiar with current guidelines for safe practice published by national and international physical education subject associations. For some time, the responsibility for this in the UK fell to the British Association of Advisers and Lecturers in Physical Education (BAALPE) and is now carried out by the newly formed Association for Physical Education (afPE). Every school should own at least one copy of the most up-to-date guidelines provided by BAALPE/AfPE and ensure that all teachers have access to the guidance. At the time of going to press, the sixth edition of *Safe Practice in Physical Education and School Sport* (BAALPE, 2004) is most current, and subject leaders must see this and future editions as an important support for their own work in school.

Supporting colleagues

We have already discussed the importance of taking a broadly collaborative approach to subject leadership in physical education. Features of the role such as policy writing and curriculum mapping and reviewing will bring the subject leader into close contact with the day-to-day practice of colleagues, and should be conducted sensitively and with some degree of empathy. In addition to these tasks, the proactive subject leader will actively seek out opportunities to strengthen relationships with colleagues and to influence the quality of physical education provision.

School:					
Teacher's name:					
Aspect	**Risk rating** **Low, Medium, High**	**What further** **action required?**	**Who** **responsible?**	**By when?**	**Completed?**
School staff *AOTTs* *Pupils* *Others* Facilities Procedures Equipment Transport Other *Preparation* *Class organization* *Teaching style* *Accident* *procedure* *Progression and* * challenge* *Other*					

Signed:.. (Headteacher)

Signed:.. (Subject leader)

Date risk assessment conducted:........../........../..............

Reviewed:........../........../.............. (Date) Signed:...

Reviewed:........../........../.............. (Date) Signed:...

Reviewed:........../........../.............. (Date) Signed:...

Reviewed:........../........../.............. (Date) Signed:...

Figure 8.4 Example physical education risk assessment template (adapted from BAALPE, 2004)

For the newly appointed and (in many cases) inexperienced subject leader, establishing a presence in staff meetings can be daunting and something that needs to be strategically planned. A new subject leader should ask the headteacher for time within a regular meeting or specific INSET session to be dedicated to physical education with a view to sharing thoughts, beginning the review process and providing some input. It is advisable that a degree of thought is given to how such meetings are best facilitated so that a confrontational or didactic approach can be avoided. If colleagues are not confident in physical education they are unlikely to change their practice simply because somebody new says they should! Our experience suggests that colleagues are most likely to respond to a subject leader's input when:

- they are included in developments from the start;
- they receive regular communication and updates;

- all opinions are valued and respected;
- teachers' subject knowledge, skills and understanding is improved;
- changes to practice result in very quick results in:
  - Pupil achievement
  - Pupil behaviour
  - Pupil and teacher enjoyment within the lessons concerned.

It is important that the subject leader considers the role that he or she will adopt during meetings (facilitator, chair, secretary, listener, presenter, organizer and so on) and that this fits in with existing procedures and practice. Above all else, colleagues need to feel as though they are effectively supported and valued and have access to mentoring within physical education that will help improve practice. The subject leader must be ready to disseminate up-to-date information gleaned from attendance at local, regional or national events and translate this into practical implications relevant to the immediate school setting.

Budget management

Although a primary school physical education budget is unlikely to be too alluring, a subject leader should ensure that resource management procedures include short- and long-term planning for replacing, repairing and upgrading equipment and resources. All physical education materials have a shelf-life, particularly when they are well used; worn, damaged and broken items can also carry a safety risk. A subject leader must have a full understanding of the amount of annual budget allocated and how this compares to that for other curriculum subjects. Where necessary, a case for increased funding can be based on:

- maintaining standards in line with health and safety requirements;
- the number of children accessing equipment (i.e. all children in the school);
- specific, identified learning needs of pupils;
- the need to spend money on staff development where subject knowledge and confidence is low;
- the need to buy or prepare resources to support colleagues' teaching;
- relative spend compared to other curriculum subjects in the past.

In the likely event that the budget will be limited, subject leaders must ensure that money is spent wisely and that purchases are relevant and directly linked to enhancing the quality of teaching and learning in curriculum physical education. The cost of a football strip for the school team, for example, can pay for a range of physical education equipment for use throughout the school and an informed decision regarding the relevance of any spend should be taken with an appropriate underpinning rationale. It is also imperative that all allocated monies are spent each year, and that accurate records of purchases (included all delivery notes and copies of invoices) are filed effectively within school records. Central to budget management will be the need for annual or termly stock-taking, identification of spending need (including identification of likely suppliers and costs) and prioritizing spending requirements. It is unlikely that a full 'wish list' can be purchased each year, so a phased approach to buying is often required.

Subject leaders must also remember that other avenues are open for attracting funding. We have recently seen schools effectively use supermarket vouchers donated by parents to upgrade stocks of physical education equipment. The school's Parent–Teachers Association, or equivalent, will also want to support one-off purchases and parents and governors will be valuable allies when fund-raising events are required. Links with local community organizations, sports governing bodies and clubs will create further opportunities for funding bids and local sports development officers will be able to provide further guidance in this regard.

We firmly believe, however, that high quality, developmentally appropriate physical education can be delivered without expensive facilities and equipment. We have recently seen primary physical education in a number of less developed countries where improvised materials and spaces are used to good effect. New, colourful and visually stimulating resources can, however, provide learners with additional learning support and motivation and help to present the subject in schools in the best possible way. All subject leaders are therefore encouraged to seek out budgetary increases and to manage spending wisely so that the state and status of primary physical education can be protected and improved.

Running large events

In addition to being an accomplished accountant and stock-taker (see above), it is likely that the physical education subject leader will be charged with organizing large-scale events such as school 'sports days'. Whilst we do not see this as the most important aspect of the role, we find that many subject leaders are expected to invest an enormous mount of time, energy and goodwill in ensuing that such events run smoothly. As a consequence, this task often becomes a bigger priority than the more fundamental aspects of subject leadership described above.

The subject leader must first of all consider his or her own view of such events and identify content that would be most developmentally appropriate for the ages of children concerned. The developmental physical educator will question the relevance of one-off events where few links to curriculum learning are made and which ask children to perform and compete within activities with little or no opportunity for practice. For many schools, the annual sports day is the 'public face' of school physical education and, as such, must fit with the policy and rationale for curriculum physical education.

Consequently, the subject leader should, as an early priority, identify his or her expected role within whole school events and formulate an action plan to:

1 Confirm that the content of large events is developmentally appropriate, suitable and relevant within overall school physical education policy.
2 Identify specific roles in the planning and preparation for the event.

3 Recruit sufficient colleagues to contribute to this process and enable the subject leader to delegate responsibility for many specific actions.

4 Allow the event to become a celebration of pupil learning in physical education as an acceptable 'public face' for the subject.

The wider role

Through carrying out the roles highlighted above, the subject leader must also become a role model for others, demonstrate what is possible in the subject and maintain a personal commitment to the subject. This cannot be done in isolation and all subject leaders are encouraged to seek support through local, regional and national networks. Membership of local cluster groups, discussion forums and professional bodies will help in this regard. Subject leaders should aim to become actively involved within the wider profession. This will help the subject leader to stay informed and up to date in a dynamic subject area and reduce the chances of feeling isolated; it is likely that any problems facing the subject leader are being faced by somebody else at the same time, particularly when government initiatives seem to be focused on the subject. Subject leaders are encouraged to:

- become members of professional subject associations such as AfPE;
- seek opportunities to attend local, regional and national physical education conferences;
- make immediate contact with borough or county personnel (advisory teacher, partnership development manager, school sports coordinator and so on);
- make immediate contact with local secondary school physical education department;
- begin to build up a range of contacts in local community clubs;
- make contact with local HEI ITT provider and engage in locally delivered CPD opportunities;
- maintain a keen interest in issues relevant to physical education such as health of children, inclusion and government policy statements.

Summary

The need for primary physical education subject leaders to be advocates, champions and enthusiasts for the subject is clear. The performance of this role is undoubtedly impossible without a degree of personal commitment, together with a clear underpinning rationale for the subject. Without a strong sense of *why* the subject is important, a subject leader will be unable to fully articulate *how* standards in the subject can be raised. The subject leader my be a relatively inexperienced teacher and should consider how the development of personal qualities and professional skills can support the role. Of late, we have seen many recently qualified teachers begin to work within subject leadership in our local schools and the potential for impact is clear. Those who have made the most of early leadership opportunities have provided us with the following additional tips that we hope will be of use to others in similar circumstances.

10 tips for the newly appointed physical education subject leader

1 Get to know your colleagues and their professional development needs.

2 Engage with local networks and seek support from others.

3 Be confident with your own rationale for primary physical education and be prepared to stand by your principles.

4 Build effective channels of communication and proactively seek out opportunities to use them regularly.

5 Identify opportunities for an early 'quick win' (such as facilitating a staff INSET, or sharing teaching resources).

6 Try to implement small changes – colleagues who have been teaching physical education in a particular way for a number of years will not change their practice overnight.

7 Be a reflective practitioner and show others that you are also engaging in professional development opportunities.

8 When reviewing and mapping the school physical education curriculum, take a 'bottom-up' approach and build high quality from the Foundation Stage and/or Key Stage 1.

9 Demonstrate the holistic benefits of high quality physical education and provide colleagues with strategies to utilize the physical domain in learning.

10 Remain alert to new initiatives and policies that can be used as leverage for raising the status of physical education in school.

Key Questions

1 What approach do you think is most suited to physical education subject leadership in the primary school?

2 What evidence is required to begin a curriculum audit?

3 What different approaches can be taken when mapping a physical education curriculum?

4 If you had £500 to spend on physical education equipment, what would you buy?

5 What is meant by risk management and how is this achieved?

Learning tasks

1 Reflect on the role of the subject leader within your most recent school experience placement. Was the leader an advocate for the subject? What other qualities can you identify?

2 What particular leadership style will suit you if you were deployed in this role in the future? Can you identify a small number of specific actions that you would seek to complete in the first term of being a subject leader?

3 During a school-based practice, conduct a mock curriculum audit and identify one area of weakness.

With support from the subject leader or an academic tutor, consider what an action plan would look like.

4 Collect long-term plans and the school physical education policy in your next school-based practice. Consider whether the plans reflect the policy statement and to what extent the curriculum map is developmentally appropriate.

5 Consider health and safety requirements in one or more specific activity areas of the NCPE. Devise a checklist that can be used by teachers and pupils to ensure practice is appropriate.

6 Identify your own professional development needs in relation to a possible future role of subject leader

7 Write your own ideal job description for a primary physical education subject leader. What tasks do you think are the most important and why?

Links to the Framework of Professional Standards for Teachers

The content and focus of this chapter have direct relevance to the following Qualified Teacher Status (QTS) standards (TDA, 2007) for those training to teach in primary schools: Q1, Q2, Q3, Q4, Q6, Q7, Q11b, Q17, Q18, Q25, Q27.

Useful websites

www.afpe.org.uk

The Association for Physical Education. Contains general information about membership and links to specific services, such as relevant health and safety guidance, and links to professional development opportunities.

www.qca.org.uk

The Qualifications and Curriculum Authority Website contains a wealth of information regarding planning, teaching and assessing.

The following link outlines principles of assessment for learning: http://www.qca.org.uk/downloads/4031_afl_principles.pdf.

www.ofsted.gov.uk

The Office for Standards in Education. This website contains links to all subject reports. The following link is to the 2004/5 report for primary physical education: http://www.ofsted.gov.uk/publications/annualreport0405/4.1.10.html

References and further reading

Assessment Reform Group (2002) *Assessment for Learning: 10 Principles*. Available at: http://www.qca.org.uk/downloads/4031_afl_principles.pdf [accessed 1 August 2006].

BAALPE (2003) *Achieving Excellence: Subject Leader in Physical Education* (2nd edn). Leeds: Coachwise.

BAALPE (2004) *Safe Practice in Physical Education and School Sport* (6th edn). Leeds: Coachwise.

Bailey, R. (2001) *Teaching Physical Education: A Handbook for Primary and Secondary School Teachers*. London: Kogan Page.

Bailey, R. and MacFayden, T. (eds) (2000) *Teaching Physical Education* 5–11. London: Continuum.

Bell, D. and Richie, R. (1999) *Towards Effective Subject Leadership in the Primary School*. Buckingham: Open University Press.

Chedzoy, S. (1996) *Physical Education for Teachers and Coordinators at Key Stages 1 and 2*. London: David Fulton Publishers.

Costa, A. L. (1991) 'The Search for Intelligent Life', in A. L. Costa (ed.) *Developing Minds: a resource book for teaching thinking, Volume 1 (revised edition)*. Alexandria, USA: Association for Supervision and Curriculum Development.

DfES (2003) *The National Physical Education and School Sport Professional Development Programme, Primary Resource Pack, Section 3*. London: DfES Publications.

Easton, C., Golightly, J. and Oyston, M. (1999) *Coordinating the Curriculum in the Smaller Primary School*. London: Falmer Press.

Flamholtz, E. G. and Randle, Y. (2000) *Growing Pains: Transitioning from an Entrepreneurship to a Professionally Managed Firm*. San Francisco: Jossey-Bass, p. 259.

Fletcher, L. and Bell, D. (1999) 'Subject Leadership in the Primary School: Views of Subject Leaders', Paper presented at the British Educational Research Association Annual Conference, University of Sussex at Brighton, 2–5 September 1999. Available at: http://www.leeds.ac.uk/educol/documents/00001211.htm [accessed 1 August 2006].

Gadsby, P. and Harrison, M. (1999) *The Primary Coordinator and Ofsted Re-inspection*. London: Falmer Press.

Gallahue, D. (1996) *Developmental Physical Education for Today's Children* (3rd edn). Dubuque, IA: Brown and Benchmark.

Goleman, D., Boyatzis, R. E. and McKee, A. (2002) *Primal Leadership: Learning to Lead with Emotional Intelligence*. Boston, MA: Harvard Business Press.

Graham, G., Holt-Hale, S. A. and Parker, M. (2004) *Children Moving: A Reflective Approach to Teaching Physical Education* (6th edn). Boston, MA: McGraw Hill.

Gronn, P. (2003) 'Leadership: Who Needs It?', *School Leadership & Management*, **23**(3), August, 267–90.

Hall, J. (1999) *The Primary Physical Education Handbook*. London: A&C Black.

Hersey, P. and Blanchard, K. (1984) *Managing Organizational Behavior*. Englewood Cliffs, NJ: Prentice-Hall.

Lester, G. (2002) *Protecting Children: A Guide for Sportspeople*. Leeds: NSPCC and Sports Coach UK.

MacGilchrist, B., Myers, K. and Reed, J. (2004) *The Intelligent School* (2nd edn). London: Sage.

Ofsted (1999) *Handbook for Inspecting Primary and Nursery Schools*. London; HMSO.

Ofsted (2005a) *Guidance on the use of evidence forms*. London: HMI. (Available from: http://www.ofsted.gov.uk/publications/index.cfm?fuseaction=pubs.displayfile&id=3857&type=pdf) [accessed 30 August 2006].

Ofsted (2005b) *The Annual Report of Her Majesty's Chief Inspector of Schools*, 2004/5. London: HMI. (Publication available at: http://www.ofsted.gov.uk/publications/annualreport0405/4.1.10.html [accessed 3 August 2006].

PEAUK and Tacklesport (2003) 'Observing Children Moving' (CD Rom), London: PEUAUK, Tacklesport.

Pollard, A. (2005) *Reflective Teaching* (2nd edn). London: Continuum.

Raymond, C. (1998) *Coordinating Physical Education Across the Primary School*. London: Falmer Press.

Scott, S., Jackson, S. and Backett-Milburn, K. (2001) 'Swings and Roundabouts: Risk Anxiety and the Everyday World of Children', in A. Jones (ed.) *Touchy Subjects: Teachers touching children*. Dunedin, New Zealand: University of Otago Press.

Severs, J., Whitlam, P. and Woodhouse, J. (2003) *Safety and Risk in Primary School Physical Education*. London: Routledge.

Tishman, S., Jay, E. and Perkins, D. N. (1993) 'Teaching Thinking Dispositions: From Transmission to Enculturation', *Theory into Practice*, **32**, Summer, 147–53.

Waters, M (ed.) (1999) *Coordinating the Curriculum in the Smaller Primary School*. London: Falmer Press.

Whitlam, P. (2005) *Case Law in Physical Education and School Sport: A Guide to Good Practice*. Worcester: BAALPE.

Appendix 1 Medium-term planning example

A Unit of Work for Key Stage …

Year:	Key Stage:	Time (number of lessons):	Title of Unit:	Learning Outcome:

Cross Curricular Elements:

Lesson	Lesson 1	Lesson 2	Lesson 3	Lesson 4	Lesson 5	Lesson 6
Focus on:						
Warm up/Introduction:						
Concluding activity:						
Relationships:						
Resources needed:						

Attainment targets – Level descriptors
Level:
Level:

Criteria for assessing attainment

General requirements across all Key Stages:

NC Knowledge and understanding
Pupils should be taught to:

NC Breadth of study (activity speak)
Pupils should be taught to:

Appendix 2 Short-term planning example – Tabular approach to lesson planning

Lesson phase and timing	Task	What am I looking for?	Progression(s)	Differentiation (STEP)	Movement vocabulary/focus for FB	Teaching style/ strategy to support learning	Equipment and resources
1. Warm up to learn							
2.							
3.							
4.							
5. Cool down and plenary							

Immediate post-lesson evaluation:
Pointers for next lesson:

Appendix 3 Overview of Qualified Teacher Status (QTS) Standards and links to primary physical education.

The standards used here are those deemed to be 'draft' by the Training and Development Agency for Schools (TDA) in January 2007.

The table below provides examples of how a trainee primary teacher can use experience of teaching physical education as evidence towards achieving QTS. It should also be noted that the 'Q' standards are clearly linked to induction, post-threshold, excellent and advanced skill teacher standards and all teachers are encouraged to reflect on their practice to identify areas for professional development in physical education.

1. PROFESSIONAL ATTRIBUTES	Example of trainee practice in physical education.	Chapter link
Q1. Have high expectations of children and young people and a commitment to ensuring that they can achieve their full educational potential and to establishing fair, respectful, trusting, supportive and constructive relationships with them.	A trainee volunteers to accompany his Key Stage 2 class on a residential Outdoor Adventurous Activities trip. He works alongside the subject leader, class teacher and centre staff and parents to clarify expectations for children's learning during this trip and uses the experience to develop trusting, supportive and constructive relationships with the children.	1, 2, 3, 6
Q2. Demonstrate the positive values, attitudes and behaviour they expect from children and young people.	A trainee shows enthusiasm by changing into PE kit for lessons and ensures that learning is at the heart of every PE lesson through detailed planning.	5, 8
Q3. (a) Be aware of the professional duties of teachers and the statutory framework within which they work. (b) Be aware of the policies and practices of the workplace and share in collective responsibility for their implementation.	A trainee meets with the PE subject leader to clarify the PE health and safety policy. She is especially concerned with teaching off site (games activities is usually taught in the local park) and, after reading current BAALPE recommendations, carries out a risk assessment for the upcoming block of work.	5, 8
Q4. Communicate effectively with children, young people, colleagues, parents and carers.	After speaking with the headteacher, a trainee uses the school intranet website to celebrate the work of his Year 4 class during the spring term. Examples of pupil peer-assessments are uploaded to the site and shared with colleagues who use the information to inform future planning.	8, 5
Q5. Recognize and respect the contribution that colleagues, parents and carers can make to the development and well-being of children and young people and to raising their levels of attainment.	A trainee asks parents and carers to suggest ideas and materials that could be used as starting points for dance activities during the autumn term. At the end of the unit of work, the same parents and carers are invited into school to celebrate the achievements of their children.	2, 3, 8

Q6. Have a commitment to collaboration and co-operative working.	During teaching practice, a trainee works as part of the whole school team to plan and facilitate 'sports day'. She ensures that all children in her class can participate in the event and creates a programme for the day using her desktop publishing skills.	5, 8
Q7. (a) Reflect on and improve their practice, and take responsibility for identifying and meeting their developing professional needs. (b) Identify priorities for their early professional development in the context of induction.	Following a limited exposure to the PE curriculum during Stage 1 teaching practice, a trainee identifies the need to gain experience in teaching gymnastic activities. She negotiates an opportunity to plan, teach and assess a sequence of linked lessons and to apply knowledge acquired in a recent college-based course. The same trainee identifies that professional development during induction year is important and, following appointment to post, makes an early contact with the local Lead Development Agency in order to access CPD courses.	1, 6, 7, 8
Q8. Have a creative and constructively critical approach towards innovation, being prepared to adapt their practice where benefits and improvements are identified.	A trainee attends a whole school INSET course that is delivered by a local authority 'lead trainer.' The course examines inclusion in PE and the trainee seeks to apply the strategies introduced in the course within her teaching. She is especially keen to seek ways of engaging the most able children and begins to use ICT to support pupils' work in the 'evaluate and improve' aspect of NCPE.	1, 2, 3, 4, 5, 6, 7
Q9. Act upon advice and feedback and be open to coaching and mentoring.	Following a 'satisfactory' PE lesson, a trainee acts on feedback from the school experience mentor (who observed the lesson) to try and improve specific aspects; in particular, the assessment and recording of pupils' learning is an agreed focus for the next lesson in sequence and the trainee creates an assessment grid that is clearly linked to the stated learning intentions.	4, 5, 6

2. PROFESSIONAL KNOWLEDGE AND UNDERSTANDING	Example of trainee practice in physical education.	Chapter link
Q10. Have a knowledge and understanding of a range of teaching, learning and behaviour management strategies and know how to use and adapt them, including how to personalize learning and provide opportunities for all learners to achieve their potential.	Having made some initial observations and assessments of pupils' work in PE, a trainee plans carefully differentiated tasks within a games activities lesson which focuses on invasion games. Tasks are set for different groups of children and variation is achieved by using different equipment, space and numbers in teams.	1, 3, 5, 6

Q11. Know the assessment requirements and arrangements for the subjects/curriculum areas they are trained to teach, including those relating to public examinations and qualifications.	A trainee proactively seeks opportunities to work alongside class teachers who are preparing end of term reports for pupils. Although he finds this demanding, the ensuing discussion with class teachers is valuable and informative to all. In particular, comments based on the '4 aspects' of NCPE are included in each pupil's report.	4, 5, 6, 8
Q12. Know a range of approaches to assessment, including the importance of formative assessment.	A final stage trainee uses a system of 'formative assessment' during a six week series of dance activities with a Year 5 class. By the end of the unit of work, each pupil has collected a range of photographs, skill analysis grids, video clips and peer assessment information. The trainee meets with the class teacher to discuss how this information can be sued to inform subsequent planning.	4, 5, 6, 8
Q13. Know how to use local and national statistical information to evaluate the effectiveness of their teaching, to monitor the progress of those they teach and to raise levels of attainment.	A trainee uses information provided by the Local Education Authority regarding children's attainment in 'physical development' at the end of the Foundation Stage to plan and assess her pupils' work in a year 1 class. She thinks that the majority of pupils are exceeding expectations and plans tasks that will continue to provide appropriate challenge.	4, 5
Q14. Have a secure knowledge and understanding of their subjects/curriculum areas and related pedagogy to enable them to teach effectively across the age and ability range for which they are trained to teach.	A trainee works with school and college-based staff to ensure that (over the duration of her undergraduate degree) she gains practical experience within games, gymnastic and dance activities. She also completes a written PE assignment in the second year of her course which focuses on the 'acquire and develop' aspect of NCPE.	1, 2, 3, 4, 5, 6
Q15. Know and understand the relevant statutory and non-statutory curricula and frameworks, including those provided through the National Strategies, for their subjects/curriculum areas, and other relevant initiatives applicable to the age and ability range for which they are trained.	A trainee works alongside the class teacher and other colleagues to ensure that the national PSA target of 2 hours per week of high quality PE and sport is achieved for her pupils. She also seeks to make connections between PE and other subjects and encourages children's creative skills through the teaching of literacy alongside dance activities.	3, 5, 6, 7
Q16. Have passed the professional skills tests in numeracy, literacy and information and communication technology (ICT).	N/A	N/A
Q17. Know how to use skills in literacy, numeracy and ICT to support their teaching and wider professional activities.	A trainee uses a variety of simple software packages to manage his own plans and records of pupils' work. He uses a database to keep a record of formative assessments in physical education, linked to NCPE level descriptors, which is shared with other colleagues to help plan for individual need.	5

Q18. Understand how children and young people develop and that the progress and well-being of learners are affected by a range of developmental, social, religious, ethnic, cultural and linguistic influences.	By taking a 'developmental approach', a trainee plans tasks in PE that are specifically matched to meet individual needs. During a teaching practice, the class includes children from a variety of ethnic groups; the trainee draws on this to support learning in dance activities drawing on a wide range of cultural influences.	1, 2, 3, 6
Q19. Know how to make effective personalized provision for those they teach, including those for whom English is an additional language or who have special educational needs, and how to take practical account of diversity and promote equality and inclusion in their teaching.	A trainee focuses on using task cards to 'scaffold' children's learning in swimming activities and water safety. For some children in the Year 2 class, English is an additional language, and the trainee works with the TA to use two languages on each card.	1, 2, 3, 5, 6, 7
Q20. Know and understand the roles of colleagues with specific responsibilities, including those with responsibility for learners with special educational needs and disabilities and other individual learning needs.	A trainee meets with the 'SENCO' to discuss policy and practice with particular reference to the pupil in her class identified with 'ADHD.' The trainee is particularly concerned that PE experiences can build on this child's seemingly limitless desire to move while not compromising safety for the whole class.	5, 7, 8
Q21. (a) Be aware of current legal requirements, national policies and guidance on the safeguarding and promotion of well-being of children and young people.	A trainee completes a college-based directed task that shows how the five outcomes of 'Every Child Matters' link to National Curriculum requirements in Key Stage 1. She attempts to reflect this in her teaching of PE and specifically includes learning intentions that relate to health and the fostering of self-esteem amongst the children through meaningful and enjoyable activities.	1, 2, 3, 4, 7, 8
(b) Know how to identify and support children and young people whose progress, development or well-being is affected by changes or difficulties in their personal circumstances, and when to refer them to colleagues for specialist support.	A trainee is concerned that an 8-year-old child in her class suddenly appears to have little energy and struggles to remain active in PE for sustained periods of time. The trainee consults with the class teacher who in turn speaks with the head teacher and an associated health professional; in collaboration with the pupil's parents, guidance is offered concerning dietary intake and sleep requirements.	3, 7

3. PROFESSIONAL SKILLS	**Example of trainee practice in physical education.**	**Chapter link**
Q22. Plan for progression across the age and ability range for which they are trained, designing effective learning sequences within lessons and across series of lessons and demonstrating secure subject/curriculum knowledge.	A student in her final stage of ITT seeks an opportunity to plan, teach and assess a sequence of lessons in Athletic Activities. She finds out the level of prior experience in this activity area and attempts to map out a unit of work that will challenge her Year 5 pupils. In her planning, she identifies clear learning intentions which will extend the pupils' knowledge and understanding to include new and different ways of throwing a range of objects for distance and accuracy.	5, 6

Q 23. Design opportunities for learners to develop their literacy, numercay and ICT skills.	Following a gymnastic activities lesson with a Year 2 class, a trainee uses video clips of the pupils moving to focus on 'movement vocabulary'. The pupils use the interactive whiteboard in the classroom to suggest appropriate words that are then written next to 'still' images of their actions.	5
Q.24. Plan homework or other out-of-class work to sustain learners' progress and to extend and consolidate their learning.	A trainee uses questioning during a PE warm up to check understanding about short term effects of exercise on the body. She uses existing knowledge to link to ongoing work in science and asks children to measure heart rates across a 'normal' day, including time at home and before and after school. She helps the children to create a heart rate log and uses this data (particularly that gathered over a weekend) during maths lessons.	5, 6
Q.25. Teach lessons and sequences of lessons across the age and ability range for which they are trained in which they:		
(a) use a range of teaching strategies and resources, including e-learning, taking practical account of diversity and promoting equality and inclusion.	Despite initial concerns regarding maintaining 'control' of the pupils, a trainee adopts a 'guided discovery' style when teaching a 'floorwork' gymnastic activity in Key Stage 2. She prepares task cards to engage the pupils in the planning and evaluation of their own work.	4, 5, 6
(b) build on prior knowledge, develop concepts and processes, enable learners to apply new knowledge, understanding and skills and meet learning objectives.	During a placement with a Year 4 class, a trainee uses the knowledge accrued by pupils in a concurrent sequence of geography lessons to good effect in an Outdoor and Adventurous Activities context. The trainee plans activities where the pupils can apply navigation skills in teams, within the school grounds, in variety of 'orienteering' challenges.	5, 6
(c) adapt their language to suit the learners they teach, introducing new ideas and concepts clearly, and using explanations, questions, discussions and plenaries effectively.	During a dance activities lesson, a trainee works with a small group of Year 1 pupils to explore the 'use of space'. The trainee is surprised with how quickly the children are able to work skilfully in their own space and extends the pupils learning by introducing partner and trio work. The trainee uses discussion to prompt the pupils to work at different levels and to compliment each others' work. The trainee asks the children to demonstrate their work to the rest of the class during the plenary and asks the observers to suggest what they like about the observed actions.	5, 6
(d) demonstrate the ability to manage learning of individuals, groups and whole classes, modifying their teaching to suit the stage of the lesson.	A trainee uses 'exploration' and 'guided discovery' teaching styles to engage the whole class at the start of a games activity lesson. As the lesson progresses, the trainee provides individuals and small groups with appropriate and specific feedback whilst maintaining a careful watch over the whole class.	5, 6

Q26. (a) Make effective use of a range of assessment, monitoring and recording strategies.	A trainee uses principles of 'assessment for learning' to design four systems for assessing and recording pupils' progress in gymnastic activities. Simple formats for individual, group, peer and self-assessment are used across a unit of work to create a portfolio of achievement.	4, 5, 6, 7, 8
(b) Assess the learning needs of those they teach in order to set challenging learning objectives.	During the early stages of school-based practice, a trainee observes Year 3 pupils working in a games activity context. It is evident that many pupils are unable to demonstrate a range of sending and receiving skills and that some are restricted by competitive practices. The trainee plans the following lesson to include differentiated tasks and to allow all pupils more time and space 'on the ball'.	4, 5, 6
Q27. Provide timely, accurate and constructive feedback on learners' attainment, progress and areas for development.	A trainee plans a Year 1 PE lesson with a learning intention of 'acquire and develop sending and receiving skills.' At the planning stage, she thinks through the appropriate movement vocabulary required to give instructions and provide feedback. During the lesson the trainee uses this language (using a prompt card to remind her) to give constructive feedback, particularly in relation to body position and arm action within ball rolling and throwing actions for accuracy.	4, 5, 6
Q28. Support and guide learners to reflect on their learning, identify the progress they have made and identify their emerging learning needs.	A trainee uses questioning to check pupils' understanding within the main activity in a Year 6 athletic activities lesson (the lesson is focusing on evaluating and improving each others' work in running activities). She challenges the pupils to analyse travelling actions and to consider the changes to technique that can be made to cover various distances in less time. Each child completes a self-assessment log that includes a focus for subsequent lessons.	5, 6
Q.29. Evaluate the impact of their teaching on the progress of all learners, and modify their planning and classroom practice where necessary.	A trainee evaluates all lessons, including those in PE. In the early stages of ITT, these comments reflect largely on health and safety and behaviour management issues. As the trainee becomes more experienced in teaching physical education, evaluations become more focused on quality of learning and small changes that can be made to strengthen the experience of each child.	4, 5, 6
Q.30. Establish a purposeful and safe learning environment conducive to learning and identify opportunities for learners to learn in out-of-school contexts.	A trainee follows school-based and national best practice guidelines for health and safety in PE. He involves the children in preparing a health and safety poster for the upcoming unit of work taking place in a swimming pool at a local sports centre and prepares laminated resource cards that provide visual learning stimuli.	5, 6

Q.31. Establish a clear framework for classroom discipline to manage learners' behaviour constructively and promote their self-control and independence.	A trainee who is working with a Year 2 class is concerned about the children becoming boisterous during gymnastic activities in the school hall. She sets early learning tasks that emphasise control, accuracy and neatness of body actions and encourages each child to work in their own defined space (initially using individual mats and hoops as a guide).	5, 6
Q.32. Work as a team member and identify opportunities for working with colleagues, sharing the development of effective practice with them.	A trainee attends a whole school INSET course that is delivered by a local authority 'lead trainer'. The course examines inclusion in PE and the trainee seeks to apply the strategies introduced in the course within her teaching. She is especially keen to seek ways of engaging the most able children and begins to use ICT to support pupils work in the 'evaluate and improve' aspect of NCPE. This is successful and she is asked to feedback to colleagues at the end of term staff meeting.	5, 7, 8
Q.33. Ensure that colleagues working with them are appropriately involved in supporting learning and understand the roles they are expected to fulfil.	A trainee makes effective use of her teaching assistant (TA) in PE. During a unit of work in dance activities, the TA scaffolds pupils' work with appropriate feedback and feed forward, using movement vocabulary that the trainee has written on a prompt card and discussed before the lesson.	5, 6, 7

Index